THE CONSTITUTIONAL CONVENTION OF 1787

Constructing the American Republic

OTHER TITLES IN THIS SERIES

Greenwich Village, 1913: Suffrage, Labor, and the New Woman
> Mary Jane Treacy

Kentucky, 1861: Loyalty, State, and Nation
> Nicolas W. Proctor and Margaret Storey

Patriots, Loyalists, and Revolution in New York City, 1775–1776, Second Edition
> Bill Offutt

Red Clay, 1835: Cherokee Removal and the Meaning of Sovereignty
> Jace Weaver and Laura Adams Weaver

Rousseau, Burke, and Revolution in France, 1791, Second Edition
> Jennifer Popiel, Mark C. Carnes, and Gary Kates

The Threshold of Democracy: Athens in 403 BCE, Fourth Edition
> Josiah Ober, Naomi J. Norman, and Mark C. Carnes

Also Available

Charles Darwin, the Copley Medal, and the Rise of Naturalism, 1861–64
> Marsha Driscoll, Elizabeth E. Dunn, Dann Siems, and B. Kamran Swanson

Confucianism and the Succession Crisis of the Wanli Emperor, 1587
> Daniel K. Gardner and Mark C. Carnes

Defining a Nation: India on the Eve of Independence, 1945
> Ainslie T. Embree and Mark C. Carnes

Henry VIII and the Reformation of Parliament
> John Patrick Coby

The Trial of Anne Hutchinson: Liberty, Law, and Intolerance in Puritan New England
> Michael P. Winship and Mark C. Carnes

The Trial of Galileo: Aristotelianism, the "New Cosmology," and the Catholic Church, 1616–33
> Michael S. Pettersen, Frederick Purnell Jr., and Mark C. Carnes

W. W. Norton & Company has been independent since its founding in 1923, when William Warder Norton and Mary D. Herter Norton first published lectures delivered at the People's Institute, the adult education division of New York City's Cooper Union. The firm soon expanded its program beyond the Institute, publishing books by celebrated academics from America and abroad. By mid century, the two major pillars of Norton's publishing program—trade books and college texts—were firmly established. In the 1950s, the Norton family transferred control of the company to its employees, and today—with a staff of four hundred and a comparable number of trade, college, and professional titles published each year—W. W. Norton & Company stands as the largest and oldest publishing house owned wholly by its employees.

Editor: Justin Cahill
Associate Editor: Scott Sugarman
Project Editor: Jennifer Barnhardt
Editorial Assistants: Kelly Rafey, Rachel Taylor
Managing Editor, College: Marian Johnson
Production Manager: Ashley Horna
Marketing Manager, History: Sarah England Bartley
Design Director: Rubina Yeh
Book Design: Alexandra Charitan
Permissions Manager: Megan Schindel
Composition: Jouve International
Illustrations: Mapping Specialists, Ltd.
Manufacturing: Sheridan Books, Inc.

Library of Congress Cataloging-in-Publication Data

Names: Coby, Patrick, 1948- author.
Title: The Constitutional Convention of 1787: constructing the American
    Republic / John Patrick Coby.
Description: First edition. | New York: W. W. Norton & Company, [2017] |
    Series: Reacting to the past | Includes bibliographical references.
Identifiers: LCCN 2017042260 | ISBN 9780393640908 (pbk.)
Subjects: LCSH: United States. Constitutional Convention (1787) |
    Constitutional conventions—United States—History. | United States.
    Constitution. | Constitutional history—United States. | United
    States—History.
Classification: LCC KF4510 .C63 2017 | DDC 342.7302/92—dc23 LC record available at https://lccn.loc.gov/2017042260

W. W. Norton & Company, Inc., 500 Fifth Avenue, New York, NY 10110

W. W. Norton & Company Ltd., 15 Carlisle Street, London W1D 3BS

1 2 3 4 5 6 7 8 9 0

REACTING TO THE PAST

THE CONSTITUTIONAL CONVENTION OF 1787

Constructing the American Republic

John Patrick Coby, Smith College

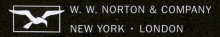

W. W. NORTON & COMPANY
NEW YORK · LONDON

BARNARD
REACTING TO THE PAST

ABOUT THE AUTHOR

JOHN PATRICK COBY is Esther Booth Wiley 1934 Professor of Government at Smith College, where he teaches courses in political theory and American political thought. He is the author of five books and of numerous scholarly articles and reviews. His books include *Socrates and the Sophistic Enlightenment: A Commentary on Plato's Protagoras; Machiavelli's Romans: Liberty and Greatness in the Discourses on Livy; Thomas Cromwell: Machiavellian Statecraft and the English Reformation;* and the Reacting to the Past game *Henry VIII and the Reformation Parliament.* He is the recipient of three teaching prizes: the Smith College Faculty Teaching Award, the Sherrerd Prize for Distinguished Teaching, and the Board of Trustees Honored Professor Award.

CONTENTS

PART 4: ROLES (STANDARD VERSION)   58

Factions   59

Delegates   60

PART 5: CORE TEXTS   66

Aristotle, FROM *Politics*, 335–323 B.C.E.   67

John Locke, FROM *Second Treatise of Government*, 1690   76

Montesquieu, FROM *The Spirit of the Laws*, 1748   79

David Hume, *Essays Moral, Political, and Literary*, 1758   94

Thomas Paine, FROM *Common Sense*, 1776   103

Thomas Jefferson, FROM *Notes on the State of Virginia*, 1785   108

APPENDIX A: THE GAME (EXPANDED VERSIONS)

THE CONSTITUTIONAL CONVENTION OF 1787

Constructing the American Republic

 PART 1: INTRODUCTION

BRIEF OVERVIEW OF THE GAME

The Constitutional Convention of 1787: Constructing the American Republic has as its subject the most fundamental political-legal event in American history. Students in the game, playing delegates to the convention, gather in "Philadelphia" to write a new constitution for the United States. Or is it that they gather to amend the already existing constitution, the Articles of Confederation, ratified a mere six years earlier? The job at hand is itself a matter of controversy. Informing the debates are two competing theories of republican government: *Country republicanism*, with roots in the Classical and Renaissance worlds and in the thought of Aristotle, Machiavelli, Rousseau, etc.—but called confederalism at the convention; and *Court republicanism*, arising from a "new science of politics" developed by authors such as Locke, Montesquieu, Hume, etc.—but called nationalism at the convention. The game attempts to teach the entire founding period, and not just the four-month convention, by allowing, where appropriate, the thought of the ratification period to filter in—e.g., Federalist and Antifederalist writings. Sectional interests, backroom deal-making, personal rivalries, foreign intrigue, and the danger of leaks all work to add drama to the proceedings. The game ends in a vote to accept or reject the constitution.

Multiple Game Versions

The "Constitutional Convention" game is different from other games in the Reacting to the Past series in that it comes in three fully developed versions: Standard, Expanded Mid-Size, and Expanded Full-Size. The Standard version aims for simplicity, brevity, and accessibility. It attempts no faithful rendition of the convention but instead focuses debate on four large convention issues, three of them institutional and one of them socioeconomic. The resulting constitution is therefore much abridged. Both individual and factional roles are employed, although factional identity is more important here. The Expanded versions follow the course of the convention and set students to the task of constructing fairly complete constitutions, working from the Virginia Plan (Mid-Size is like Full-Size only shortened by the removal of some constitutional issues). For both versions the roles are individualized; factional affiliations, while present, are of secondary importance. All versions use the same game book, published by W. W. Norton, but each has its own instructor's guide and its own role sheets. Norton will distribute the instructor's guide and role sheets for the Standard version; files for the Mid-Size and Full-Size versions exist on the Reacting to the Past Consortium Library site, available to registered faculty; downloading the files is free. (Go to https://reactingconsortiumlibrary.org.)

Related Short Game

Also available on the Reacting Consortium Library site is a one-week short game titled *Raising the Eleventh Pillar: The New York State Ratifying Convention of 1788*. The purpose of the short game is to introduce faculty and students to the Reacting pedagogy, without much up-front investment of time and effort or subtraction from the coverage requirements of a lecture course. The game's subject is representation.

PROLOGUE: SOVEREIGNTY

At the Indian Queen

"elaware, my good man, is a SOV-RUN state and will not be dictated to or trifled with by the likes of Pennsylvania!"

The angry bellow catches your notice and ends momentarily the conversation at your table. You and your companions, fellow delegates to the grand convention, have been exchanging views on the state of the country—though mostly just marking time, waiting for the convention to commence its business. Many an afternoon has been whiled away as this one has, in idle talk over a tankard of Philadelphia brew. Perhaps a tankard too many was responsible for the outburst at the other end of the tavern.

The tavern is the Indian Queen, located on Fourth Street, between Market and Chestnut, near Benjamin Franklin's residence. A number of the delegates have their lodgings at the Indian Queen, a large and rambling establishment built in 1759. They appreciate its proximity to the State House, where the convention is to be held; its well-appointed rooms at reasonable rates; its fine dining and imported wines; and its corps of uniformed servants, who, at no extra cost, stable horses, carry luggage, fetch barbers, and provide copies of the latest London magazines. With more delegates arriving every day, the inn, and its competitors—Mary House's boarding house, the City Tavern, the George, the Black Horse, and others—are all fast filling up, and rooms are being shared. The Society of the Cincinnati, a fraternal organization of Revolutionary War officers, is also in town, holding its triennial convention, as are the Presbyterian Synods of Pennsylvania and New York. So the city is crowded and lodging is tight. Perhaps the bad temper at the tavern's far end was the product of the cheek-by-jowl accommodations now forced on many.

Whatever its cause, the noisy spat continues with the Pennsylvanian gleefully responding that during the bulk of colonial rule—for about one hundred years—puny

Delaware was but a province of Pennsylvania (called the Three Lower Counties). "Not until 1776," he avows, "when all the country was rushing toward independence, did Delaware enjoy its first real taste of autonomy. And now, a mere eleven years later, it purports to being Pennsylvania's SOV-RUN equal. Why should Pennsylvania—or Virginia, or Massachusetts, or any of the great states—give heed to this self-declared equality?" he demands to know.

Inevitably the topic from afar overtakes the conversation near at hand, listless as it was. One of your tablemates picks up where the Pennsylvanian leaves off. "Why, indeed," he wonders, "do small states expect to wield as much power as their larger neighbors? Do small states contribute an equal share to the country's treasury? We know they do not, but a share proportionate to their size and wealth. Are their citizens somehow more worthy, such that, though fewer in number, they deserve a vote equal to those greater in number? Nothing," he asserts, "in republican thinking or in American history justifies the claim."

The last remark provokes a knowing response from another delegate at the table. "How can you not be aware," he snidely asks, "that the Continental Congress seated in New York votes by states, with each state, regardless of size, casting the same, one vote."

"Which is exactly why," comes the confident retort, "the Congress is badly constructed and the Articles of Confederation needs replacing by a wholly new charter of union."

The talk before was about crop production and trade with foreign countries. All agreed that more of both would be desirable. But now, with this new topic, agreement vanishes. Some stand firm in defense of the independence and sovereignty of the thirteen states; others disparage the states as vestiges of the colonial past, mere accidents of history, which should be discarded to make way for a single nation in fulfillment of the promise of the Revolution. Says one of the Nationalists, "We must remember the language with which we began the Revolution: 'Virginia is no more, Massachusetts is no more, Pennsylvania is no more. We are now one nation of brethren; we must bury all local interests and distinctions.'"

"But if states are no more," queries a delegate from the opposing camp, "will not liberty and self-government disappear with them? Does history provide any examples of republics existing outside of small states? Rome ceased to be a republic," he observes, "when it grew into an empire."

The Delawarean, overhearing this talk of small states as the true home of republican government, hollers across the room, contending that Delaware is not too small, that rather all the other states are too large. He then proposes that a map of the country be laid out and that state boundaries be erased and new states created, each the size of Delaware. When finished, he orders another tankard of beer.

Others at your table are unpersuaded. History cannot be the only guide, they reason, because republics of the past were spectacular failures—feeble, factious, feckless, and, worst of all, short-lived. "It will be the glory of America," one of them proclaims, "to show the world how republics are properly made—and not as confederations with no direction from the center, but as consolidated unions capable of great enterprises."

State pride now wells up in the breast of one delegate, who warmly declares his allegiance to his home state, a sovereign power, as he describes it, which by treaty is allied with other states for limited purposes. "When sovereign bodies enter into agreements," he explains, "they do so as equals, their respective populations being a matter of no consequence. Thirteen sovereign states contracted to create a confederal union under the Articles of Confederation. Delegates from these same states are assembling in Philadelphia to consider alterations to the plan of confederation. As before, they will deliberate and decide as equal partners—or they will go home!"

An incredulous listener at the adjacent table begs leave to dissent. "My good sir," he remarks, "I must tell you that you are mistaken. The states are not sovereigns in the sense you contend for. They do not possess the peculiar features of sovereignty. They cannot make war, or peace, or alliances, or treaties. Considered as political beings, they are dumb, for they cannot speak to any foreign sovereign whatever. They are deaf, for they cannot hear any propositions from the same. They have not even the organs of defense or offense, for they cannot of themselves raise troops or equip vessels of war. Now contrast their status, if you will, with that of the national Congress, which can act alone without the states and against instructions from the states. If the Congress declares war, war is de jure declared—captures made in pursuance of it are lawful; no acts of the states can vary the situation or prevent the judicial consequences. I do concede," he allows, "that the union of states, in some respects, comprises the idea of confederation; but it comprises as well the idea of consolidation; for the union of thirteen states is first a union of men composing these states, from whence a national character results to the whole. If the states therefore retain some semblance of sovereignty, they have certainly divested themselves of the larger and more essential portion."

His companion seated opposite congratulates him on his well-argued and finely delivered oration. The companion confesses himself fatigued by the adulation heaped on states, "metaphysical entities" and "imaginary beings," as he styles them, which distract from the fact that individuals are the first object of government's care. He adds that no colony ever presumed itself sovereign before independence was declared, or once thought that independence could be achieved without the coordinated action provided by union. The claim to sovereignty only emerged with the securing of peace and has since served as a pretext for the thirteen states to do as they please.

Mention of consolidation renews the anxiety that liberty will perish if a subordinate status is forced on the states. "In small associations people exert control over their own affairs; in large associations, a ruling class, separate from the people, takes over; and the people are crushed." The delegate speaking these words—and heard from already—calls himself a Confederalist.

To this concern another delegate offers this assurance: that Massachusetts, once consisting of three provinces—Massachusetts Bay, Plymouth, and Maine—has united into one without discernible harm to the liberties of any.

"No harm!" shouts a disbelieving patron standing nearby. "All this past winter our *Pennsylvania Gazette* reported on a mighty rebellion taking place in the western part of that state. I reckon those rebels fight'n with Captain Daniel Shays have a different opinion as to whether their liberties have suffered any harm."

"Is it liberty to defraud one's creditors, borrowing in specie and repaying in paper," asks an irate delegate who, too, has wandered over. He claims that Massachusetts's farmers—and the farming poor in most other states—have pressured their legislatures to pass paper-emissions bills that serve to depreciate the currency, making money repaid worth less than money borrowed. The rebellion occurred, he maintains, because the legislature there had the courage to deny these unjust demands. But elsewhere state legislatures have generally buckled under the pressure, causing the collapse of credit and investment.

Another delegate with similar views traces the country's problems to the plague of demagogues that has descended on state capitals, practicing the low arts of glad-handing and vote buying. "No good will ever come from state government," he predicts, "so long as local electorates return to office these incompetent scalawags."

"Agreed," says that reader of the *Gazette*, "but not because legislators are intimidated by the poor. Whoever heard of such a thing! Rather because legislators are in the pockets of bondholders, who want taxes high in order to ensure regular payment of the interest due on their government securities." By his lights the Shaysites rebelled in protest of taxes that *could not* be paid because the money to pay them *did not* exist. "Only hard currency is accepted in payment of taxes," he explains, "but hard currency is nowhere to be found, since it is sent abroad in exchange for manufactured goods purchased by the rich. Moreover, the continued harassment of debtors and the time they waste in court appealing foreclosures take them away from their labors and deprive them of the tools and livestock by which they make a living. The country's economic troubles," he contends, "have their origin in burdensome taxes passed by legislators indifferent to the plight of their constituents. The remedy," he insists, "is a government whose officials are tightly bound to and closely watched by the people."

The irate delegate continues irate: "And what about the time wasted by honest creditors who must go to court to collect money justly owed them? A debt is a contract freely entered into. Why be so forgiving of people who go back on their word?" There is more to his lecture: "Debt relief and tax forgiveness—policies pursued by nearly every state legislature—cause the common man to despise his labors; and his resulting indolence, combined with his taste for refinements and luxuries, are the real reason he wants for cash and borrows what he cannot repay." He ends by quoting verses of the Hartford Wits, published under the title *Anarchiad*:

> The crafty knave his creditor besets,
> And advertising [brandishing] paper pays his debts;
> Bankrupts their creditors with rage pursue,
> No stop, no mercy from the debtor crew.[1]

A thunderous clamor from the street diverts the attention of all. General Washington's carriage is passing by, and a crowd forms to applaud his Excellency. A man from the street bursts into the tavern breathlessly reporting that some persons in the crowd have resolved to chase after and halt the carriage, unhitch its horses, and pull the vehicle themselves in honor of the man who won the Revolution. "Monarchy," mutters the delegate next to you.

The ruckus without quiets the debate within. You take your leave of the delegates and venture outside to see what the shouting is all about.

Apparently not everyone is enamored of his Excellency or of conditions prevailing in the land: Washington whipped the British; no, Washington lost every battle he fought. The war ended with the defeat of the country's enemies and their surrendering of all claims in North America; hardly, because the British are still in possession of forts in the Northwest and the Spanish in possession of the Mississippi. The wartime officers performed valiantly and are deserving of the nation's gratitude; except that they once mutinied and threatened the civilian power and now pose a continuing danger to the Republic. Life is better with independence secured; but taxes are higher and the economy depressed. The manufacturing states are right to demand tariffs; on the contrary, they are selfish and short-sighted and will ruin the agrarian states with their protectionist policies. The national government has managed the transition from dependent colonies to independent states and is all the government a confederation needs; but how can a government be judged adequate that is powerless to raise revenues, regulate trade, or enforce law? The best government is a simple government with a single legislature and a weak executive; exactly wrong, as the best government is a complex government with separated and independent powers.

There is little order to and no resolution of the numerous points advanced. Even matters of fact are disputed because memories are hazy and affected by interest. A crowd member identifies you as a delegate to the convention. Excitedly, he appeals to you—a man of experience, sagacity, and deep learning, he supposes—to help them sort through this mélange of opinion. You are embarrassed, profess humbly your incompetence, and plead not to be put on the spot. But others join in, asking that you explain how the country arrived at where it now is, staging a constitutional convention barely half-a-dozen years after adoption of its first charter of union.

Seeing no respectable way out, you accede to their request. A stool is provided for your comfort, while the crowd arranges itself on the tavern's spacious side porch. At least you have calmed them, you think to yourself, but will they hear what you have to say? You begin your narrative in 1781, upon the close of hostilities.

WHAT IS REACTING TO THE PAST?

Reacting to the Past is an innovative classroom pedagogy that teaches history and related subjects through a series of immersive role-playing games. Students in Reacting read from specially designed game books that place them in moments of heightened historical tension. The class becomes a public body or private gathering; students assume the roles of particular persons from the period or fictionalized members of factional alliances. Their purpose is to advance an agenda and achieve victory objectives through formal speeches, informal debate, negotiations, vote taking, and conspiracy. After a few preparatory sessions, the game begins, and the students are in charge. The instructor serves as an adviser and arbiter. The outcome of the game sometimes differs from historical events; a debriefing session sets the record straight.

HOW TO PLAY A REACTING GAME

The following is an outline of what you will encounter in Reacting and what you will be expected to do.

Game Setup

The instructor will explain the historical context of the game before it formally begins. During the setup period, you will read several different kinds of materials:

- This game book, which includes historical background, rules and features of the game, core texts, and essential documents

- A role sheet describing the historical person you will play in the game and, when applicable, the faction to which you belong

- Supplementary documents or books that provide additional information and arguments for use during the game

Read all or as much of this material as possible before the game begins and reread it throughout the game. A second and third reading while *in character* will deepen your understanding and alter your perspective. Students who have carefully read the materials and are familiar with the rules of the game will do better than those who rely on general impressions.

Game Play

Once the game begins, usually one student will be randomly chosen, elected, or identified by role to preside over the game sessions. The instructor will then become the Gamemaster (GM) and take a seat at the back of the room. While not directing the play of the game, the GM may do any of the following:

- Pass notes to individuals or factions

- Announce important events, some of which may be the result of students' actions, others instigated by the GM

- Perform scheduled interventions, sometimes determined by die rolls

- Interrupt proceedings that have gone off track

- Arbitrate play-related controversies

There are usually two types of roles in Reacting games: members of factions and Indeterminates, individuals who operate outside the established factions. Each sheet includes an individualized description of the player's biography, personal responsibilities, powers, and objectives. If you are a member of a faction, you may also receive a faction advisory, which outlines the concerns and objectives of the faction as a whole. Indeterminates provide factions with obvious sources of extra support. One faction will never have the voting strength to prevail without allies, so cultivating their loyalty is, therefore, in the interest of every faction. Collaboration and coalition building are at the heart of every game, but Indeterminates who recognize their power may drive a hard bargain.

The classroom may sometimes be noisy, because side conversations, note passing, and players wandering around the room are common and accepted practices in Reacting. But these activities are also disruptive and can spoil the effect of formal speeches, so players should insist on order and quiet before proceeding.

Always assume when a fellow student speaks to you in or out of class that he or she is speaking to you in role. If you need to address a classmate out of role, employ a visual sign, like crossed fingers, to indicate your changed status. It is inappropriate to trade on out-of-class relationships when asking for support or favors.

Work to balance your emotional investment in your role with the need to treat your classmates with respect. Some specific roles may require you to advocate beliefs with which you personally disagree. While such assignments may seem difficult at first, careful study of your role sheet and the readings should help you develop a greater understanding of why this person thought and acted as he or she did. In a few cases, you may even need to promote ideas that are viewed today as controversial or offensive. Again, always go back to the sources: analyze why those ideas made sense for that person in that particular time and place, and then advocate those beliefs as persuasively and effectively as you can. If you ever feel uncomfortable or uncertain about your role, feel free to speak with your instructor. Remember also that you will have an opportunity during the debriefing session to discuss the differences between your game character and your personal beliefs and values.

Game Requirements

The instructor will lay out the specific requirements for the class. In general, though, a Reacting game will ask students to perform three distinct activities:

Reading and Writing. This standard academic work is carried out more purposefully in a Reacting game because what you read is put to immediate use and what you write is meant to persuade others to act in certain ways. The reading load (including both preparation and research) may vary with each role; the writing requirement is typically a set number of pages per game. In both cases the instructor is free to make adjustments. Papers are often policy statements but can also take the form of autobiographies, poems, newspaper articles, clandestine messages, or after-game reflections, all of which may provide the basis for formal speeches.

Public Speaking and Debate. In most games every player is expected to deliver at least one formal speech (the length of the game and the size of the class will affect the number of speeches). Debate occurs after a speech is delivered. Debate is impromptu, raucous, and fast paced, and is often followed by decisions determined by voting.

Strategizing. Communication among students is a pervasive feature of Reacting games. You will find yourselves writing emails, texting, attending out-of-class meetings, and gathering for meals with your classmates on a fairly regular basis. The purpose of these communications is to lay out a strategy for advancing your agenda and thwarting that of your opponents and to hatch plots that ensnare the individuals who are working against your cause.

Skill Development

A Reacting role-playing game provides students with the opportunity to develop a host of academic and life skills:

- Effective writing
- Public speaking

- Problem solving

- Leadership

- Teamwork

- Adapting to quickly changing circumstances

- Working under pressure

- Meeting deadlines

 PART 2: HISTORICAL BACKGROUND

CHRONOLOGY

1781
- *March*   Articles of Confederation ratified
- *March 1–November 3*   First meeting of "Confederation" Congress, Philadelphia
- *May*   Bank of North America chartered
- *June–September*   Slavery informally ended in Massachusetts by court decisions
- *October*   Surrender of Cornwallis at Yorktown
- *November 5, 1781–November 2, 1782*   Second meeting of Congress, Philadelphia
- *December*   5 percent impost voted by Congress, but defeated by opposition of Rhode Island and Virginia (1782)

1782
- *March*   Resignation of Lord North as British prime minister
- *November 4, 1782–June 21, 1783*   Third meeting of Congress, Philadelphia

1783
- *March*   Newburgh conspiracy put down by Washington
- *April*   5 percent impost voted by Congress, plus 3/5 rule for counting of slaves in assessment of taxes, but defeated by opposition of New York (1786)
- *June*   Mutiny of Pennsylvania militia and flight of Congress from Philadelphia
- *June 30–November 1*   Third meeting of Congress continued, Princeton
- *September*   Treaty of Paris signed, formally ending Revolutionary War
- *November 3–4*   Fourth meeting of Congress, Princeton
- *November 26, 1783–June 3, 1784*   Fifth meeting of Congress, Annapolis
- *December*   William Pitt the Younger appointed British prime minister
- *December*   Resignation of Washington as commander-in-chief

1784
- *January*   Treaty of Paris ratified by Congress
- *April*   Land Ordinance of 1784 passed by Congress
- *April*   Spain's closing of Mississippi River to American trade
- *August*   Secession of eastern Tennessee from North Carolina and creation of state of Franklin
- *November 1–December 24*   Sixth meeting of Congress, Trenton

1785
- *January 11–November 4*   Sixth meeting of Congress continued, New York
- *March*   Mt. Vernon conference on navigation of Potomac River and Chesapeake Bay
- *May*   Jefferson in Paris as American ambassador to France, replacing Franklin

- *May*   Land Ordinance of 1785 passed by Congress
- *June*   Adams in London as American ambassador to Great Britain
- *November 7, 1785–November 3, 1786*   *Seventh meeting of Congress, New York*

1786
- *August–February 1787*   Shays' Rebellion in Massachusetts; scattered resistance until June
- *September*   Annapolis convention held to discuss trade
- *September*   Exeter Rebellion in New Hampshire
- *November 6–October 30, 1787*   *Eighth meeting of Congress, New York*

1787
- *February*   Constitutional Convention authorized by Congress
- ***May 25–September 17***   **Meeting of Constitutional Convention, Philadelphia**
- *July*   Northwest Ordinance passed by Congress
- *November 5–October 21, 1788*   *Ninth meeting of Congress, New York*

1788
- *June*   Formal adoption of Constitution with ratification by New Hampshire, the ninth state
- *November 3–March 2, 1789*   *Tenth meeting of Congress, New York*

1789
- *March–September*   Opening session of Congress of United States, New York
- *April*   Inauguration of Washington as first president of United States under new Constitution

AMERICA UNDER THE CONFEDERATION

Peace of Paris

Major fighting in the Revolutionary War ended at Yorktown in October 1781. British general Charles Cornwallis, surrounded by land and by sea, surrendered his army of eight thousand to the American and French forces besieging him. British hopes of final victory collapsed at once; and the expense of conducting a multifront war against rebellious colonies and continental powers—France, Spain, and the Netherlands—caused a change of government the following spring. The long-serving ministry of Lord North (1770–82) was replaced by the ministries of Lord Rockingham and then of Lord Shelburne, both advocates of peace and reconciliation. King George III, though opposed to the change and humiliated by it, was obliged to go along. Peace negotiations began soon after. Meanwhile, British forces in America withdrew slowly from the cities they occupied, leaving New York last in November 1783.

Independence had been won but under what terms? As colonists, Americans enjoyed certain trading privileges inside of Britain's empire. Would these privileges return, particularly the right to trade freely with the British West Indies? Would confiscations of **loyalist** property continue unobstructed or would these traitors to the cause—as **patriots** viewed them—be protected, indemnified, and permitted repatriation?

Loyalists were those Americans who remained loyal to the British crown. They were sometimes called Torries. **Patriots** were those Americans who embraced the cause of independence and revolution.

Would Americans be required to pay debts owed to British creditors? To some, such debts seemed nonbinding because they had been contracted under governments dissolved by the Revolution. Also, what ongoing presence would Britain (and France and Spain) have in the New World, and what would be America's borders? Those living in and migrating to the West beyond the Alleghenies wanted guarantees of unimpeded navigation of the Mississippi; those living in the Northeast wanted access to the fisheries of Newfoundland.

The Continental Congress (discussed later) named five commissioners to negotiate peace with the British: John Adams, John Jay, Benjamin Franklin, Thomas Jefferson, and Henry Laurens. Of the five, only the first three mattered, as Jefferson stayed home in America (attending to a dying wife) and Laurens sat prisoner in the Tower of London. Adams arrived late to Paris, the site of the negotiations, because he was in the Netherlands finishing work on a commercial treaty. Jay was ambassador to Spain and arrived in June 1782. Franklin, the ambassador to France, was already in Paris and began informal talks in April with the British representative, Richard Oswald.

Congress had instructed its commissioners to conduct negotiations in accordance with French wishes and to keep nothing secret from its trusted ally in the war. Franklin was willing enough, but Jay quickly suspected a Franco-Spanish agenda detrimental to American interests. Spain had entered the war in 1779 as an ally of France but not as an ally of America. For its troubles Spain expected the return of Gibraltar, and with the help of France it laid siege to the island. The siege, however, was unsuccessful, and Spain was unsatisfied. Because America's alliance with France required fighting the British as long as France was at war, Jay feared that France would prolong the war for the sake of Spain, or alternately, that France would offer Spain territory in the American West in compensation for the loss of Gibraltar. Eventually, Jay persuaded Franklin that separate and secret negotiations with Britain were in America's interest and that their instructions from home had to be ignored. The argument they made to their negotiating partner was that favorable terms accorded Britain's former colony (whose status Jay insisted be that of an independent state) would sever the cord that tied America to France, Britain's perennial foe.

Favorable terms, indeed, were what America received in the Peace of Paris signed in September 1783. The boundaries agreed to were, along the north, the Great Lakes and the southern stretch of the St. Lawrence River, but with some uncertainty regarding the top of Maine; along the west, the Mississippi River; and along the south, everything but Florida, a Spanish possession that then extended westward across the Gulf of Mexico, but again with some uncertainty as to how far north the border went. The one difficulty was Spain's continuing occupation of both sides of the Mississippi at its mouth, a position enabling Spain to open up or shut off navigation as it wished.

On the point of fair treatment of the loyalists, the most the commissioners would give was the promise of a good faith effort by Congress to persuade the states to return confiscated properties and to cease the persecutions. Likewise, on the point of debt repayment, all that Britain received was the assurance that Congress would pass no law impeding the collection of debts incurred before the outbreak of hostilities. Outside the peace negotiations, Britain, otherwise compliant, dug in its heels, denying American ships access to West India; but smugglers soon made a mockery of the restriction.

First Fruits of Independence

America's triumph was near complete: independence plus ample territory in which to expand. The population grew rapidly, fueled in part by immigration. Work was plentiful and wages appreciably higher than those paid in Europe. Property values and new construction were on the rise. By any measure, life was good and the future promising. One token of revived optimism was the explosion of spending on imported products, mostly British. Americans reasoned that with the period of forced austerity finally over, now was the time for comfort and ease. But within a year they had exhausted their supply of specie (gold and silver coins), and recession set in.

Not all areas suffered equally. Bostonians were hardest hit. Boston merchants faced discrimination in shipping regulations that required use of British bottoms, while Boston consumers were keenest for imports and the first to run out of cash. Other seaports suffered less, such as Philadelphia and Charleston, and Baltimore enjoyed a boom. In general, farmers fared better than townspeople, and the South fared better than the North.

The attitudes and actions of different occupations and regions reflected the various interests of each. Artisans and mechanics demanded tariffs on manufactured goods coming into the country. Farmers, whose purchases became more expensive with tariffs, demanded their elimination; farmers also demanded government credit, paper money, and debt relief. Creditors, conversely, insisted on sound money and strict collection of debts. The mercantile North wanted preference given to American shipping, while the agrarian South wanted free trade and the option to ship with the lowest bidder. Economic interest caused the regions to wonder whether fellow Americans or foreigners and erstwhile enemies were their true friends.

As a case in point, merchants, forbidden by Britain to carry British goods anywhere but to America, petitioned state governments to pass anti-British legislation in reprisal. Some states did as bidden, while others refused, causing Britain to ship to states with less onerous duties (i.e., taxes laid on imports and exports), and causing the merchants there to send the imported goods across state lines. In response, states tried taxing incoming trade from their neighbors, only to suffer like taxes on their own. Before long, many states were in a commercial war with each other.

A second problem concerned revenue. The Congress had three ways to raise it: Congress could requisition (i.e., ask for) contributions from the states; it could borrow from foreigners; or it could print notes in the hope that they would circulate as money. During the war Congress did all three, and with abandon. As a result, these sources of funds were now largely tapped out (or never materialized), and the postwar debt stood at $35,000,000, with interest accruing. To pay down the debt, Congress in 1783 requested the power to levy a small import duty for twenty-five years. The states denied it the authority, as they had done two years earlier when a similar request was made. And the situation seemed to be worsening because the states through the mid-1780s paid a declining proportion of the sums requisitioned, despite steady improvements in their fortunes. Moreover, so few states sent delegations to Congress that rarely did the legislative body have a quorum to do business. Plainly something was wrong at the national level.

One powerful indication of disarray was the situation of the Continental Army. Until the treaty was signed and the British were gone, the war was not assuredly over; keeping the army intact was, therefore, a national priority. It was camped at Newburgh, New York, in 1783, waiting on Congress to pay its soldiers their overdue wages and to pay its officers their promised pensions. Money, though, was slow in coming, and the worry at Newburgh was that if discharge came first, payment might never follow. Some officers under Washington's command joined with national creditors in a scheme to force the states to cede more power to Congress to raise taxes and pay debts. Though sympathetic to their cause, Washington stopped short of endorsing it, and in a dramatic, personal confrontation, he reprimanded the plotters, some of whom were contemplating mutiny, if not a coup d'etat. Embarrassed by Washington, they renounced their plans and reaffirmed their loyalty. A short time later, Pennsylvania militiamen gathered in Philadelphia to press similar demands. Congress became so unnerved by their menacing demeanor that it removed itself to Princeton, Annapolis, and then Trenton, before finally lighting in New York, where it remained.

Another glaring deficiency was Congress's inability to enforce the treaty or to manage foreign relations. The British forts along the Canadian border were to be vacated at the war's end, but Britain held on to them for many years, citing American harassment of loyalists and failure to repay debts in violation of the treaty. Fur trading, however, was the real reason, as well as instigating Indian attacks along the frontier—for who then knew if America had been lost to Britain forever.

Spain was a second, and greater, cause for concern because it felt itself even less bound by the treaty than did Britain and because it still had an empire in the New World and was determined to maintain it against pressure from American settlers moving west. To hold back the tide, Spain resorted to arming Indian tribes, bribing regional leaders, and encouraging immigrants to secede from the union. The Mississippi River was its trump card, which it played deftly to alienate westerners from easterners. The latter cared little about navigation rights on the river since their interests were oriented toward trade with Europe. Expansion westward, they reasoned, would depopulate the East and reduce the value of its lands. Westerners, on the other hand, cared most about access to the Mississippi because without that right they could not move goods to market and be economically independent. The Spanish ambassador, Don Diego de Gardoqui, in his negotiations with the Congress's Foreign Secretary, John Jay, offered trade concessions to eastern shippers in exchange for America's abandonment of the Mississippi to Spain; and he offered western settlers union with Spain as the only remaining means of gaining navigation rights to the Mississippi. Gardoqui almost succeeded (Congress voted in August 1786 to instruct Jay to put off the Mississippi demand for a period of twenty-five or so years, but the vote was sectional and by a margin too narrow to secure ratification of a treaty. In addition, a former Revolutionary War officer plotted in April 1787 to have Kentucky become a vassal state of Spain). In failing, Spain kept the Mississippi closed, and western settlers soured on a government that had so mishandled their vital interests.

Angered by the Tea Act of May 1773, Bostonians threw hundreds of crates of British tea into Boston harbor in an event known as the **Boston Tea Party**. Parliament retaliated by passing the **Coercive Acts** (March 1774), referred to in the colonies as the Intolerable Acts. These acts, four in number, closed the port of Boston, curtailed local self-government, protected British officials from prosecution in American courts, and commandeered private homes for the quartering of British troops.

Continental Congress

When Britain, in response to the **Boston Tea Party** (December 1773), passed the **Coercive Acts**, the colonies, in defense, sent delegates to the First Continental Congress convened in Philadelphia. The delegates finished their work of remonstrating with the king (Declaration and Resolves) in October 1774 and arranged for a second meeting of the Congress the following spring. But before delegates could assemble, fighting flared up in Massachusetts at Lexington and Concord (April 1775). Efforts to broker a cease-fire were unavailing (Olive Branch Petition), and so the Second Continental Congress continued in session as the wartime government of the colonies. One of its early acts was to write a constitution to legalize its existence. Called the Articles of Confederation, this first constitution of the new nation was approved by Congress in 1777 and sent to the states for ratification. All states ratified quickly, excepting Maryland, which withheld its assent until 1781, only months before the war's conclusion.

Maryland was one of a half dozen states not to have claims to territories beyond their present borders. All others did. Massachusetts, for instance, believed itself in possession of Maine, western New York, and the southern portions of what later would become the states of Michigan and Wisconsin. Connecticut asserted title to the northern tiers of Pennsylvania, Ohio, Indiana, and Illinois; New York laid claim to Vermont; North Carolina to Tennessee; South Carolina to a narrow stretch of land below Tennessee; and Georgia to Alabama, Mississippi, and Louisiana. But the biggest claimant by far of western and disputed lands was Virginia, which regarded southwestern Pennsylvania, Kentucky, and all the territory north of the Ohio River and east of the Mississippi River as part of a greater Virginia created by the colony's original charter. Maryland demanded that these lands outside of state borders be ceded to the Confederation government. When Virginia agreed in 1781, the logjam broke, and Maryland ratified the constitution. It also helped that the French ambassador signaled his country's reluctance to fight the British navy in the Chesapeake Bay if Maryland waited any longer.

Why was the confederation of twelve states held hostage to the approval of a reluctant thirteenth? Because, by the terms of the Articles, unanimity was required for creating the association and for amending any of its provisions.

Articles of Confederation As the name suggests, the Articles provided government for a confederation of separate states and not for a union of a single people. Historically, confederations served limited purposes, particularly defense, and respected the sovereignty of their members. Each member was counted equal, regardless of size, and the consent of each member was judged necessary, regardless of inconvenience. The Articles was a confederation of this sort with most of the real business of governing left to the individual states.

Accordingly, the Continental Congress (usually called just Congress after ratification of the Articles) lacked three essential powers: taxation of states, regulation of trade, and enforcement of law. It could requisition funds, using land values to determine amounts due (though no assessment was ever taken), but it relied on the states to raise the funds through taxes levied on their citizens. It could enter into commercial treaties with foreign governments, but states retained the right to impose custom duties and restrictions on imports and exports. It also could assert command over the member parts, stating confidently that the "Articles of Confederation shall be inviolably observed by every state." But unless it was prepared

United States and Its Western Territory, 1787

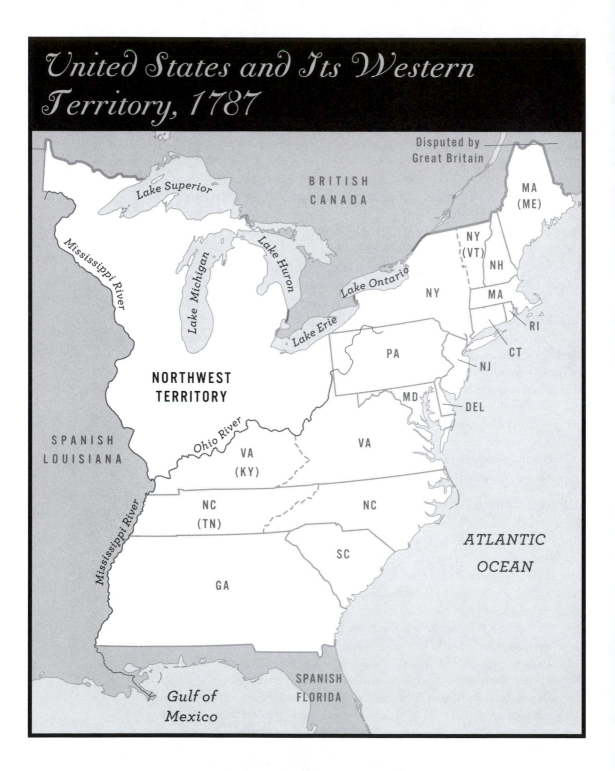

Disputed by Great Britain

BRITISH CANADA

Lake Superior

Lake Michigan

Lake Huron

Lake Ontario

Lake Erie

Mississippi River

NORTHWEST TERRITORY

SPANISH LOUISIANA

Ohio River

Mississippi River

MA (ME)

NY (VT)

NH

NY

MA

RI

CT

NJ

PA

MD

DEL

VA (KY)

VA

NC (TN)

NC

SC

GA

ATLANTIC OCEAN

Gulf of Mexico

SPANISH FLORIDA

to go the war against noncomplying states, it had no means of compelling their obedience, nor had it clear authority.

The objective was to keep this central government firmly tethered to the states, lest it become a successor to King George and the British Parliament. Numerous provisions were aimed at achieving just this purpose. First, the "sovereignty, freedom, and independence" of each state was solemnly declared, as was their retention of "every power, jurisdiction and right" not "expressly delegated" to the Congress. Second, congressional members were elected annually, paid by their home states, and subject to rotation (no more than three years of service out of six) and to recall (no fixed term of office preventing early removal); they thus functioned more as ambassadors to a diplomatic body than as legislators expected to deliberate and pass laws. Third, important matters (e.g., engaging in war; entering into treaties; coining, borrowing, or appropriating money; provisioning an army; appointing a commander-in-chief) required a majority of nine delegations; and, as mentioned, amendments to the constitution required the unanimous consent of the states.

This government had no executive, other than the Committee of States, which served when Congress was not in session. The committee consisted of one delegate from each state (state delegations contained between two and seven members—state's choice—but they cast a single vote no matter the delegation's size or the state's population). The committee exercised only those powers that a nine-delegation majority chose to bestow on it, provided that no power given was of the sort that required a nine-delegation majority for the Congress itself to exercise (e.g., those powers listed earlier); plus a majority of nine committee members was required before undertaking action. With supermajorities needed both for the granting and for the exercising of power, the Committee of States was an interim executive distinguished by its enfeeblement.

The weakness of the Continental Congress was therefore by design, plain for all to see, and a cause of regular complaint by those who had a war to run or a peace to organize. But from another perspective, the government was amazingly strong and a radical departure from confederations past. For example: (1) The Confederation's purpose was, per usual, the common defense, but it was additionally concerned with the security of liberty and the promotion of the general welfare. Toward the end of promoting the general welfare, Congress created a national bank, even though the power to do so was nowhere "expressly delegated." (2) The Confederation guaranteed the free citizens of each state the same "privileges and immunities of the free citizens of the several states"; and it guaranteed that "full faith and credit" would be given by each state to the "records, acts, and judicial proceedings" of every other state. (3) Prohibitions were imposed on the states respecting foreign and military policy, while the debts of the states were assumed by the Confederation. (4) The Continental Congress was unicameral rather than bicameral, with no second-chamber senate to halt or delay the work of a first-chamber house. (5) Congress established courts to adjudicate international and interstate disputes, but nothing like a separate and independent court system existed outside of Congress's control; furthermore, Congress supervised the selection of commissioners to ad hoc courts of final appeal. Finally, (6) the ceding of western territories made the settlement of these territories the Confederation's business. This enlargement of purpose and this concentration of power could, over time, result in the Congress's overawing the states, and those who wished the central government to be subordinate worried that it potentially was supreme.

That development did not come to pass, however, because decentralizing forces prevailed and because the career of the Congress was cut short. In all areas but two, Congress was seen by its critics as too weak for its responsibilities. The two exceptions were the organization of the western territories and the creation of a national bureaucracy.

Northwest Ordinances The West—or Northwest—was organized by a series of ordinances. The first was authored by Thomas Jefferson in 1784, after Virginia renewed its 1781 cession of land, dropping many of the restrictions that had made acceptance and implementation of the cession impossible. By the terms of this ordinance, the land northwest of the Ohio River was to be divided into ten territories, to be governed democratically by their inhabitants, and to be admitted to the Confederation upon reaching populations equal to the smallest state. Congress approved Jefferson's draft with some revisions, including elimination of Jefferson's suggested territorial names (e.g., Assenissipia) and removal of a provision prohibiting slavery after 1800. The '84 Ordinance was, however, incomplete legislation, as it stopped short of providing for the survey of the territories or for the sale of lands.

The Ordinance of 1785 filled this gap. It created townships six-square miles in size, divided into thirty-six one-square mile sections. The central section of each township was set aside for public education, and other sections were reserved for war veterans. Both whole townships and individual sections were sold at auction at the floor price of $1 an acre. Under Jefferson's ordinance land was to be free to settlers. But no longer was Congress that generous because it needed money, and speculators were gathering with cash in hand.

Between the '85 Ordinance and the Ordinance of 1787, the last of the three, western settlement was driven by land speculators, most especially by New Englanders organized as the Ohio Company. They offered to buy up a million dollars of war certificates in exchange for a million and a half acres of southeastern Ohio, just beyond where the surveyors had gone. Congress agreed, once some of its members were included in a subsequent land deal. In the meantime, Indian tribes, weakened by the war, were prevailed on to surrender their titles (which they never supposed they had) through a series of one-sided treaties.

But outpacing both the Congress and the speculators were settlers unwilling to wait for titles or to buy the land they already occupied. So alarmed was Congress by the inflow of squatters and the lawlessness reputed of them that its Ordinance of 1787 altered the plan for territorial government, replacing immediate democratic self-rule with temporary colonial administration. Congress appointed a governor, secretary, and three judges to administer the respective territories of the North-west, reduced in number from Jefferson's proposed ten to between three and five (five states were eventually created). An assembly was allowed once the territory reached a free adult male population of five thousand, but its lawmaking power was restricted, first by a legislative council chosen by the Congress from nominees supplied by the assembly, and second by the governor exercising an absolute veto. The ordinance invited admission to statehood for territories with populations of sixty thousand or more. It also included a bill of rights with guarantees of religious freedom, habeas corpus, trial by jury, and so on; and, most important—for the country's future politics—it prohibited slavery, going beyond Jefferson's original proposal by eliminating the sixteen-year delay.

The three ordinances did not apply to lands south of the Ohio and east of the Mississippi rivers. Because these territories were ceded late to the Congress, state governments and enterprising settlers effectively made policy there. Otherwise, the organizational model developed by the Northwest Ordinances governed west-ward expansion all the way to the Pacific.

National Bureaucracy. In the early years of the Revolution, before ratification of the Articles, Congress tried serving as its own bureaucracy. Administrative affairs were handled directly by committees of delegates or by employees under their close supervision. The burden was overwhelming (John Adams served on eighty or so committees), and those less anxious about executive power urged appointment of single executives to oversee departments already in oper-ation. By the end of 1781 their objective was achieved. Robert Livingston was appointed secretary of foreign affairs, Benjamin Lincoln secretary of war, and Rob-ert Morris superintendent of finance. The post office department had existed since 1775; its first postmaster general was Benjamin Franklin, who had served in that capacity during colonial days. Livingston and Lincoln resigned soon after their appointments, to be replaced by John Jay and Henry Knox, respectively, each a more consequential successor devoted to the cause of strengthening the national government. But the most ardent nationalist and most consequential of the early secretaries was easily Robert Morris, whose financial genius kept the war effort solvent and the army supplied, in part by persuading Congress to char-ter the **Bank of North America**. After the war he was a strong voice in favor of taxation, debt management, and new borrowing to tie credi-tors to the government, but he was thwarted by his political enemies who accused him (with some cause) of corruption. When he resigned in 1784, a board of commissioners replaced him, because his immense influence reminded people of why they feared executive power and centralized government.

Established in 1781, the **Bank of North America** was a commercial bank funded by the sale of shares to private stockholders. It was the country's first central bank, receiving government deposits and issuing promissory notes redeemable for gold or silver.

State Constitutions

As indicated by the fact that Congress rarely could muster a quorum, political energy in the war and postwar years focused on the states. Even before independence was declared, and long before it was won, the colonies turned to the business of drafting constitutions and setting up governments.

Three types of constitutions were attempted, with Pennsylvania, Virginia, and Massachusetts serving as models for other states. The Pennsylvania constitution, adopted in September 1776, came nearest in form to the Articles, insofar as it paired a unicameral legislature with a twelve-person executive council. It extended voting privileges widely to all taxpaying males and their adult (nontaxpaying) sons, and it eliminated property qualifications (though not religious qualifications) for office holding. Annual elections, rotation in office (i.e., term limits), and proportional representation kept the government bound tightly to the people. An unusual element was the Council of Censors, an institution revived from the republics of the ancient world. Charged with defending the constitution inviolate, this elected body met every seven years to review the performance of the government, censuring officials and ordering impeachments in cases of perceived abuse; to recommend the repeal of legislation deemed unconstitutional; and to call for a convention to amend the constitution if changes were in order. Liberal Europeans lauded the democratic purity of the Pennsylvania constitution, and years later French revolutionaries copied its unicameralism when writing their constitution of 1791. By then, however, Pennsylvania had adopted a new constitution, one with bicameralism and a governor and without the Council of Censors.

Pennsylvania represented the democratic extreme, and only Georgia and the territory of Vermont followed its lead. Virginia provided the more common model. Legislative supremacy (a principle taken from John Locke) was the defining feature of its constitution, with executive and judicial power placed in decidedly subordinate positions. There was a single governor, but he was dependent on the legislature for his election and reelection and encumbered by a body of advisers, called the Council of State. Elected annually, the governor was eligible to serve for no more than three years out of seven, and he had no veto. Colonial experience associated executive office with the tyranny of the royal governors and the British Crown. Most state constitutions, therefore, erected barriers against executive power and looked to legislatures as guardians of the people's liberties. Judicial power, though less suspect than executive power, was also constrained. High court judges in Virginia were appointed by the legislature, and the legislature routinely intruded into controversies that were properly judicial. While the Virginia constitution paid homage to the principle of separated powers and divided its legislature into two chambers, the concentration of power in the legislature's hands was so conspicuous that Thomas Jefferson, writing in his *Notes on the State of Virginia,* called the Virginia General Assembly an elective despotism in the making ("One hundred and seventy-three despots would surely be as oppressive as one").

Jefferson criticized the similarity of the two houses of the assembly (claiming that homogeneous chambers defeated the point of having two), denounced the unrepresentative character of the assembly's composition, and worried over the assembly's subsequent practice of altering the constitution by ordinary statute and of reducing the number required for a quorum.

The Massachusetts constitution came several years later (1780), after experience had revealed the shortcomings of state constitutions in effect elsewhere. John Adams was its principal author; a special convention, democratically based, voted its adoption; and the citizens assembled in town meetings ratified it. In respect of the principle that concentrated power is a danger to liberty (even when vested in the people), the Massachusetts constitution separated power among three branches of government and safeguarded the independence of each:

> In the government of this Commonwealth, the legislative department shall never exercise the executive and judicial powers, or either of them: The executive shall never exercise the legislative and judicial powers, or either of them: The judicial shall never exercise the legislative and executive powers, or either of them: to the end it may be a government of laws and not of men.

The legislature, called the General Court, was divided into a senate and a house, chambers that the constitution differentiated inferentially as the representative bodies of wealth and numbers, respectively. The apportionment of senators among electoral districts varied according to the taxes they paid, and **property qualifications** were in place for voters (£60 estate) as well as for officeholders (£600 estate). While the same threshold defined the electorate for representatives, a much smaller threshold was needed for office holding in the lower house (£200). Elections were annual for both houses. The governor (whose property qualification stood at £1,000) was elected annually by the people (not by the legislature) and was eligible for indefinite reelection (without any consecutive-term restriction). He possessed a qualified veto and was empowered to summon and adjourn the legislature. There was a governor's council to serve as an advisory board, but it met, or not, at the governor's discretion. Judges were appointed by the governor for life terms (though subject to impeachment) and received fixed salaries not reducible by the legislature.

By such measures as these did Massachusetts institute stable, if not entirely popular, government. It might fairly be said that the constitution of Massachusetts provided the prototype for the Constitution of the United States, just as the constitution of Pennsylvania provided the prototype for the Articles of Confederation.

Legislative Abuses

Beneath the celebrated work of founding lay the less glamorous task of governing, and if the states were uneven framers of constitutions, they were incompetent makers of law. Such at least was the opinion of James Madison. In his "Vices of the Political System of the United

Property qualifications and other assorted details for all state constitutions are provided in Appendix D.

States," a memorandum written on the eve of the Constitutional Convention (April 1787), Madison charged the states with three vices related to their lawmaking power: multiplicity of laws, mutability of law, and injustice of laws. The states had engaged in a "luxuriancy of legislation," said Madison, creating in the few years since independence as many new laws as in the entire century preceding. Because law imposes limitations on personal freedom, the number of laws should be few, not many; unnecessary laws—beyond those required to prescribe the duties of citizens and to circumscribe the discretion of magistrates—are a "nuisance," he contended. Frequent changes in laws deprive legislators of the wisdom born of experience and deceive and ensnare citizens subject to their penalties. Finally, the injustice of laws Madison traced to human selfishness and majority rule in polities the size of America's states (about which see "Court Republicanism," later in this part).

The special problem of the mid-1780s was currency. It came in many forms (pounds, doubloons, dollars, crowns, pistoles, johanneses, moidores), it was easily counterfeited, and there was too little of it. Especially burdened were farmers, who needed to borrow, and debtors, who needed specie to satisfy their creditors. Failure to pay often meant sentence to **debtors' prison**. To the degree that state governments fell into the hands of the farming and debtor interests, pressure built to provide relief through paper-money issues. Seven states were so afflicted, none more so than Rhode Island. In 1786 the legislature there ordered the emission of bills of credit worth nominally £100,000 to be divided among towns according to taxes levied and loaned out to freeholders in equal shares. This paper money was designated legal tender, and creditors were obliged to accept it in payment of debts owed. When creditors refused, closing shops and hiding out to avoid being paid in inflated scrip, the legislature passed a "tender law" regulating offers to pay money. By this act, borrowers could use the county courts to remit their debts, and lenders were required to accept the deposits or have their loans declared repaid and the deposits appropriated by the state. In subsequent legislation, noncooperating creditors were fined and denied their right of trial by jury. The legislature even attempted using this scrip to pay congressional requisitions, but the Continental Congress rejected the payment. Finally a test case was brought before the state supreme court (*Trevett v. Weeden*, 1787), which pitted an indebted meat lover against his credit-extending butcher. In what was one of the first exercises of judicial review, the court ruled that the legislature had acted unconstitutionally in denying the butcher his right of trial by jury. A Rhode Island delegate to the Continental Congress expressed disgust on learning that he would be paid his salary in the state's paper script, worth in New York one sixth its face value: "A more infamous set of men under the Character of a Legislature, never, I believe, disgraced the Annals of the World."

Rhode Island was the most egregious case and became the butt of jokes told throughout the nation. Other states electing to issue paper

On court order, persons who had fallen into debt could be incarcerated in **debtors' prison** until, by their forced labor or their raising of outside funds, they paid back all of what they owed.

money proceeded more deliberately, avoiding backlash and depreciation of the currency. The Pennsylvania State House was partly financed by paper money.

Annapolis Convention

In his "Vices of the Political System," Madison listed paper money as an instance of one state's trespassing on the rights of another. Also on that list were commercial regulations showing favoritism to local manufacturing and placing the products of neighboring states on a par with those of foreign countries. Hostility of this sort, he lamented, was contrary to the spirit of union.

Washington was likewise alarmed by the failure of states to cooperate even on matters of mutual interest. To address this problem as it affected Virginia and Maryland, he offered his home at Mount Vernon for a conference to discuss navigation and fishing rights on the Potomac River and Chesapeake Bay (1785). Resolutions were agreed on by negotiators and then by the states represented, including Pennsylvania, which was invited late to the meeting. Pleased by the result, Maryland proposed hosting a conference to address wider commercial questions, with Delaware included. This group of four neighboring states subsequently grew to all thirteen on the urging of Virginia, whose legislature was moved to think nationally by Madison. September 1786 was the chosen date for the conference; Annapolis, Maryland, the chosen site. But only five states sent delegations. Even Maryland stayed away, as sentiment in the state swung back in a localist direction. The conference was therefore stymied from the start. But Alexander Hamilton, representing New York, used the disappointing turnout to propose a still wider conference—a constitutional convention in fact—to be held the following spring in Philadelphia, its stated purpose being "to render the constitution of the federal government adequate to the exigencies of the Union."

Shays' Rebellion

Enthusiasm for a constitutional overhaul was not immediate. Congress waited until February before grudgingly giving its blessing. Even among nationalists, support was sluggish until galvanized by events in Massachusetts that winter. The paper-money craze had been resisted by the Massachusetts legislature, where Boston merchants exerted much influence. In the western counties, however, and among the state's farming poor, paper money and other debt-relief measures enjoyed considerable popularity. Such people came increasingly to view the government in Boston as the reincarnation of the British Parliament, its laws and taxes enacted tyrannically without effective representation of "colonists" living at a distance. They petitioned this "foreign" government, as they had the Parliament in the **resistance years**, only to have their pleas, once again, go unheeded. When the legislature adjourned

The **resistance years** were 1764 to 1774 (and just beyond), when Americans were in open protest against British colonial policy but before serious fighting had begun.

its 1786 session without providing tangible assistance, mob violence erupted in numerous towns across the state. Courts were closed in Northampton, jails broken open in Great Barrington, and judges forced to sign pledges not to proceed with foreclosures in Taunton and elsewhere. These anarchic outbursts turned insurrectionary when a band of twelve hundred farmers descended on the Springfield armory seeking munitions. Their leader was Daniel Shays, a war veteran suffering, like many others, from debts and taxes. The armory, though, withstood Shays' assault, as the local militia scattered the attackers with a single shot of cannon fire. Boston had organized a much larger force under the command of Benjamin Lincoln, who succeeded in tracking down the insurgents and arresting their leaders (Shays excepted, who had taken refuge in Vermont). By spring, the uprising was mostly over. Afterward, the legislature decided to deal leniently with all involved and to accede to some of their demands.

Outside of Massachusetts the alarm was sounded with equal urgency, the point made excitedly that Congress had failed to assist Massachusetts in its hour of need. George Washington was among those whose mind fixed on national remedies in response to the peril posed by Shays' Rebellion; and James Madison used the insurrection to persuade Washington to attend the convention in Philadelphia.

There was, of course, some dissension from the building belief that dissolution now threatened the country. Benjamin Franklin, recently returned from Europe, made light of the disturbance in Massachusetts, as did Thomas Jefferson, who wrote breezily from Paris (where he was serving as America's ambassador) that "The tree of liberty must be refreshed from time to time with the blood of patriots and tyrants."

Critical Period

Opinion was divided over the condition and prospects of the country—over whether, as a later historian put it, the 1780s had been a "critical period" in the new country's history.[2] Most people acknowledged that the federal government under the Articles was "[in]adequate to the exigencies of the Union." They differed as to whether a modest repair or a radical transformation was required to set matters straight. The optimists noted that Americans had adjusted to hard economic times and that material life was now improving, partly as a result of the virtuous habits developed; that the western territories were being settled and the national debt was being paid down (albeit slowly) with proceeds from the sale of lands; that crop prices were rising and trade was expanding (all the way to China), despite diplomatic setbacks and embarrassments like ship seizures by the Barbary pirates; and that colleges were being established (a quick doubling of the number), literature was being written, dictionaries and spellers were compiled (Noah Webster's *American Dictionary* and *American Spelling-Book*), religion was being reformed, and arts and sciences were taken up. Perhaps this progress to date did not constitute a renaissance, but neither did it signal a dark ages.

The pessimists emphasized the weakness of the Continental Congress and the record of failed attempts to make it even marginally stronger; the fiscal irresponsibility of state governments run by factious and small-minded politicians; their disregard for treaties and the contempt in which the country was held by foreign powers, who anticipated dismemberment and the opportunity to pick over the carcass of what to them appeared to be a wholly improbable union; and the danger of armed minorities making common cause with the disfranchised poor to impose their will on lawful majorities to the defeat of the republican principle. One contemporary expressed his disappointment thus:

> The commencement of peace was likewise the commencement of our distress and disgrace. Devoid of power, we could neither prevent the excessive importations which lately deluged the country, nor even raise from that excess a contribution to the public revenue; devoid of importance, we were unable to command a sale for our commodities in a foreign market; devoid of credit, our public securities were melting in the hands of their deluded owners, like snow before the sun; devoid of dignity, we were inadequate to perform treaties on our own part, or to compel a performance on the part of a contradicting nation.[3]

The two camps, therefore, differed in their assessments and predictions. But underlying these opposing sets of fact and speculation were opposing opinions regarding the nature and requirements of republican government.

REPUBLICAN THEORY AT THE TIME OF THE FOUNDING

Empowering Government and Safeguarding Liberty

The word *republic* is from the Latin *res publica*, meaning "the public business." A republic is generally any regime that makes the common good its public business and in which the public business is not the exclusive province of a prince. A republic is best defined therefore by what it is not: it is not a despotism in purpose or an absolute monarchy in form. But neither is it quite a democracy. *Democracy* is Greek for "people power." A democracy, strictly speaking, is a regime in which the people make and execute law directly and where the people assembled have final say and are the sovereign power. During America's founding period, democratic government was in bad order, thought to be a proven failure of the past and a certain recipe for disaster in the present. Americans typically avoided the term, preferring to call their governments "republics" instead, though the designation had as yet no precise and settled meaning. It merely implied a measure of popular control over the actions of government, not government by the people.

What Americans wanted and defined themselves by was not democracy but liberty. It was for liberty that they had sacrificed, fought, and died. Liberty meant to them, first, personal independence, which rested, they believed, on ownership of private property (the freehold farm especially); and secure property, they reasoned, required protection from taxes imposed by parties not accountable to the people taxed ("No Taxation without Representation"). Liberty, second, meant individual rights against the predatory power of others. Such predators might be strangers or neighbors engaged in acts of aggression or trespass, in which case government existed to provide protection and redress. Or predators might be agents of the government itself, in which case liberty meant, third, the public right of supervising government. The British government, during the Seven Years' War (1756–63), defended American colonists from the aggression of the French army and its Indian allies. But after the war, the actions of that same government, Americans concluded, were what put their liberties most at risk. They looked about for protection from their putative protector only to discover that no effective protection availed. In the process they discovered the central problem of republican theory: *having enough power for safety while preventing that power from endangering liberty.*

How did the Americans attempt to resolve this problem? They began with a statement of first principles, declaring as self-evident truths of natural law "that all men are created equal; that they are endowed by their Creator with certain inalienable rights; that among these are life, liberty, and the pursuit of happiness." From this opening insight regarding human nature and divine benefaction came luminous clarity as to the true purpose and origin of government. For it is "to secure these rights," they proclaimed, "that governments are instituted among men, deriving their just powers from the consent of the governed." It thus follows, they deduced, that government's power is for the sake of people's rights; also that government's power originates in people's consent—because equal people cannot be made obligated and subordinate except by their free agreement. And even though government and people remain separate and unequal entities (the one invested with the power, the other endowed with rights), the people's enduring sovereignty is nonetheless affirmed, insofar as the people remain the judges of whether any form of government has become destructive of society's ends; at which point—the point of revolution—"it is the right of the people to alter or to abolish it, and to institute new government, laying its foundation on such principles, and organizing its powers in such form, as to them shall seem most likely to effect their safety and happiness."

These pronouncements from the Declaration of Independence echoed arguments in John Locke's *Second Treatise*, a book written in justification of the English people's revolt against their own form of government. But the fact that both the Declaration and the *Second Treatise* moved from idealized principles of political theory to the desperate measure of revolution, meant that the dual problem of empowering government and of controlling government had not been fully addressed. What was there between words and war to achieve republicanism's overarching objective?

In the American context two solutions presented themselves, and they largely determined the factional split that emerged around the framing of the Constitution.

Country Republicanism

Country republicanism constituted one of the factions. The term *country* comes from English thought and politics. It was coined during the reign of Charles I, second of the Stuart kings, to identify and disparage persons of a "backward" turn of mind who objected to centralized government and its ever-expanding powers. The term later attached to the Whig party when in the 1670s it formed to prevent James, the Catholic brother of Charles II, from ascending to the throne. This effort, called the Exclusionary Crisis, failed in its immediate purpose, but it succeeded soon after, deposing James in a bloodless coup known as the Glorious Revolution. Opposing the Whigs were the Tories, who supported the Stuart monarchy in Parliament.

In the eighteenth century, the Whig party was ascendant, the Tories having been reduced to minority status because of their resistance to the Hanoverian succession, which cost them the backing of the monarchy, their natural ally. The Hanovers were a German branch of the royal family, brought in to reign when the Stuart line came to an end with Queen Anne. The first of the Hanovers was George I. He and his successor son, George II, ceded operational control of the government to a minister named Robert Walpole, who held office (as Britain's first de facto prime minister) from 1721 to 1742. Those in opposition to the Walpole ministry and adopting an outsiders' mentality toward government were called the Country faction of the Whig party. Those in support of the ministry and enjoying the spoils of patronage were called the Court faction. Country politicians were often of the landed gentry, while Court politicians represented the mercantile and financial classes resident in London.

These facts from long ago and faraway mattered in late-colonial America because the writings of Country oppositionists supplied the patriots with many of their arguments for independence. And the case patriots made in the resistance years to prove corruption and tyranny in the British government was in turn applied prospectively to

STUART DYNASTY

James I (r. 1603–25)
Charles I (r. 1625–49)

CIVIL WARS AND COMMONWEALTH

Oliver Cromwell, Lord Protector (1653–58)

STUART RESTORATION

Charles II (r. 1660–85)
James II (r. 1685–88)

GLORIOUS REVOLUTION

William and Mary of Orange (r. 1688–1702)
Anne (r. 1702–14)

HANOVERIAN DYNASTY

George I (r. 1714–27)
George II (r. 1727–60)
George III (r. 1760–20)...
...Elizabeth II (r. 1952–)

the American government of the Confederation era, with supporters warning of dangers sure to follow from concentrated power and imperial ambition. More precisely, a group of patriots issued these warnings, those persons previously denominated Confederalists.

From the Country perspective, society is composed of an undifferentiated populace and the government that rules over it. The government is pointedly not *of* the people or *by* the people; and while it might claim to be *for* the people, it more commonly is viewed as a foreign body and oppressor power. The English monarchy at the time of George III was a lineal descendance of Norman invaders who conquered the island and imposed their alien rule on the Anglo-Saxon population (Battle of Hastings, 1066). That rule was near absolute until a century and a half later when the people's lost liberties were slowly reclaimed. Magna Carta (1215) marked the beginning of the process; the English Civil Wars (1642–51) and the Glorious Revolution (1688) marked the triumph, for with these latter events, Parliament emerged as a power equal to the monarchy. Government by kingly prerogative thus gave way to "king-in-parliament" constitutionalism by which the assent of both bodies was needed for the making of law. The practice also took hold, during this roughly five-hundred-year period, of stipulating the people's (or social classes's) rights against the government.

This story of liberty lost and regained is called the Whig Theory of History. It reads as a cautionary tale warning of an eternal war between the people's liberty and the government's power. It begins by postulating the uniformity of human nature and the selfishness of all human beings. But it then adds the qualifier that uniform humanity divides into groups of few and many because of differing opportunities for gain. The governing classes, positioned to acquire and oppress, are distinct from the common poor, confined to procuring daily necessities in the struggle for existence. The few, typically, are depicted as privileged and greedy, the many as honest folk wanting not to be oppressed. Machiavelli, a sixteenth-century Italian political philosopher, was the source of these insights (e.g., his *Discourses on Livy*, I.3; *The Prince*, 9), and Country writers cited him frequently. From Machiavelli they also learned that the people must be vigilant in defense of their liberties, must develop, in other words, a "Don't-Tread-on-Me" sense of pride and prickliness, because the ruling great are persistently "malignant" (Machiavelli's word), conspiring for domination even when appearing to be generous and public minded. Accordingly, the true republican spirit is suspicious and jealous of power, quick to believe that conspiracy is afoot and that base motives actuate persons in office. The American patriots interpreted Parliament's passing of the Sugar Tax, Stamp Tax, and Townshend Duties, not as sensible attempts to pay off war debts with the revenues raised, but as steps in a comprehensive strategy designed to subject Americans to arbitrary power.

The remedy proposed by the Declaration of Independence—that of overthrowing oppressive government and instituting new government—is no real solution because the same antithesis obtains. It matters little that consent has replaced coercion, for those holding power will just as surely be corrupted by it. "Power corrupts, and absolute power corrupts absolutely," says a nineteenth-century adage out of the same school of thought. Thus, safeguards are always needed, especially against the executive. Containing the executive by elevating the legislative is the first precaution to take, as it was for Locke (*Second Treatise*, XI, sec. 134; XIII, secs. 150–52). But legislators are also wielders of power, so they too must be closely watched. Annual elections in small electoral districts, rotation in office, and instruction and recall of delegates are proven ways of tying lawmakers to the citizenry. Another way is the convention that supplants the legislature or even the crowd without that intimidates the representatives within (e.g., the Pennsylvania militiamen). And because the people's vigilance requires a clear understanding of who is in charge and who bears responsibility, simple government with a unicameral legislature might be the wiser way to go.

Above all, government must not entertain grand ambitions of conquest, splendor, and glory, because these aspirations are incompatible with liberty. A liberty-loving people want to be left alone to work their farms, raise their families, and enjoy life's simple pleasures. They trade their liberty for servitude if obliged to pay the taxes and accept the regimentation required for national greatness (a modification of Machiavelli developed by republican writers, or "commonwealthmen," of the English Civil War period).

The Country Whig saw history as moving in cycles of growth and decay (this too an inheritance from Machiavelli and, before him, from the Greek historian Polybius). Progress is always followed by decline, because civic virtue (duty, sacrifice, piety, obedience) is always corrupted by societal success. As people succeed at guarding against danger and necessity, they let down their guard against their own vices. In other words, the more secure and prosperous a society becomes, the more selfish and complacent become its citizens; and losing the virtue that once made it vigorous and whole, society slides ineluctably into dissipation and disarray. A society is healthy at or near its beginning, when necessity is palpable and working to make people good. Society reaches meridian when strength combines with virtue to produce moderate, sustainable growth. This civilizational highpoint cannot be maintained in perpetuity, however; the cycle prevents it. But it can be prolonged by periodic returns to first principles—that is, by renewals of the patriotic spirit alive when the political community was fresh and young. Constitutional conventions, or a council of censors, as tried in postcolonial Pennsylvania, can be the instruments by which departures from founding principles are corrected, or the instruments by which adjustments are made to fit institutions of government to the declining virtue of the people (*Discourses on Livy*, I.18, III.1). A healthy society is suited for republican institutions because these depend directly on the people's virtue. An unhealthy society must eventually

> *History is cyclical—rise and decline—not linear and progressive, and returning to one's past is the proper way of building one's future.*

submit to despotism because widespread wickedness can only be suppressed by absolute power. Ancient Rome is the model: republican in its rise to eminence; caesarian in its decline and fall.

Country republicanism evinces, therefore, a preference for the primitive. The rustic traits of simplicity, frugality, fortitude, perseverance, industry, common sense, and self-reliance are highly prized as manifestations of civic virtue; whereas the urbane traits of sophistication, luxuriance, gentility, innovation, leisure, learning, and interdependence are reprobated as tokens of societal corruption. America was never more virtuous than when the thirteen colonies protested British tyranny by choosing to boycott British imports (Non-Importation Agreement, 1774). Conversely, America experienced a quick waning of its virtue when military victory and economic prosperity gave license to selfish indulgence. If America was to have a republican future, thought Country republicans, it needed, first, to break free of decadent Europe; and it needed, second, to maintain the political integrity of the small, homogeneous, agrarian community, such as was guaranteed to the states under the Articles of Confederation.

The small republic is the only polity conducive to virtue and compatible with liberty. History proved as much, with no examples of extensive republics to offer. So too did theory, particularly in the writings of the celebrated Montesquieu (*The Spirit of the Laws*). Montesquieu was everyone's authority on the subject of separated powers, but he was the authority of Country republicans on the subject of confederation and associational size. According to the Montesquieuian formula, an empire requires despotic government, a moderate state monarchical government, and a small state republican government (VIII.16–17, 19–20). Pertinent statements regarding size are these: "It is natural for a republic to have only a small territory. . . . In an extensive republic, the public good is sacrificed to a thousand private views. . . . In a small one, the interest of the public is more obvious, better understood, and more within reach of every citizen" (VIII.16). The common good is thought to be the special benefit of republics and the special obligation of republican citizens, whose virtue consists precisely in their devotion to the commonweal and their willing sacrifice of private interests. Preferring the public to the private, always a difficult undertaking for naturally selfish human beings, is greatly facilitated if one's private good approximates the public good by being common to others. Subsistence farmers have similar interests, few in number; consequently an agrarian community, if kept small, is easily united and ruled. Factions there do not jockey for advantage and strive against each other, because in such a community factionalism does not much exist, only the one public interest shared in equally by all. Rousseau offered a similar vision of republican society in his *On the Social Contract*.

No American state, however, was so small as to be democratically governed, since democracy is direct rule by the people assembled. Nothing larger than a city-state can accept democracy, so defined, and even Rhode Island was larger than that. But some portion of popular rule can still be salvaged by use of representation. In fact, representative democracy was one definition of a republic current at the time. New problems do emerge with representation, but the solution to these problems points again to small republics.

Country republicanism propagates the **agent** theory of representation—that is, elected officials bound to the people and acting in their place.

For example, a free people live under laws to which they give their consent. To be free, while lawmaking indirectly, the people require representatives who think like themselves, representatives with similar backgrounds, sentiments, and interests—that is, representatives who are their **agents**. Firsthand acquaintance with the characters of representatives and with the lives of constituents is needed, respectively, by each. The number of representatives therefore matters because too few can never know so much or be known by so many. On the other hand, a legislative multitude cannot deliberate productively. An extensive republic will either have too few representatives for proper understanding of and sympathy with the people's interests or too many representatives for efficient lawmaking. Only a small republic can satisfy this requirement of liberty.

Representatives who resemble the people better command the people's confidence, and a trusting public more willingly obeys laws enacted by them. While trust is always a danger, it is less so when rulers and ruled are substantially alike. And when they are alike, or to the degree that they are, the ready obedience offered by the people permits a reduction in the coercive force applied by the government. An uncoerced population is free; a coerced population is servile. One sure measure of liberty's demise is the presence of a standing army in times of peace. Large states have recourse to standing armies and are despotically governed; small states rely on citizen militias and are free republics.

Large states have governing offices attractive to the ambitious, and they have governing officers too concealed from the people's oversight. As the distance widens between rulers and ruled, supervision of rulers decreases as does their removal and replacement with others, while opportunities for deceit and oppression increase. Once again, liberty depends on keeping the republic small.

But small republics, so a counterargument goes, are defenseless against larger states, and because defeat in war will cost a people their liberty just as surely as will oppression by a tyrant, smallness is not a practical option. There is, though, a remedy, known and practiced by the ancients: to wit, a confederation of small republics, where the united whole provides protection from

A free republic is small and agrarian, has a government like its people, and is defended by a citizen militia with help from other republics joined in a defensive alliance.

dangers without, and the independent parts provide governance consistent with liberty within. Furthermore, Montesquieu concurred, saying: "As this government [confederation] is composed of petty [small] republics, it enjoys the internal happiness of each; and with regard to its external situation, by means of the association, it possesses all the advantages of large monarchies" (IX.1).

In sum, America under the Articles of Confederation already possessed the regime that theory and practice had shown to be best at preserving the people's liberty. If the Confederation fell short on the point of providing security, a few amendments would suffice to correct the problem.

The greatest peril lay in overcorrection, in discarding the confederation model of small republics tied loosely together and replacing it with one extensive republic presided over by a power-hungry government. Nothing in theory or practice suggested that this novel form of union and governance was compatible with liberty.

Country republicans in America, at the time of the convention, went by no one name, but were alternately called localists, states' rights advocates, or confederals (changed to "Confederalists" for the game). After the convention they were called Antifederalists (see "Terms in Use" in Appendix C).

Court Republicanism

Those persons previously referred to as Nationalists—and soon to be known as Federalists—made up the Court faction in America. Not that there was a court in America, or anyone who favored creating one—all were patriots espousing republican principles. Still, this British appellation identified parties whose experience during the Confederation era argued strongly in favor of strengthening the central government: officers in the Continental Army, bureaucrats attached to the Congress, delegates whose horizons reached beyond the states. In Britain, the Court faction consisted of Whigs who had reconciled to the necessity of augmented executive power and who were unfazed by, or less apprehensive about, the corruption that attended upon monarchy—for example, parliamentarians in the pay of the Crown. Charged by Country oppositionists with backsliding from the settlement of the Glorious Revolution, they thought of themselves as realists and modernizers who understood the value of public debt funded by taxes, chartered banks with monopoly privileges, and professional armies able to prosecute the nation's wars. Their American counterparts, not yet so "modern," wanted simply a federal government more competent than the Continental Congress. In the 1790s, when the faction matured, they more closely resembled the Court party in Britain and were called "monocrats" by their opponents.

Court republicans were less inclined to rail against power or to view it as the enemy of liberty. After all, power was now in the hands of the people, whose sovereignty, while dormant in the matter of lawmaking, was active in the matter of electing, renewing, and cashiering lawmakers. Constant suspiciousness of officeholders regularly accountable to the people, they argued, is nearer to paranoia than to vigilance. One Court republican, of considerable repute, put the matter thusly:

> It is agreed on all hands that no government can be well administered without powers; yet the instant these are delegated, although those who are entrusted with the administration are no more than the creatures of the people . . . amenable for every false step they take, they are, from the moment they receive it, set down

as tyrants; their natures, one would conceive from this, immediately changed, and that they could have no other disposition but to oppress.[4]

Court republicans conceded some truth to the maxim that power corrupts, but they also noted that power can ennoble when placed in the hands of meritorious individuals. These talented few—or "natural aristocrats" as both Jefferson and Adams called them—deserve the people's confidence and deference, not their jealousy and ingratitude. The nation requires the services of its finest citizens, whose ambition and love of fame ought to be viewed as honorable qualities useful to the public. Representatives should be a cut above the electorate they represent—not, as the opposition says, the same as and no better than—because their task is to deliberate about the public good and to fashion sensible programs by which to achieve it. Country republicans contradicted themselves when they posited a homogenous, faction-free community in love with the common good and then demanded the selection of populist representatives committed to the advancement of local interests. A more consistent republicanism, supposing this commonality of interests, would disconnect representatives from electoral districts and from responsibility toward particular groups of constituents. Such representatives would be **trustees** of the commonweal.

> Court republicanism propagates the **trustee** theory of representation—that is, elected officials entrusted to use their own judgment in advancing the common good.

The better way of guarding against corruption and abuse is through separation of powers in a complex government. Most Americans acknowledged the value of separated powers—genuflecting before the altar of Montesquieu—but many Americans, in particular Country republicans, thought that separation was sufficiently accomplished with prohibitions on multiple office holding—that is, no magistrate who is also a legislator, no legislator who is also a judge. In fact, real separation requires institutional independence, which Country republicans effectively prevented by insisting on subservience of the executive and judicial branches to the legislative power. Being nearest to the people and most worthy of trust, the legislative enjoyed preeminence among Country republicans and was proclaimed by them supreme. But experience had shown that state legislators were no less susceptible to abusing their offices and that to guard against this corruption the citizenry was obliged to exhibit and sustain an impossible degree of vigilance. Hostility toward commerce, prosperity, refinement, and national power followed necessarily because these societal achievements were thought to be corrosive of civic virtue. Frugality, equality, and contrariness were the only qualities allowed to republicans of the Country persuasion. But if institutions could be made to check and balance one another, then the responsibility for watching government need not fall solely on the shoulders of the people. Such institutions, argued Court republicans, can in fact be constructed, by adopting a "new science of politics" that supersedes the virtue-dependent republicanism of old. This new science protects liberty by means of written constitutions, bicameral legislative bodies, independent courts, elected representatives, and

> *Power is more reliably checked and liberty safeguarded when the branches of government watch each other than when a vigilant populace watches the whole.*

enlargements of the association. It does not postulate inevitable decline slowed only by periodic returns to beginnings; it rather is progressive and at peace with cultural development.

The protection of liberty depends both on popular vigilance and on government vigor. But so focused were Country republicans on guarding against government oppression, that they tended to forget the Declaration's stated reason for instituting government—"to secure these rights." Strong, energetic government, properly constituted, is a friend of liberty, because bodies other than government endanger liberty and need government to hold them in check.

In a republic, where voting majorities determine election outcomes, majority rule presents a separate danger to the rights of individuals and minorities. Country republicans failed to notice the problem because they conceived of the people as an undifferentiated mass standing opposite the government. But "all civilized societies," wrote Madison in his "Vices" memorandum, "are divided into different interests and factions, as they happen to be creditors or debtors; rich or poor; husbandmen, merchants or manufacturers; members of different religious sects; followers of different political leaders; owners of different kinds of property, etc., etc." Once a majority forms around a common interest or passion, minorities are defenseless against it and can hope only that the majority somehow controls itself. Self-control, Madison noted, could in theory issue from any of three sources: (1) "a prudent regard to their own [the majority's] good as involved in the good of the general and permanent good of the community," (2) "respect for character," and (3) religion. But these restraints, more often than not, fail to ensure virtuous behavior even in individuals; and in multitudes, Madison cautioned, they are practically useless. No multitude is concerned with reputation, because praise and blame, when spread among so many, dilute to insignificance and because public opinion—that is, majority rule—is the lone arbiter and judge of righteous conduct and so is certain to excuse its own wickedness. Madison posed this question: "Place three individuals in a situation wherein the interest of each depends on the voice of the others, and give to two of them an interest opposed to the rights of the third? Will the latter be secure? . . . . Will two thousand in a like situation be less likely to encroach on the rights of one thousand?"

The remedy for majority tyranny cannot then be supplied from within majorities themselves. But from the outside a remedy avails—for the enlarged size of the republic and the diversity of its interests preclude factions from acting in concert or from attracting enough citizens to achieve majority status. In extended republics (unlike city-states), people live at great distances and are unaware that their passions are felt by others; or they lack the ready means of communicating with others and coordinating actions. Also, in "civilized societies" with diverse interests, no single faction likely equals a majority of the community's population; it therefore must reach out to other parties with whom to form a winning coalition. But the essential instability of coalitions prevents constructed majorities from becoming permanent majorities, and the give-and-take on which coalitions depend prevents the success of agendas that are narrowly selfish and conspicuously unjust.

Now it is the case that where majorities control the lawmaking process, the liberty of the majority is not endangered and is not the problem. The problem rather is the liberty of individuals and of minorities. Republican government, reflecting majority interest, imperils these liberties. But they can be safeguarded by the multiplication of factions, as brought about by the size of the republic, because then no faction exists that is a natural and permanent majority. Country republicans and past political theory thought exactly the opposite—that liberty depended on small republics free of factions. "It may be inferred," Madison suggested, "that the inconveniences of popular states, contrary to the prevailing theory, are in proportion not to the extent, but to the narrowness of their limits."

> *The cure for faction is more of it, not less, as Country republicans propose, hoping in vain to achieve a faction-free republic through simplicity, uniformity, and compactness.*

The role of government, Madison went on to explain, was that of an honest broker or neutral umpire: "The great desideratum in government is such a modification of the sovereignty as will render it sufficiently neutral between the different interests and factions, to control one part of the society from invading the rights of another; and at the same time sufficiently controlled itself, from setting up an interest adverse to that of the whole society." Monarchies achieve the former objective (neutrality respecting groups) but not the latter (prevention of a government interest at variance with the common good); small republics achieve the latter objective (subordination of government to the people's sovereignty) but not the former (protection against majority tyranny). Only a republic existing in an extended sphere can achieve both.

In a word, liberty in America would be better preserved in a continental union with a complex national government, than in a confederation of states where the rights of citizens are at the mercy of local majorities. American republics need not remain small in order to remain free. Quite the opposite is true.

Court republicans in America were called Nationalists at the time of the convention. After the convention they were called Federalists (see "Terms in Use" in Appendix C).

Summary

Country republicanism rested on the following assumptions about government and society:

1. Rulers and ruled belong to different classes, notwithstanding the democratic restraints (e.g., elections) that tie them together.

2. The ruled (i.e., the people) are a single, undifferentiated whole in their opposition to the rulers (the government).

3. The government has power, whereas the people have liberty, which functions as a limitation on power.

4. Liberty is primarily the independence of the individual; only secondarily and reactively is it the sovereignty of the collective, when, in an effort to defend liberty against power, the people act politically.

5. Liberty needs defending because those entrusted with power are corrupted by it.

6. The political defense of liberty requires small republics with representatives similar to and removable by the people, perhaps also simple governments with unicameral legislatures that are easily supervised by the people.

7. Public supervision counts additionally as the moral defense of liberty, insofar as vigilance relies on the civic virtue of the people, meaning their patriotism, law-abidingness, and willingness to sacrifice for country.

8. The small, homogeneous, agrarian community is the social environment most conducive to virtue and most protective of liberty.

9. Human nature, seeking aggrandizement and indulgence, is ordinarily discontent in this social environment. Consequently, temptations to extravagance, taking the forms of commerce, manufacturing, luxury, and so on, must be rejected in favor of economies and practices supporting moderation.

10. Resistance to corruption is a delaying action, which periodic returns to first principles can assist, thereby prolonging the life and health of society. Arresting the cyclical movement of history, however, is not possible because all societies must suffer eventual decline and fall.

11. Societies die also when conquered by states greater than themselves, but confederations of small republics can guard against outside dangers while preserving liberty within.

Court republicanism worked from different assumptions, though sometimes the differences were subtle:

1. The old antithesis between the people and their government no longer obtains, or obtains with its previous force (i.e., the resentment of native populations toward foreign domination) because by revolutionary action the people have taken over government and made it their servant.

2. The rulers, now dependent on the ruled, can be partly trusted to apply their special talents to the public good because ambition in the finest of citizens is a virtue not to be disparaged and dismissed as personal vanity.

3. Distrust of rulers (still a sensible precaution, because power often does corrupt) is better practiced by the rulers themselves, jealous of each other, than by the ruled, jealous of government as a whole. Put differently, a complex government with separated powers checking and balancing each other is a more reliable guardian of liberty than a virtuous people focused on public affairs.

4. The institutional remedies of the "new science of politics," being better suited to selfish human nature, cooperate with, rather than stand athwart, the natural progress of society.

5. Human selfishness, coupled with human diversity, divides the people into separate and distinct factions.

6. The largest of these factions, or the majority, presents a threat to individual and minority liberties outside the threat posed by government.

7. The number of people feeling a passion or sharing an interest exacerbates the problem of human selfishness to the point that nothing in politics, morality, or religion suffices to control majorities from within themselves.

8. Controlling majorities from without, by government action, is frustrated if electoral majorities capture government and use it to serve factional ends.

9. The size and character of society provide the best safeguard against tyranny of the majority because in a large, diverse society, no single faction (economic, political, religious, etc.) is likely to contain a majority of the whole.

10. In the absence of a natural and permanent majority, all factions, being but natural minorities, are perforce obliged to build coalitions to achieve electoral and lawmaking success.

11. Justice is provided and liberty guarded (if only inadvertently) by the need of governing coalitions to represent the interests of many factions and not just one. The upshot is that having more factions (the expected byproduct of size and diversity) rather than having fewer factions (or, unrealistically, having no factions) is the counterintuitive remedy for majority tyranny.

12. Government, protected from easy capture by natural majorities, functions then as a referee among all groups of society.

13. National government—in order to loom over its rivals, the state governments—must be granted powers requisite to its liberty-preserving mission.

 PART 3: THE GAME (Standard Version)

NOTICE

The Constitutional Convention of 1787 can be played in any of three versions: Standard, Expanded Mid-Size, and Expanded Full-Size. All versions use the same game book, but the sections titled "The Game" and "Roles" are different for the Standard version from those for the other two. For the Standard game, those sections are provided next; for the other two, they are found in Appendices A and B. Read only the sections that fit the version your Gamemaster has selected. Also, not all of the core texts are for use with the Standard version. The Gamemaster knows which selections to assign. The game agenda, which varies depending on game version, will be distributed by the Gamemaster.

SETTING: STATE HOUSE, PHILADELPHIA

The date is summer 1787, or late May to mid-September. The place is Philadelphia, Pennsylvania, the largest city in America at the time (forty thousand). The building in which you gather, where the Declaration of Independence was written and signed, is the State House, known later as Independence Hall. You sit as individual delegates convened to decide on the structure of a new national government stronger than the Congress under the Articles of Confederation. But how strong and how different from the current government, in operation since 1781, are the questions facing you.

You may meet additionally in coffeehouses, in dining halls, or in any other convenient place. Such out-of-class sessions may be convivial or serve as venues in which convention business is discussed.

FRAMING A CONSTITUTION

Your job is to create *a* constitution, not to re-create *the* Constitution. Whether you depart from the original—and the extent to which you do depart—is entirely for you to decide. But you must address the same structural problems and respond to the same historical contingencies as confronted the delegates in Philadelphia. Thus your freedom of action is bounded.

Before you are questions of constitutional architecture: the branches of government, their respective compositions, the relationship of national to state government, and the limitations on each. Meanwhile, above these problems of structure and organization are the rival theories of republican government, each striving to have its precepts reflected in the final charter. Finally, there is slavery, an inheritance of colonial America that seems so out of place in a republic espousing the rights of man.

The historical environment in which you operate is complicated by three factional divides: Nationalists versus Confederalists, with moderate versions of each; large states versus small states; and North versus South, or freedom versus slavery. The first of these groupings is the most important, going the furthest toward determining identity.

STORY OF THE CONVENTION

In the correspondence of the day, contemporaries referred to a meeting of states occurring in Philadelphia "May next." The opening session of this historic event was set for May 14, 1787. When May 14 arrived, however, very few of the elected delegates were present, too few to make a quorum, and the first meeting of the Constitutional Convention adjourned without action—indeed, without actually convening. But the Virginia delegation was there, and the Pennsylvania delegation, too, whose many members all lived in or near Philadelphia. Together they composed a plan of government consisting of fifteen resolutions; and on May 29, a few days after the convention finally did make a quorum, they presented this plan, known as the Virginia Plan (because it was mainly written by Virginia delegate James Madison), for the consideration of the delegates.

The Virginia Plan envisioned a national government consisting of three branches—legislative, executive, and judicial; a national legislature divided into two chambers; popular election of members to the lower chamber (House of Representatives) and election by the lower chamber of members to the upper chamber (Senate); unspecified lawmaking power granted to the national legislature ("in all cases to which the separate states are incompetent") plus a veto ("negative") over state laws; proportional representation in both houses based on the free populations of states; a single executive serving a single term of to-be-determined years, elected by the national legislature, exercising a qualified veto over its laws and subject to impeachment; a national judiciary with judges appointed by the upper chamber of the national legislature, serving lifetime, or "good behavior," terms; and a system of inferior tribunals, or district and circuit courts, created by the national legislature. The remaining resolutions discussed the admission of new states, amendments, and ratification.

Most of this—indeed all of this—represented a radical departure from the Continental Congress under the Articles of Confederation. Surprisingly, the Virginia Plan sailed through a first reading by the convention, passing with little alteration on June 13. But the convention was then organized as a Committee of the Whole (a parliamentary device allowing for provisional voting), so nothing decided was final. And acceptance, notwithstanding the vote, was far from complete.

On June 15, an alternate plan of government was presented. Called the New Jersey Plan, it proposed reforms to the Articles (e.g., an executive, likely multiperson; an independent taxing power; authorization to coerce noncomplying states), but importantly it maintained the unicameral Congress and the representation of states as equals—in other words, it was still a confederation of semi-sovereign states. After a day of defense and attack, Alexander Hamilton, on June 18, took the floor, stupefying the convention with a day-long presentation of a plan of his own, one that, judging by the reaction, most delegates judged to be a tiny bit monarchical (a president for life), a mite aristocratic (senators for life), and less than friendly to the states (away with them!). No comment followed; instead, there was a return to the deconstruction of the New Jersey Plan and a vote of recommitment to the Virginia Plan, expanded now to nineteen resolutions.

The convention again took up the Virginia Plan, commencing a second review on June 19. But discontent was building, waiting to explode when the convention reached the resolution respecting state suffrage in the national legislature (postponed when first encountered). This was the issue that pit large-state delegates, wanting representation proportionate to population, against small-state delegates, wanting representation equal for all states regardless of size. For close to a month, the convention wrestled with this issue. At a moment of extreme tension, Benjamin Franklin suggested that the convention seek divine guidance by hiring a chaplain to lead the delegates in prayer. Of a different temper, a delegate from Delaware threatened to call on foreign assistance if the convention denied small states their equal vote. On July 16 an agreement composed of four parts was finally reached.

As this protracted debate over state suffrage unfolded, another issue, equally divisive, came into play. This was slavery—not the practice of, so much, but the inclusion or exclusion of slaves in the population counted for representation. Under the Articles of Confederation, with each state casting a single vote, slavery could be regarded as a local matter, and the Articles in fact said nothing about it. But with the lower house constituted on the principle of proportional representation, the slave issue became a national matter affecting everyone. Southern states wanted slaves counted equally with free inhabitants; northern states wanted them counted not at all.

Even more contentious was the issue of importing slaves, because importation not merely tolerated an existing evil but actively and purposefully made it worse. For some, the offense was moral (slavery violates God's law and natural law); for others it was self-interested (their representation diminishes my representation). A grand bargain affecting representation, taxation, and commerce eventually brought the matter to a successful resolution.

The convention adjourned for ten days in late July and early August to provide time for a Committee of Detail to write a report. The committee was charged with organizing past decisions and resolving delayed matters, but it took the liberty of venturing into new territory, especially the powers to be exercised by the national legislature. Some of the above debate was in response to the committee's report, which, presented on August 6, ran to twenty-three resolutions.

Another committee of consequence was the Committee on Postponed Matters, which reported three times in early September. Among the items handed to the committee was the election of the president. The composition of the executive branch consumed more of the convention's time than any other issue. Repeatedly did the subject come up, defying all attempts at resolution. The difficulty was not so much caused by conflicting ideas of executive power. Republican theory, with its emphasis on legislative power, said too little about this. Rather, the difficulty lay in the fact that the executive branch consisted of many elements, most of them interconnected. As a result, an agreement about one element would dissolve in the face of a disagreement about another. The committee, though, devised a compromise acceptable to most.

Once it was clear that the convention was not going to fail over the state-suffrage question, the delegates applied themselves with renewed energy to completing a constitution in all its manifold parts—too numerous and detailed even to list, much less to discuss.

On September 17, all but three of the delegates still in attendance put their signatures to the Constitution. Many others had left before, either because they were opposed to what was transpiring or because they were exhausted by the effort.

COUNTERFACTUALS

Delegates to the historical convention voted collectively as representatives of their states. Each delegation, no matter its size, cast a single vote. At the high end, states were represented by eight delegates, at the low end by only two. But whether eight or two, or any number in between, the state had just one vote cast by the majority of its delegation. You, however, vote individually. This procedural change is in place to simplify the voting process. The change does advantage the Nationalists, so to compensate, more Confederalists are included than were actually present at the convention.

A second change is substantive, rather than procedural. Once the Constitution was drafted, in September 1787, and sent to the states for their consideration and approval, a second round of debates immediately ensued. The full story of the making of the American Constitution includes the debates occurring at both stages of the contest, and books on the subject typically carry the narrative into the summer of 1788. The game will do something of the same, incorporating elements from the ratification debates into the debates of the convention proper. The writings of Federalist and Antifederalist authors, as they soon were called, are available for use by delegates who respectively support and oppose the constitution. The consequence should be a more principled debate around battle lines more clearly drawn.

Finally, all delegates are present and seated for the entire convention, even though historically many arrived late and left early. There could be a few exceptions, however, depending on game developments.

MAJOR ISSUES FOR DEBATE

The convention will debate and resolve nine issues pertaining to the lower and upper houses of the national legislature, to the presidency, and to slavery.

House of Representatives

1. The Character of the Representative The first issue concerns the lower house, or what in time will be called the House of Representatives. A question at the center of the Country republican–Court republican debate is the nature of representation—whether its purpose is to replicate the thinking of the people, were they assembled and fully informed, and to enact their wishes into law; or whether its purpose is to refine and enlarge public opinion, often misinformed and localistic, toward the end of achieving national objectives and common goods. The former position is called *agent* representation and is espoused by Country republicans; the latter position is called *trustee*, or *elite*, representation and is espoused by Court republicans.

2. The Size of the Lower House This theoretical debate is made practical with a decision respecting the size of the lower house, with a large house seen as accomplishing agent representation and a small house as accomplishing trustee representation. Are sixty-five members a sufficient number to start with, and is a maximum of one representative per forty thousand inhabitants the right ratio to keep the house from growing too large in the future while still fulfilling its representational function?

Senate

3. The Mode of Electing Senators How to elect the members of the upper house, or senators, provides a second opportunity for Country and Court republicanism to enter the convention. Country republicans see Montesquieuian small republics as essential to the exercise of political and personal liberty, and they see the thirteen existing states as the American equivalent of small republics. The states, therefore, are needed components of constitutional order (not accidents of history), and using their legislatures to elect the senate is a practical way for the states to exert influence and protect themselves. Court republicans are centralizers who think the states should stay out of national affairs.

4. The Suffrage of States in the Upper House The signature debate of the Constitutional Convention was over the suffrage, or representation, of states in the upper house—whether proportional to population or equal for all states. This issue will break apart the usual factional divide of Country and Court republicans because what matters most here is the size of a delegate's state. Large-state delegates view the matter differently than do small-state delegates.

Presidency

5. The President's Term of Office The Continental Congress has no executive worthy of the name. All delegates to the convention acknowledge the need for an executive, one of whose functions is to check the legislature—the dominant branch in a popular government, able, like a vortex, to suck into itself all other governmental branches. But how to achieve executive independence and how to prevent the president from becoming a monarch and then a despot are the questions before the delegates. Term of office is one institutional factor affecting independence and power. Should the term be long, short, or something in between?

6. The President's Eligibility for Reelection Depending on the length of the term, the issue of reeligibility is more or less important—for a short term of one, two, or three years would seem to require reeligibility; a long term of six or seven years not nearly so much; and a term of life, or during "good behavior," not at all. But even if the term is long, a president, without the hope of reelection, might lack the motivation to perform at his best, and the experience gained in office would be lost to the nation. On the other hand, would not a president eligible for reelection be unduly dependent on the body that reelects him? A conundrum, to be sure!

7. The Mode of Electing the President Tightly connected to issues 5 and 6 is the issue of the mode of election. With reeligibility, executive independence would be compromised if the national legislature, the dominant branch, were the body that elects and reelects the president. The same, though, would be true if state legislatures were the electing bodies. So why not let the people elect, for a president popularly elected would then have an independent base of support and be as much a representative of the people as is the legislature? But how can the public ever become informed about candidates living in distant states? Will they not simply favor candidates near to them ("favorite sons"), and won't this parochialism advantage large states over small states? Would electors popularly elected make a difference? Yet another conundrum!

Slavery

8. The Importation of Slaves Slavery is a stain on the country's reputation and an institution wholly incompatible with republican government. Even southerners agree. But that hypocrisy notwithstanding, slavery is deeply entrenched in the South, essential to its plantation economy organized for the production and export of cash crops. The South will not come into the union if its livelihood is put at risk. But will it allow slavery to be placed on a path of ultimate extinction by agreeing to end the importation of new slaves? Some southerners might; others, with more to lose, probably not.

9. The Inclusion of Slaves in the Population Counted for Representation and Taxation It would be easier to end the importation of slaves if slaves did not add to the population counted for representation in the legislature (and the game assumes proportional representation for the lower house). But the slave population is a sizable portion of the overall population of the southern states, which, if not included, would leave the South hopelessly outvoted in the legislature. Might the solution then be to tax the states for their slaves in the same proportion that states are represented for their slaves? Perhaps, but a population tax might be equivalent to a requisition laid upon the states by the national government; when tried by the Continental Congress, states found ways not to pay the tax. In any event, this issue of representation and taxation, like the issue of importation, will cause some delegates to divide by region rather than by party principles.

RULES AND PROCEDURES

Organization

The convention will have two officers: a president and a secretary/president pro tempore combined into one.

The president is George Washington, delegate from Virginia. The president determines the order in which speeches are presented, calls on people in debate, and makes necessary rulings (see "Convention President's Powers," later in the game book).

The secretary/president pro tempore is any delegate chosen by the convention to serve in this capacity. Interested parties nominate themselves for the post and offer brief speeches in support of their candidacy. In case of a tie, a run-off election is conducted. As secretary, the elected delegate records all motions and all votes; as president pro tempore, the delegate serves as acting president in the event of the president's absence.

Committees

If the convention bogs down over particularly thorny issues, the president may choose to create an ad hoc committee. These committees will consist either of five members (the leaders of each faction plus one other, selected randomly, to prevent ties) or of nine members (two from each faction, including the leader and whomever the leader chooses, plus a ninth selected randomly). The president will determine the committee's size and perform the random selections (applied to the factions, with the leader of the winning faction choosing an extra member from the ranks). Time pressure and chance of acceptance of a committee's recommendations may be factors in the president's decision, for a small committee will work more expeditiously, while a large committee will be more representative of the body.

In cases when the committee is united, a presumption exists in favor of its work. Altering or rejecting its proposal(s) can be done only with a **two-thirds majority of the convention**. If a committee is divided (meaning that no consensus emerged and that the minority opposes the proposal being presented), it will supply the convention with a majority and a minority report. No changes are allowed, nor may both reports be rejected. The convention adopts whichever of the two garners more votes, even if neither obtains a majority. This fail-safe device is meant to prevent the convention from coming to a full stop. If necessary, more than one minority report is allowed from a committee, but with the same rules in operation: no changes on the floor, take-it-or-leave-it votes on all plans, largest plurality prevailing.

Voting

Voting, as noted earlier, is done by individuals, not by state delegations. A majority of voting delegates is needed for positive action.

Proposals require a second. The president rules on any motion to amend, unless it is acceptable to the person whose proposal would be amended. A "friendly" amendment, so called, should at once be incorporated into the text of the original proposal. An "unfriendly" amendment, if allowed by the president, is considered after the original proposal and only in the event of its defeat. The president rules also on seconded motions to table (i.e., suspend consideration) or to call the question (i.e., have a vote).

If this simple procedure does not work—because in the course of debate a flurry of unfriendly amendments and rival proposals comes pouring fourth—the president is free to decide the order of consideration (whether first proposed, first considered, or estimated odds of success).

The Gamemaster has information regarding an alternate method of voting and may choose it instead to expedite the process.

Revoting Any measure may be revisited but only with the approval of the president. The clock is ticking, and the president is responsible for ensuring that the work of the convention is completed on time. A revote requires only **majority approval** for passage (but see "Final Vote," next).

Final Vote Through a series of votes over the course of the game, the convention slowly writes its constitution. Before the last class, the convention learns from the Gamemaster what sort of constitution it has heretofore produced (whether weighted toward the Nationalist position, the Confederalist position, etc.). The convention is free to make last-minute adjustments in response to delegates' wishes. These proposed amendments, however, may be subject to a two-thirds vote requirement. **A die roll taken before the proposing of amendments will determine whether a simple majority or a supermajority is required**. The purpose is to discourage issue-by-issue voting done in the belief that until the last class the convention's work is merely provisional and easily changed. The convention then proceeds to a **final vote** to accept or reject the constitution as amended, where a **simple majority** is needed for passage. The game ends with this vote.

Extra Vote, Lost Votes A number of actions taken, some of these affected by die rolls or other forms of chance determination, can double a delegate's final vote or eliminate it altogether. Delegates may also lose their votes at other times in the convention. This device of vote enhancement/removal is meant to replicate the fact that at Philadelphia some delegates arrived late, left early, or left and returned after having been absent for a time.

Convention Walk-In

One of the actions that affects the vote is called a convention "walk-in" (the opposite of a walk-out, which was many times threatened by delegates in Philadelphia). A walk-in is an attempt to increase the convention's size by persuading elected delegates, who have not yet left their home states, to appear in Philadelphia (in fact, nineteen delegates elected by their state legislatures never attended, some of them having declined their appointments). A letter sent to state legislatures is the mechanism of persuasion (though no letter is actually sent). Two issues can occasion a walk-in: suffrage in the senate and slavery in the South. If attempted (by delegates invited to consider a walk-in), a die roll determines whether persons answering the call are friendly or unfriendly to the delegate issuing it. No new delegates actually arrive; rather, the final vote of the delegate issuing the call is doubled, if the delegates answering are friendly; if the delegates are unfriendly, the vote is eliminated. The odds of success are affected by the size of the party supporting the appeal. Supporters gain or lose victory points depending on whether the die roll goes for or against them.

Loan Agreements

Another such action affecting votes—final and otherwise—is a loan agreement. Role descriptions identify those delegates who are in financial arrears and who must secure a loan from the leader of another faction or possibly face the consequences of having their debts come due. In exchange for a contract providing the needed cash (the amount is not a factor), the indebted delegate delivers a proxy ballot to the faction leader stipulating how the delegate's vote is to be cast and on what issue. Chance determines who among these unfortunates will be required to pay up; likewise, chance determines which of three penalties will apply for failing to produce a contract showing a loan. The penalties include loss of the first vote of a game session, loss of all votes of that game session, or loss of the game's final vote.

Convention President's Powers

The president has the following powers:
1. Setting the order of speeches and calling on delegates

2. Establishing committees and determining their size

3. Ruling on requests to caucus before votes

4. Ruling on unfriendly amendments

5. Ruling on motions to table and to call the question

6. Ruling on requests to revisit decisions

7. Determining other rules, such as due times for website postings of papers, but with the convention's approval

The president may not make or second a proposal, and the president does not serve on committees. The president does, however, vote.

Behavior

Proper decorum is expected of all members. Side conversations and note passing while another is speaking at the podium are impolite behaviors and may bring reprimands from any of the delegates, but especially from the president. Still, side conversations and note passing are regular features of Reacting games; so it remains to be seen what will be tolerated and what can be gotten away with.

Even your most detested enemy is to be addressed with respect. "The Right Honorable Mr. . . ." will do.

You are advised to remember that a Reacting game is only a game and that resistance, attack, and betrayal are not to be taken personally because game opponents are merely doing as their roles direct.

VICTORY

The game employs a two-tiered scoring system. Points are awarded to the factions passing a constitution reflective of their principles and interests. For one faction, defeating the constitution can be a path to victory. In addition, individual characters have points assigned to their roles. Factions can win a maximum of 5 points (and possibly lose a maximum of 3); individuals can win 6 or more. But only the Gamemaster knows exactly how many points attach to various constitutions and personal objectives.

Victory is mainly individualized. It requires that a particular character win a majority of the combined faction points and delegate points available to him. Because the delegate points outnumber the faction points, it is possible for a faction to lose and a faction member to win; the opposite is true as well.

For the factions, victory is a game win, defeat a game loss—that is, passage or rejection of a constitution identified as favoring or disfavoring the factions' interests. The Gamemaster has a table for rating constitutions. The faction scoring the most points comes in first; the next in line is second, and so on. Ties are possible. **No faction can win without help from another**.

ASSIGNMENTS AND GRADING

Game Quiz and Study Guide Questions

The instructor may distribute a fill-in-the-blank quiz before the game starts. Serving less as a test than as a study guide, the quiz should be answered as you read through the assigned material. To play the game well, you need to absorb as much factual information about the period as you can, and you need to do so quickly. The quiz is intended to assist with the work of absorption and retention. If distributed, the quiz, or a portion of it, will then be taken by the class before the game proper begins. As an incentive to do well, the winners, or winner, will receive bonus victory points worth 10 to 15 percent of their individualized, role sheet's total. The instructor may also choose to treat the quiz as a test, by assigning to it some small percentage of the course grade.

Separate from the quiz are the Study Guide Questions provided at the end of each of the core texts. You are advised to read the questions before, or as, you read the text and to write down the answers as you come across them. These questions may be used to structure the class discussions about the readings. In addition, the instructor may decide to include some of these questions on the quiz.

Fun-Facts Competition

Before the opening of every convention session, the Gamemaster will pose a multiple-choice question. During the course of the game, you are obliged to answer one such question correctly or suffer the loss of a victory point at the game's end. No penalty is incurred for wrong answers. Those succeeding early and protecting themselves from loss can gain a victory point by answering a second question correctly, and by answering a third, they can gain one more. Two positive points are the maximum allowed. But in the pursuit of positive points, wrong answers do matter, causing those seeking a first point to return to the start where a correct answer is needed just to prevent a loss, and causing those seeking a second point to forfeit the one point already earned. Furthermore, you must commit to the contest before hearing the question.

As an inducement to compete, students who have committed to answering a question (and these students only) may consult the Internet using any electronic device in their possession. Students have about one minute to answer unless the Gamemaster changes the time limit.

Papers

A Reacting game ordinarily requires ten pages of writing spread over an indefinite number of papers. In this version of the game, you write one or two papers (at most three), depending on the role you receive. Because of the shortened length of this game version, the page requirement may be reduced. By how much is a decision the instructor will make.

To know when a paper is due, you should compare the "Assignments" section in your role sheet with the game agenda and the course syllabus (distributed by the instructor). When ambiguities occur (because the class has fallen behind or has gotten ahead), you should ask the Gamemaster and the convention president. It is always better, for obvious reasons, to be ready early than to be ready late.

Class Preparation

Once the game begins, you have no regular reading assignments other than the reading you do as research for your papers. But for each class there is work to be done. You should reread the pertinent sections of your role description, especially the paragraphs under "Issues and Sources," because the information provided there will enable you to participate in debate, even when not delivering a paper. You should read the speeches your fellow delegates post on the class website, for this way you will be ready with supporting comments, queries, or rebuttals. And when appropriate, you should meet or communicate with faction members in advance of class sessions.

Grades

Though the instructor is free to make adjustments, written work normally accounts for two-thirds of your grade and participation one-third—formal speeches from the podium (likely graded higher if spoken and not read) and informal debate from the floor, plus caucusing, negotiating, and strategizing, to the extent that these activities are known to the instructor. It is the instructor's option whether to award a bonus for winning and impose a penalty for losing, as it is the instructor's option whether to factor in quiz performance as part of the course grade.

 PART 4: ROLES (Standard Version)

FACTIONS

Republican principles determine the main factional divide and provide the game with its four ideological parties, each with its own group role description. Court republicans are either Nationalists or Moderate Nationalists; Country republicans are either Confederalists or Moderate Confederalists. Of secondary importance are the distinctions between large states and small states and between northern states and southern states. These distinctions come into use when the issues are senate suffrage, on the one hand, and slavery, on the other.

Nationalists

Nationalists are united in the belief that state governments possess too much power, exercise it badly, and pose serious danger to the peace, prosperity, and continued unity of the country. Some Nationalists would even do away with the states, except as administrative units. They despair of solving the country's problems by patched-up reforms of the Articles of Confederation. At most points they work to invigorate the national government at the expense of the state governments. They particularly oppose use of state legislatures as electoral bodies for national offices. They tend to favor a strong executive and the constitutional devices to bring it about. Legislatures they regard less as the palladium of liberty than as hothouses of parochial selfishness.

In general, Nationalists take a realistic (i.e., low) view of human nature and are inclined to use corruption as much as guard against it. They appreciate the special talents of the political elite and spare no effort to draw them into national service.

Moderate Nationalists

This milder variant of the Nationalist position holds that the Congress under the Articles of Confederation is a proven failure, too strong in structure (e.g., a unicameral legislature) to be trusted with power and too lacking in power to accomplish national objectives (e.g., the regulation of trade). But Moderate Nationalists, unlike some of their Nationalist kin, value the states as a check-and-balance on the federal government. They therefore are open to constitutional provisions that include and protect the states.

Confederalists

Confederalists are Country republicans who have all the small-republic reasons for defending the states. They therefore worry that the push to nationalize will end in despotism and the destruction of liberty. They agree that the Articles of Confederation falls short of expectation, and they welcome amendments to fix problems widely recognized. But the framework, they insist, should remain that of a confederation of states, not a consolidated union.

Confederalists accept a national government competent within its sphere, so long as that sphere is kept strictly limited. Therefore, they will tolerate no encroachments on the states' "police power," an imprecise concept covering an assortment of responsibilities, including criminal justice, slave codes, militias, taxes, land ownership, manufacturing, transportation, education, religion, and marriage.

The great fear of Confederalists is that a single American nation under a centralized government may one day emerge to obliterate the identities of the states. Their goal, in reaction, is to defend the rights of states and to enhance their profile and importance within the union. Confederalists, accordingly, support such constitutional provisions as annual elections to keep officeholders accountable and dependent, their election by state legislatures, and voting in the national legislature by states.

Confederalists evince some wariness of ambitious individuals talented enough and/or wealthy enough to operate on a national stage. This suspiciousness marks them as democrats. But Confederalists, like Nationalists, hail from the wealthy elite, and most fancy themselves talented; plus their attachment to states outpaces their regard for the poor and the powerless. Hence their democratic bona fides are a little shaky, if not a thing of convenience.

Moderate Confederalists

Moderate Confederalists support the Country republican premise that the small republic is the place where people are freest and happiest, and they suppose that the thirteen states—notwithstanding the size of some—are a close approximation of small republics. Thus the states must be preserved. But they must also be reined in because they have behaved badly during the Confederation period and threaten the integrity of the union. Moderate Confederalists hope (they don't quite assert) that reforms to the Continental Congress will suffice to solve the problem.

DELEGATES

Fifty-five men representing twelve states participated in the Constitutional Convention (Rhode Island sent no delegation). Of these fifty-five, forty were present for most of the debates; and of these forty, perhaps twenty-five made significant contributions. Thirty-nine signed the final document.

Along with the four group roles, the game contains thirty-two individualized roles (class size will determine how many are in use). All of these are based on historical figures, but liberties have been taken with some to serve game needs, including the addition of one character who was not a delegate to the convention (identified by an asterisk).

The thirty-two included delegates are arranged by factions. Their public descriptions are as follows.

NATIONALISTS

James Madison (Virginia)

Son of a Virginia planter; Princeton graduate and student of John Witherspoon; state legislator; delegate to the Continental Congress; main author of the Virginia Plan and driving force behind the Virginia delegation, though young at age thirty-six.

George Washington (Virginia)

Virginia planter, surveyor, and soldier; commander of American forces during the Revolutionary War; unanimous choice for convention president, though a reluctant attendee.

James Wilson (Pennsylvania)

Scottish immigrant, arriving before the Revolution; important pamphleteer; lawyer-jurist; signer of the Declaration of Independence; opponent of the Pennsylvania constitution; land speculator and financier.

Charles Pinckney (South Carolina)

At twenty-nine, one of the youngest of the delegates, and proud of the fact; war veteran; state legislator; delegate to the Continental Congress; cousin to John Rutledge and Charles Cotesworth Pinckney; slave owner.

Alexander Hamilton (New York)

Revolutionary War veteran on Washington's staff and hero of Yorktown; pamphleteer; organizer of the Annapolis Convention; gifted lawyer married into a prominent political family; not native born but from the Caribbean and an orphan.

Gouverneur Morris (Pennsylvania)

Transplanted New Yorker from an aristocratic family; young, talented lawyer with a wooden peg leg, the original lost under mysterious circumstances; bon vivant; active in state government; master constitutional draftsman; Washington and Robert Morris his patrons.

Rufus King (Massachusetts)

Rising young man, married to the daughter of a wealthy New York merchant; important friends, including John Hancock, governor of Massachusetts.

Nathaniel Gorham (Massachusetts)

Descendant of Mayflower Pilgrims; merchant, sometimes prosperous, sometimes not; recent president of the Continental Congress.

Charles Cotesworth Pinckney (South Carolina)

Planter-aristocrat; lawyer; state legislator; war veteran rising to the rank of general; slave owner.

MODERATE NATIONALISTS

John Rutledge (South Carolina)

Planter-aristocrat and lawyer-judge; member of the Stamp Act Congress and the First and Second Continental Congresses; drafter of South Carolina constitution; state legislator and governor; war hero whose estate the British confiscated; slave owner.

John Dickinson (Delaware)

Important pamphleteer during the resistance years; member of the Stamp Act Congress; member of the First and Second Continental Congresses, inclining toward reconciliation with Britain; co-drafter of the Articles of Confederation; war veteran; former president of Delaware and of Pennsylvania; lawyer married to an heiress.

Benjamin Franklin (Pennsylvania)

Oldest delegate at age eighty-one; printer, scientist, inventor, and diplomat; architect of the Albany Plan (early attempt at colonial union, 1754); signer of the Declaration of Independence; supporter of the Pennsylvania constitution; co-drafter of the Articles of Confederation; America's most famous citizen.

Oliver Ellsworth (Connecticut)

Businessman, lawyer, and judge; former delegate to the Continental Congress; prolific consumer of snuff, given to talking to himself.

Hugh Williamson (North Carolina)

Physician and scientist; state legislator; delegate to the Continental Congress and signer of the Northwest Ordinance of 1784.

John Langdon (New Hampshire)

Self-made man; merchant with political experience in the state legislature and national Congress; recent president of the state.

Abraham Baldwin (Georgia)

Connecticut-born Congregationalist minister; attorney at law; migrant to Georgia; state legislator; member of the Continental Congress; founder of the University of Georgia; slave owner.

William Davie (North Carolina)

English immigrant, though arriving at a young age, settling with family in South Carolina; Princeton graduate; cavalry officer during the war, seeing significant action in the South; lawyer; North Carolina state legislator.

CONFEDERALISTS

John Lansing Jr. (New York)

Wealthy landowner; mayor of Albany and New York assemblyman; delegate to the Continental Congress; slave owner; follower of George Clinton, governor of New York.

Luther Martin (Maryland)

Attorney general of Maryland; a fill-in for the state's more prominent politicians who declined their appointments; alcoholic.

William Paterson (New Jersey)

Lawyer and storekeeper; state legislator; owner of a confiscated loyalist estate.

Robert Yates (New York)

Surveyor; local politician; co-author of the state constitution; justice of the state supreme court; slave owner; follower of George Clinton, governor of New York.

John Francis Mercer (Maryland)

Virginia-born planter; lawyer; Revolutionary War officer.

William Few (Georgia)

North Carolina–born farmer; lawyer; war veteran; state legislator and populist; multiple terms in the Continental Congress.

William Findley* (Pennsylvania)

Irish immigrant; backcountry farmer; populist with extensive experience in the state legislature (an important figure of the day, but not in fact a delegate to the convention).

MODERATE CONFEDERALISTS

Roger Sherman (Connecticut)
Elderly jack-of-all-trades with political experience tracing back to the First Continental Congress; signer of the Declaration of Independence; co-drafter of the Articles of Confederation.

George Mason (Virginia)
Planter-aristocrat but with democratic leanings; owner of many slaves but a supporter of abolition; author of the Fairfax Resolves (revolutionary tract, 1774); draftsman of the Virginia constitution of 1776 and of the Virginia Bill of Rights; out of politics for ten years before the convention; friends with Virginia's political elite.

Elbridge Gerry (pronounced GARY) (Massachusetts)
Merchant from a prominent family; experienced politician; signer of the Declaration of Independence and the Articles of Confederation.

Edmund Randolph (Virginia)
Current governor of Virginia at the age of thirty-three; former attorney general; former delegate to the Continental Congress and to the Annapolis Convention; from a prominent Virginia family and ex officio head of the Virginia delegation.

William Samuel Johnson (Connecticut)
Son of an Anglican minister and president of King's College; lawyer; scholar with international reputation; colonial agent in London; state legislator; reluctant revolutionary once in trouble with Connecticut authorities; member of the Continental Congress.

Gunning Bedford (Delaware)
Philadelphia-born transplant with a more notable cousin of the same name; state legislator and longtime attorney general; frequent delegate to the Continental Congress.

David Brearley (New Jersey)
Princeton educated lawyer; war veteran; chief justice of the state supreme court; state legislator.

Nicholas Gilman (New Hampshire)
Merchant and soldier, with recent service in the Continental Congress.

INDETERMINATES

Reacting games commonly assign a number of students to roles called "Indeterminate." Indeterminate roles are representative types unattached to any faction. They may have leanings and a task or two to perform, but their main function is to provide the game with a persuadable audience for arguments made by others.

No student in this game is an Indeterminate as such. All belong to one of four ideological factions (Nationalist, Moderate Nationalist, Confederalist, Moderate Confederalist), and all have individualized roles with positions to advance and objectives to achieve. To some degree, the two variants of moderate delegates function as Indeterminates, insofar as they are possible allies of the factional extremes. But for the most part, they are separately defined groups. The variety of issues, the complexity of characters, and the fluidity of factional alliances mean that indeterminacy is everywhere and so does not need to be the special responsibility of a few roles set aside for the purpose.

 PART 5: CORE TEXTS

ARISTOTLE

Politics, 335–323 B.C.E.

The selections from Aristotle's Politics *investigate regime types, their animating principles, their institutional characteristics, and their relative worth. Special attention is paid to polity, the term Aristotle (384–322 B.C.E.) employs for the good form of popular rule. A polity is a mixed regime composed of democratic and oligarchical elements. A mixed regime (also called constitutional government by the translator) aims at balancing the power of the few and the many, or the rich and the poor. These two classes exist in all societies, and in simple, unitary regimes (e.g., oligarchy, democracy) one or the other prevails; in mixed regimes they share power. Aristotle explains how well-made constitutions can mitigate factional hostilities and avert revolutionary instability. The framers of the American Constitution used Aristotelian terms and concepts, even though they did not cite Aristotle or create a mixed regime per se.*

SOURCE: *Aristotle,* Politics, *trans. Benjamin Jowett (Oxford: Clarendon Press, 1905); with minor alterations.*

BOOK III.7

We have next to consider how many forms of government there are, and what they are; and in the first place what are the true forms, for when they are determined the perversions of them will at once be apparent. The words "constitution" [*politeia*] and "government" [*politeuma*] have the same meaning, and the government, which is the supreme authority in every city or state [*polis*], must be in the hands of one, or of a few, or of the many. The true forms of government, therefore, are those in which the one, or the few, or the many, govern with a view to the common interest; but governments which rule with a view to the private interest, whether of the one, or of the few, or of the many, are perversions. For citizens, if they are truly citizens, ought to participate in the advantages of a state. Of forms of government in which one rules, we call that which regards the common interests kingship, or royalty; that in which more than one, but not many, rule aristocracy [the rule of the best]; and it is so called, either because the rulers are the best men, or because they have at heart the best interests of the state and of the citizens. But when the citizens at large administer the state for the common interest, the government is called by the generic name—constitution, or polity [*politeia*]. . . . In a constitutional government the fighting-men have the supreme power, and those who possess arms are the citizens.

Of the above-mentioned forms, the perversions are as follows: of royalty, tyranny; of aristocracy, oligarchy [rule by the few]; of constitutional government, or polity, democracy. For tyranny is a kind of monarchy which has in view the interest of the monarch only; oligarchy has in view the interest of the wealthy; democracy, of the needy; none of them the common good of all. . . .

BOOK III.8

The democratic claim rests on the distinction between free citizens and enslaved subjects. Rich and poor have in common their freedom and seem as equals in contrast to slaves.

The real difference between democracy and oligarchy is poverty and wealth. Wherever men rule by reason of their wealth, whether they be few or many, that is an oligarchy, and where the poor rule, that is a democracy. But as a fact the rich are few and the poor many; for the few are well-to-do, whereas freedom is enjoyed by all, and wealth and freedom are the grounds on which the oligarchical and democratic parties respectively claim power in the state.

BOOK III.9

Let us begin by considering the common definitions of oligarchy and democracy, and what is justice oligarchical and democratic. For all men cling to justice of some kind, but their conceptions are imperfect, and they do not express the whole idea. For example, justice is thought by them to be, and is, equality, not, however, for all, but only for equals. And inequality is thought to be, and is, justice; neither is this for all, but only for unequals. When persons are omitted, then men judge erroneously. The reason is that they are passing judgment on themselves, and most people are bad judges in their own case. And whereas justice implies a relation to persons as well as to things, and a just distribution [distributive justice] . . . embraces alike persons and things, they acknowledge the equality of the things, but dispute about the merit of the persons . . . because both the parties to the argument are speaking of a limited and partial justice, but imagine themselves to be speaking of absolute justice. For those who are unequal in one respect, for example wealth, consider themselves to be unequal in all; and any who are equal in one respect, for example freedom, consider themselves to be equal in all. But they leave out the capital point. For if men met and associated out of regard to wealth only, their share in the state would be proportioned to their property, and the oligarchical doctrine would then seem to carry the day. It would not be just that he who paid one mina should have the same share of a hundred minae,[1] whether of the principal or of the profits, as he who paid the remaining ninety-nine.

---

1. A mina was a silver coin worth two or three months of a skilled worker's wages.

But a state exists for the sake of good life and not for the sake of life only. . . . Nor does a state exist for the sake of alliance and security from injustice, nor yet for the sake of exchange and mutual intercourse. . . . Those who care for good government take into consideration [the larger question of] virtue and vice in states. Whence it may be further inferred that virtue must be the serious care of a state which truly deserves the name; for [without this ethical end] the community becomes a mere alliance which differs only in place from alliances of which members live apart; and law is only a convention, a "surety to one another of justice," as the sophist Lycophron says, and has no real power to make the citizens good and just.

Editorial note: Aristotle's point is that justice, properly understood, is proportional equality, not numerical equality—meaning that a just distribution is one in which reward is proportionate to merit or to contribution: equals for equals, unequals for unequals. He implies that all parties agree regarding rewards (things) but disagree regarding merit (persons). The wealthy believe that because their property underwrites the expenses of the state, they deserve power proportionate to the taxes they pay (e.g., a weighted vote). This is the oligarchical view of distributive justice. The people, whose position Aristotle formulates, dispute that the state is a business enterprise in which profits are distributed to shareholders in proportion to the number of shares each holds. The people rather see the state as a defense alliance and marketplace and thus credit their service in the military and the labor they perform as a contribution deserving of power. Hence the ideological fight that goes on inside of all states is over the meritoriousness of persons or the worth of the contributions that the classes respectively make.

The people, however, cannot always be trusted to think in terms of proportional equality (Aristotle is actually pushing them in this direction). More often they assert the justice of numerical equality (VI.2), or equal things for equal and unequal persons alike; and it is numerical equality that more often expresses the democratic notion of distributive justice (e.g., one person, one vote).

Aristotle's own position is that oligarchs and democrats are both wrong, or partial in their views, because they mistakenly suppose that mere life (prosperity, security), rather than good life (virtue, human development) is the purpose of the state. They further suppose that law is about contractual and criminal justice only, forgetting law's higher functions of education and character formation. Aristocrats, Aristotle believes, are nearer to espousing the correct view.

Delegates to the Constitutional Convention usually spoke in terms of Aristotle's democrats and oligarchs, but now and again they described politics using terms characteristic of Aristotle's aristocrats—for instance, James Wilson's remark on July 13: "He could not agree that property was the sole or the primary object of Government and society. The cultivation and improvement of the human mind was the most notable object."

BOOK IV.8

I have yet to speak of the so-called polity. . . . For polity or constitutional government may be described generally as a fusion of oligarchy and democracy; but the term is usually applied to those forms of government which incline towards democracy, and the term aristocracy to those which incline towards oligarchy, because birth and education are commonly the accompaniments of wealth. Moreover the rich already possess the external advantages the want of which is a temptation to crime, and hence they are called noblemen and gentlemen. And inasmuch as aristocracy seeks to give predominance to the best of the citizens, people say also of oligarchies that they are composed of noblemen and gentlemen. . . .

The distribution of offices according to merit is a special characteristic of aristocracy, for the principle of an aristocracy is virtue, as wealth is of an oligarchy, and freedom of a democracy. In all of them there of course exists the right of the majority, and whatever seems good to the majority of those who share in the government has authority [only aristocrats are citizens sharing power in an aristocracy, so a majority of aristocrats is sovereign]. Generally, however, a state of this kind is called a polity or constitutional government [not an aristocracy], for the fusion goes no further than the attempt to unite the freedom of the poor and the wealth of the rich, who commonly take the place of the noble. And as there are three grounds on which men claim an equal share in the government—freedom, wealth, and virtue (for good birth, the fourth, is the result of the two last, being only ancient wealth and virtue)—it is clear that the admixture of the two elements, that is to say, of the rich and poor, is to be called polity or constitutional government; and the union of the three is called aristocracy or the government of the best . . . .

BOOK IV.9

N ext we have to consider how by the side of oligarchy and democracy the so-called polity or constitutional government springs up, and how it should be organized. . . . Now there are three modes in which fusions of government may be effected. The nature of the fusion will be made intelligible by an example of the manner in which different governments legislate, say concerning the administration of justice. In oligarchies they impose a fine on the rich if they do not serve as judges, and to the poor they give no pay; but in democracies they give pay to the poor and do not fine the rich. [The purpose in each is to encourage the participation of preferred persons.] Now the union of these two modes is a common or middle term between them and is therefore characteristic of a constitutional government, for it is a combination of both. This is one mode of uniting the two elements. Or a mean may be taken between the enactments of the two: thus democracies require no property qualification, or only a small one, from members of the assembly, oligarchies a high one; here neither of these is the common term, but a mean between them. There is a third mode in which something is borrowed from the oligarchical and something from the democratic principle. For example, the appointment of magistrates by lot is democratic, and the election of them oligarchical; democratic again when there is no property qualification, oligarchical when there is. In the aristocratic or constitutional state, one element will be taken from each—from oligarchy the mode of electing to offices, from democracy the disregard of qualifications. Such are the various modes of combination.

There is a true union of oligarchy and democracy when the same state may be termed either a democracy or an oligarchy. . . . In a well-tempered polity there should appear to be both elements and yet neither; also the government should rely on itself, and not on foreign aid . . . but on the general willingness of all classes in the state to maintain the constitution. . . .

> *A well-constructed polity will be seen as a democracy by some and as an oligarchy by others and will be supported by poor and rich alike.*

BOOK IV.11

*W*e have now to inquire what is the best constitution for most states, and the best life for most men . . . having regard to the life in which the majority are able to share, and to the form of government which states in general can attain. . . . Now in all states there are three elements; one class is very rich, another is very poor, and a third in a mean. It is admitted that moderation and the mean are best, and therefore it will clearly be best to possess the gifts of fortune in moderation; for in that condition of life men are most ready to listen to reason. Of these two the one sort grows into violent and great criminals, the others into rogues and petty rascals. And two sorts of offences correspond to them, the one committed from violence, the other from roguery. The petty rogues are disinclined to hold office, whether military or civil, and their aversion to these two duties is as great an injury to the state as their tendency to crime. Again, those who have too much of the goods of fortune, strength, wealth, friends, and the like, are neither willing nor able to submit to authority. The evil begins at home: for when they are boys, by reason of the luxury in which they are brought up, they never learn, even at school, the habit of obedience. On the other hand, the very poor, who are in the opposite extreme, are too degraded. So that the one class cannot obey, and can only rule despotically; the other knows not how to command and must be ruled like slaves. Thus arises a city, not of freemen, but of masters and slaves, the one despising, the other envying; and nothing can be more fatal to friendship and good fellowship in states than this: for good fellowship tends to friendship; when men are at enmity with one another, they would rather not even share the same path. But a city ought to be composed, as far as possible, of equals and similars; and these are generally the middle classes. Wherefore the city which is composed of middle-class citizens is necessarily best governed. They are, as we say, the natural elements of a state. And this is the class of citizens which is most secure in a state, for they do not, like the poor, covet their neighbors' goods; nor do others covet theirs, as the poor covet the goods of the rich; and as they neither plot against others, nor are themselves plotted against, they pass through life safely. . . .

Middle-class persons make the best citizens and are a bridge between the arrogant rich and the envious poor, who face each other as enemies when in cities without a middle class.

Thus it is manifest that the best political community is formed by citizens of the middle class and that those states are likely to be well-administered in which the middle class is large, and larger if possible than both the other classes, or at any rate than either singly; for the addition of the middle class turns the scale and prevents either of the extremes from being dominant. Great then is the good fortune of a state in which the citizens have a moderate and sufficient property; for where some possess much, and the others nothing, there may arise an extreme democracy, or a pure oligarchy; or a tyranny may grow out of either extreme—either out of the most rampant democracy, or out of an oligarchy; but it is not so likely to arise out of a middle and nearly equal condition. . . . The mean condition of states is clearly best, for no other is free from faction; and where the middle class is large, there are least likely to be factions and dissensions. For a similar reason large states are less liable to faction than small ones, because in them the middle class is large; whereas in small states it is easy to divide all the citizens into two classes who are either rich or poor, and to leave nothing in the middle. And democracies are safer and more permanent than oligarchies, because they have a middle class which is more numerous and has a greater share in the government; for when there is no middle class, and the poor greatly exceed in number, troubles arise, and the state soon comes to an end. . . .

These considerations will help us to understand why most governments are either democratic or oligarchical. The reason is that the middle class is seldom numerous in them, and whichever party, whether the rich or the common people, transgresses the mean and predominates, draws the government to itself; and thus arises either oligarchy or democracy. . . .

BOOK IV.12

We have now to consider what and what kind of government is suitable to what and what kind of men. I may begin by assuming, as a general principle common to all government, that the portion of the state which desires permanence ought to be stronger than that which desires the reverse. Now every city is composed of quality and quantity. By quality I mean freedom, wealth, education, good birth; and by quantity, superiority of numbers. . . . Where the number of the poor is more than proportioned to the wealth of the rich, there will naturally be a democracy. But where the rich and the notables exceed in quality more than they fall short in quantity, there oligarchy arises. . . .

The legislator should always include the middle class in his government; if he makes his laws oligarchical, to the middle class let him look; if he makes them democratic, he should equally by his laws try to attach this class to the state. There only can the government ever be stable where the middle class exceeds one or both of the others, and in that case there will be no fear that the rich will unite with the poor against the rulers. For neither of them will ever be willing to serve the other, and if they look for some form of government more suitable to both, they will find none better than this, for the rich and the poor will never consent to rule in turn, because they mistrust one another. The arbiter is always the one trusted, and he who is in the middle is an arbiter. The more perfect the admixture of the political elements, the more lasting will be the state. . . .

BOOK V.8

But above all every state should be so administered and so regulated by law that its magistrates cannot possibly make money. In oligarchies special precautions should be used against this evil. For the people do not take any great offence at being kept out of the government—indeed they are rather pleased than otherwise at having leisure for their private business—but what irritates them is to think that their rulers are stealing the public money; then they are doubly annoyed; for they lose both honor and profit. If office brought no profit, then and then only could democracy and aristocracy be combined; for both the notables and the people might have their wishes gratified. All would be able to hold office, which is the aim of democracy, and the notables would be magistrates, which is the aim of aristocracy. And this result may be accomplished when there is no possibility of making money out of offices; for the poor will not want to have them when there is nothing to be gained from them—they would rather be attending to their own concerns; and the rich, who do not need money from the public treasury, will be able to take them; and so the poor will keep to their work and grow rich, and the notables will not be governed by the lower class. In order to avoid peculation of the public money, the transfer of the revenue should be made at a general assembly of the citizens . . . . And honors should be given by law to magistrates who have the reputation of being incorruptible. . . .

BOOK VI.2

The basis of a democratic state is liberty; which, according to the common opinion of men, can only be enjoyed in such a state—this they affirm to be the great end of every democracy. One principle of liberty

Liberty can mean the right to rule and be ruled in turn, or it can mean the right to be free of all rule. The former is collective liberty (perhaps better called equality) and is represented in the Declaration of Independence by the requirement that government rest on the consent of the governed. The latter is private liberty and is represented in the Declaration by the affirmation of inalienable rights.

is for all to rule and be ruled in turn, and indeed democratic justice is the application of numerical not proportional equality; whence it follows that the majority must be supreme and that whatever the majority approve must be the end and the just. Every citizen, it is said, must have equality, and therefore in a democracy the poor have more power than the rich, because there are more of them, and the will of the majority is supreme. This, then, is one note of liberty which all democrats affirm to be the principle of their state. Another is that a man should live as he likes. This, they say, is the privilege of a freeman; and, on the other hand, not to live as a man likes is the mark of a slave. This is the second characteristic of democracy, whence has arisen the claim of men to be ruled by none, if possible, or if this is impossible, to rule and be ruled in turns; and so it coincides with the freedom based upon equality [which was the first characteristic].

Such being our foundation and such the nature of democracy, its characteristics are as follows: the election of officers by all out of all; and that all should rule over each, and each in his turn over all; that the appointment to all offices, or to all but those which require experience and skill, should be made by lot; that no property qualification should be required for offices, or only a very low one; that no one should hold the same office twice, or not often, except in the case of military offices; that the tenure of all offices, or of as many as possible, should be brief; that all men should sit in judgment, or that jurors selected out of all should judge in all matters,[2] or in most, or in the greatest and most important—such as the scrutiny of accounts, the constitution, and private contracts; that the assembly should be supreme over all causes, or at any rate over the most important, and the magistrates over none or only over a very few. . . . The next characteristic of democracy is payment for services; assembly, law-courts, magistrates, everybody receives pay, when it is to be had . . . . And whereas oligarchy is characterized by birth, wealth, and education, the notes of democracy appear to be the opposite of these: low birth, poverty, mean employment. Another note is that no magistracy is perpetual, but if any such have survived some ancient change in the constitution it should be stripped of its power, and the holders should be elected by lot and no longer by vote. These are the points common to all democracies; but democracy and demos in their truest form are based upon the recognized principle of democratic justice, that all should count equally; for equality implies that the rich should have no more share in the government than the poor, and should not be the only rulers, but that all should rule equally according to their numbers. And in this way men think that they will secure equality and freedom in their state.

Democratic distributive justice is numerical, not proportional, recognizing only equal numbers as just.

---

2. Athenian courts often consisted of hundreds of jurors, usually chosen by lot.

BOOK VI.3

emocrats say that justice is that to which the majority agree, oligarchs that to which the wealthier class agree; in the oligarchs' opinion the decision should be given according to the amount of property. In both principles there is some inequality and injustice. For if justice is the will of the few, any one person who has more wealth than all the rest of his class put together, ought, upon the oligarchical principle, to have the sole power—but this would be tyranny. Or if justice is the will of the majority . . . they will unjustly confiscate the property of the wealthy minority. To find a principle of equality in which they both agree we must inquire into their respective ideas of justice.

Aristotle here states the problem of majority tyranny that Madison's Federalist #10 and #51 attempt to solve (see selections herein).

Now they all agree in saying that whatever is decided by the majority of the citizens is to be deemed law. Granted, but not without some reserve; for since there are two classes out of which a state is composed—the poor and the rich—that is to be deemed law on which both or the greater part of both agree; and if they disagree, that which is approved by the majority, that is by those who have the higher qualification. For example, suppose that there are ten rich and twenty poor, and some measure is approved by six of the rich and is disapproved by fifteen of the poor, and the remaining four of the rich join with the party of the poor, and the remaining five of the poor with that of the rich; in such a case the will of those whose qualifications, when both sides are added up, are the greatest, should prevail. . . . But although it may be difficult in theory to know what is just and equal, the practical difficulty of inducing those to forbear who can encroach, if they like, is far greater, for the weaker are always asking for equality and justice, but the stronger care for none of these things.

BOOK VI.4

he best material of a democracy is an agricultural population; there is no difficulty in forming a democracy where the mass of the people live by agriculture or tending of cattle. Being poor, they have no leisure, and therefore do not often attend the assembly, and not having the necessaries of life they are always at work and do not covet the property of others. Indeed, they find their employment pleasanter than the cares of government or office where no great gains can be made out of them, for the many are more desirous of gain than of honor. A proof is that even the ancient tyrannies were patiently endured by them, as they still endure oligarchies, if they are allowed to work and are not deprived of their property; for some of them grow quickly rich and the others are well enough off. Moreover, they have the power of electing the magistrates and calling them to account; their ambition, if they have any, is thus satisfied. . . . Hence it is both expedient and customary in such a democracy that all should elect to offices, and conduct scrutinies, and sit in the law-courts, but that the great offices should be filled up by election and from persons having a qualification; the greater requiring a greater qualification, or, if there be no offices for which a qualification is required, then those who are marked out by special ability should be appointed. Under such a form of government, the citizens are sure to be governed well (for the offices will always be held by the best persons; the people are willing enough to elect them and are not jealous of the good). The good and the notables will then be satisfied, for they will not be governed by men who are their inferiors, and the persons elected will rule justly, because others will call them to account. Every man should be responsible to others, nor should anyone be allowed to do just as he pleases; for where absolute freedom is allowed there is nothing to restrain the evil which is inherent in every man. But the principle of responsibility secures that which is the greatest good in states: the right persons rule and are prevented from doing wrong, and the people have their due.

Study Guide Questions

1. We associate election of officeholders with democracy. Aristotle, though, associates election with oligarchy and selection by lot with democracy. Why?

2. What is the secret of combining democratic elements (offices open to all) and aristocratic elements (rule by the best)?

3. Aristotle proposes a voting scheme that gives representation to rich and poor alike. How does it work and how is it a combination of democratic and oligarchic elements?

4. While democracy is a corrupted form of polity, democracy can be better or worse depending on the population composing it. What is the best population for a democracy, and why?

JOHN LOCKE

Second Treatise of Government, 1690

John Locke (1632–1704) is one of the first of the social-contract political philosophers to articulate a theory of separation of powers. Specifically, Locke separates the legislative from the executive power—and then divides the executive into domestic (municipal) and foreign (federative). But Locke is not one to regard these powers as equal and independent. On the contrary, he declares the legislative power supreme, though subordinate to the (usually dormant) sovereignty of the people.

Most Americans, in the early years of independence, followed Locke in treating the legislative power as supreme and the executive power as subordinate and ministerial. That would change with experience and under the influence of other writers.

SOURCE: *John Locke,* Two Treatises of Government, *ed. Peter Laslett (Cambridge: Cambridge University Press, 1988).*

CHAPTER XII

Of the Legislative, Executive, and Federative Power of the Commonwealth

§ 143. The legislative power is that which has a right to direct how the force of the commonwealth shall be employed for preserving the community and the members of it. But because those laws which are constantly to be executed, and whose force is always to continue, may be made in a little time, therefore there is no need that the legislative should be always in being, not having always business to do. And because it may be too great a temptation to human frailty, apt to grasp at power, for the same persons who have the power of making laws, to have also in their hands the power to execute them; whereby they may exempt themselves from obedience to the laws they make, and suit the law, both in its making and execution, to their own private advantage, and thereby come to have a distinct interest from the rest of the community, contrary to the end of society and government: therefore in well ordered commonwealths, where the good of the whole is so considered, as it ought, the legislative power is put into the hands of divers persons, who, duly assembled, have by themselves, or jointly with others, a power to make laws; which when they have done, being separated again, they are themselves subject to the laws they have made; which is a new and near tie upon them, to take care that they make them for the public good.

§ 144. But because the laws, that are at once, and in a short time made, have a constant and lasting force, and need a perpetual execution, or an attendance thereunto; therefore it is necessary there should be a power always in being, which should see to the execution of the laws that are made, and remain in force. And thus the legislative and executive power come often to be separated.

§ 145. There is another power in every commonwealth, which one may call natural, because it is that which answers to the power every man naturally had before he entered into society: for though in a commonwealth, the members of it are distinct persons still in reference to one another, and as such are governed by the laws of the society; yet in reference to the rest of mankind, they make one body, which is, as every member of it before was, still in the state of nature with the rest of mankind. Hence it is, that the controversies that happen between any man of the society with those that are out of it, are managed by the public; and an injury done to a member of their body engages the whole in the reparation of it. So that, under this consideration, the whole community is one body in the state of nature, in respect of all other states or persons out of its community.

§ 146. This therefore contains the power of war and peace, leagues and alliances, and all the transactions with all persons and communities without the commonwealth; and may be called federative, if any one pleases. So the thing be understood, I am indifferent as to the name.

§ 147. These two powers, executive and federative, though they be really distinct in themselves, yet one comprehending the execution of the municipal laws of the society within itself, upon all that are parts of it; the other the management of the security and interest of the public without, with all those that it may receive benefit or damage from; yet they are always almost united. And though this federative power in the well or ill management of it be of great moment to the commonwealth, yet it is much less capable to be directed by antecedent, standing, positive laws, than the executive; and so must necessarily be left to the prudence and wisdom of those whose hands it is in, to be managed for the public good: for the laws that concern subjects one amongst another, being to direct their actions, may well enough precede them. But what is to be done in reference to foreigners, depending much upon their actions, and the variation of designs, and interests, must be left in great part to the prudence of those who have this power committed to them, to be managed by the best of their skill, for the advantage of the commonwealth.

§ 148. Though, as I said, the executive and federative power of every community be really distinct in themselves, yet they are hardly to be separated, and placed at the same time in the hands of distinct persons: for both of them requiring the force of the society for their exercise, it is almost impracticable to place the force of the commonwealth in distinct, and not subordinate hands; or that the executive and federative power should be placed in persons that might act separately, whereby the force of the public would be under different commands; which would be apt some time or other to cause disorder and ruin.

CHAPTER XIII

Of the Subordination of the Powers of the Commonwealth

§ 149. Though in a constituted commonwealth, standing upon its own basis, and acting according to its own nature, that is, acting for the preservation of the community, there can be but one supreme power, which is the legislative, to which all the rest are and must be subordinate; yet the legislative being only a fiduciary power to act for certain ends, there remains still in the people a supreme power to remove or alter the legislative, when they find the legislative act contrary to the trust reposed in them: for all power given with trust for the attaining an end, being limited by that end; whenever that end is manifestly neglected or opposed, the trust must necessarily be forfeited, and the power devolve into the hands of those that gave it, who may place it anew where they shall think best for their safety and security. And thus the community perpetually retains a supreme power of saving themselves from the attempts and designs of any body, even of their legislators, whenever they shall be so foolish, or so wicked, as to lay and carry on designs against the liberties and properties of the subject: for no man, or society of men, having a power to deliver up their preservation, or consequently the means of it, to the absolute will and arbitrary dominion of another; whenever any one shall go about to bring them into such a slavish condition, they will always have a right to preserve what they have not a power to part with; and to rid themselves of those who invade this fundamental, sacred, and unalterable law of self-preservation, for which they entered into society. And thus the community may be said in this respect to be always the supreme power, but not as considered under any form of government, because this power of the people can never take place till the government be dissolved.

> *The natural right of self-preservation entitles the people to dissolve their government, should that government betray their trust.*

§ 150. In all cases, whilst the government subsists, the legislative is the supreme power: for what can give laws to another, must needs be superior to him; and since the legislative is no otherwise legislative of the society, but by the right it has to make laws for all the parts, and for every member of the society, prescribing rules to their actions, and giving power of execution, where they are transgressed; the legislative must needs be the supreme, and all other powers, in any members or parts of the society, derived from and subordinate to it.

Study Guide Questions

1. What two reasons does Locke give for why the executive power should be kept separate from the legislative power?

2. How does Locke define the federative power?

3. Locke's executive, possessing both executive and federative powers, both is and is not under law. Explain.

4. Why will it prove difficult confining the executive to his subordinate station?

MONTESQUIEU

The Spirit of the Laws, 1748

Montesquieu (1689–1755) links regime type to territorial size. Despotism, he argues, is appropriate to an empire; kingship, to a nation-state (e.g., a European country); and republic, to a city-state. City-state republics can, however, align with other republics in a league of friendship for the purpose of defense.

America at the time of the founding was the size of an empire, particularly with the western lands added to the Atlantic states. America, therefore, could not expect to unite as one political body (consolidation) and retain a republican form of government. According to Montesquieuian theory, it seemed that the thirteen states (which already exceeded the acceptable bounds of size) would have to remain independent in regard to sovereignty, while joined confederally for mutual defense and a few other purposes.

Montesquieu defines political liberty not as government by the people but as freedom from the violence of arbitrary power, or as "tranquility of spirit which comes from the opinion each one has of his security." That freedom or tranquility, he contends, is the product of moderate government, and moderate government results from a constitution that checks the power of the rulers. Of the numerous means for checking governmental power (e.g., elections) the one emphasized by Montesquieu is the separation of power into three branches of government: legislative, executive, and judicial.

Except for advocates of simple, unitary regimes (and there were some at the Constitutional Convention), Montesquieu was the last word on guarding liberty through the separation of powers. Controversy, though, attended discussion of the means of separation and the extent.

SOURCE: *Montesquieu,* The Spirit of the Laws, *trans. Thomas Nugent, rev. J. V. Prichard (New York: Appleton, 1900), chapter numbers are altered to conform to modern editions.*

BOOK VIII.16–17, 19–20

16. It is natural for a republic to have only a small territory; otherwise it can not long subsist. In an extensive republic there are men of large fortunes, and consequently of less moderation; there are trusts too considerable to be placed in any single subject; he has interests of his own; he soon begins to think that he may be happy and glorious by oppressing his fellow-citizens; and that he may raise himself to grandeur on the ruins of his country.

In an extensive republic the public good is sacrificed to a thousand private views; it is subordinate to exceptions, and depends on accidents. In a small one, the interest of the public is more obvious, better understood, and more within the reach of every citizen; abuses have less extent, and of course are less protected.

The long duration of the republic of Sparta was owing to her having continued in the same extent of territory after all her wars.[1] The sole aim of Sparta was liberty; and the sole advantage of her liberty, glory.

---

1. Sparta's victory over Athens in the Peloponnesian War (404 B.C.E.) marked a change in this policy that dated back to the city's legendary lawgiver, Lycurgus (ca. 700 B.C.E.). The decline of Sparta began soon thereafter.

It was the spirit of the Greek republics to be as contented with their territories as with their laws. Athens was first fired with ambition and gave it to Lacedaemon [Sparta]; but it was an ambition rather of commanding a free people than of governing slaves; rather of directing than of breaking the union. All was lost upon the starting up of monarchy—a government whose spirit is more turned to increase of dominion.

Excepting particular circumstances, it is difficult for any other than a republican government to subsist in a single town. A prince of so petty a state would naturally endeavor to oppress his subjects, because his power would be great, while the means of enjoying it or of causing it to be respected would be inconsiderable. The consequence is, he would trample upon his people. On the other hand, such a prince might be easily crushed by a foreign or even a domestic force; the people might any instant unite and rise up against him. Now, as soon as the sovereign of a single town is expelled, the quarrel is over; but if he has many towns, it only begins.

17. A monarchical state ought to be of moderate extent. Were it small, it would form itself into a republic; were it very large, the nobility, possessed of great estate, far from the eye of the prince, with a private court of their own, and secure, moreover, from sudden executions by the laws and manners of the country—such a nobility, I say, might throw off their allegiance, having nothing to fear from too slow and too distant a punishment.

Thus Charlemagne[2] had scarcely founded his empire when he was obliged to divide it; whether the governors of the provinces refused to obey; or whether, in order to keep them more under subjection, there was a necessity of parcelling the empire into several kingdoms.

After the decease of Alexander[3] his empire was divided. How was it possible for those Greek and Macedonian chiefs, who were each of them free and independent, or commanders at least of the victorious bands dispersed throughout that vast extent of conquered land—how was it possible, I say, for them to obey?

Attila's empire[4] was dissolved soon after his death; such a number of kings, who were no longer under restraint, could not resume their fetters.

The sudden establishment of unlimited power is a remedy, which in those cases may prevent a dissolution: but how dreadful the remedy, which after enlargement of dominion opens a new scene of misery!

The rivers hasten to mingle their waters with the sea, and monarchies lose themselves in despotic power. . . .

---

2. Charlemagne (742–814), king of the Franks, united much of western Europe under the Carolingian Empire.

3. Alexander the Great (356–323 B.C.E.), king of Macedonia, conquered eastern and central Asia.

4. Attila the Hun (406?–453 C.E.) ruled over vast territories bordering the late Roman Empire.

19. A large empire supposes a despotic authority in the person who governs. It is necessary that the quickness of the prince's resolutions should supply the distance of the places they are sent to; that fear should prevent the remissness of the distant governor or magistrate; that the law should be derived from a single person, and should shift continually, according to the accidents which incessantly multiply in a state in proportion to its extent.

20. If it be, therefore, the natural property of small states to be governed as a republic, of middling ones to be subject to a monarch, and of large empires to be swayed by a despotic prince, the consequence is that, in order to preserve the principles of the established government, the state must be supported in the extent it has acquired, and that the spirit of this state will alter in proportion as it contracts or extends its limits.

BOOK IX.1, 3

1. If a republic be small, it is destroyed by a foreign force; if it be large, it is ruined by an internal imperfection.

To this twofold inconvenience democracies and aristocracies are equally liable, whether they be good or bad. The evil is in the very thing itself, and no form can redress it.

It is, therefore, very probable that mankind would have been, at length, obliged to live constantly under the government of a single person, had they not contrived a kind of constitution that has all the internal advantages of a republican, together with the external force of a monarchical, government. I mean a confederate republic.

A confederate republic solves the problem of size. This form of government is a convention by which several petty [small] states agree to become members of a larger one, which they intend to establish. It is a kind of assemblage of societies, that constitute a new one, capable of increasing by means of further associations, till they arrive at such a degree of power as to be able to provide for the security of the whole body. It was these associations that so long contributed to the prosperity of Greece. By these the Romans attacked the whole globe, and by these alone the whole globe withstood them; for when Rome had arrived at her highest pitch of grandeur, it was the associations beyond the Danube and the Rhine—associations formed by the terror of her arms—that enabled the barbarians to resist her.

Hence it proceeds that Holland, Germany, and the Swiss cantons[5] are considered in Europe as perpetual republics.

---

5. The Dutch Republic, formed in 1588, was a confederation of seven provinces of the Netherlands, united in rebellion against Spanish rule. Germany was a collection of semi-independent duchies and republics, united under the nominal headship of the Holy Roman Emperor. Beginning in the fourteenth century, the eight states, or cantons, of Switzerland were aligned together in a defensive and commercial federation.

The associations of cities were formerly more necessary than in our times. A weak, defenseless town was exposed to greater danger. By conquest it was deprived not only of the executive and legislative power, as at present, but moreover of all human property.

A republic of this kind, able to withstand an external force, may support itself without any internal corruption; the form of this society prevents all manner of inconveniences.

If a single member should attempt to usurp the supreme power, he could not be supposed to have an equal authority and credit in all the confederate states. Were he to have too great an influence over one, this would alarm the rest; were he to subdue a part, that which would still remain free might oppose him with forces independent of those which he had usurped, and overpower him before he could be settled in his usurpation.

Should a popular insurrection happen in one of the confederate states, the others are able to quell it. Should abuses creep into one part, they are reformed by those that remain sound. The state may be destroyed on one side, and not on the other; the confederacy may be dissolved, and the confederates preserve their sovereignty.

As this government is composed of petty republics, it enjoys the internal happiness of each; and with regard to its external situation, by means of the association, it possesses all the advantages of large monarchies.

3. In the republic of Holland one province cannot conclude an alliance without the consent of the others. This law, which is an excellent one, and even necessary in a confederate republic, is wanting in the Germanic constitution, where it would prevent the misfortunes that may happen to the whole confederacy, through the imprudence, ambition, or avarice of a single member. A republic united by a political confederacy has given itself entirely up, and has nothing more to resign.

It is difficult for the united states to be all of equal power and extent. The Lycian republic[6] was an association of twenty-three towns; the large ones had three votes in the common council, the middling ones two, and the small towns one. The Dutch republic consists of seven provinces of different extent of territory, which have each one voice.

The cities of Lycia contributed to the expenses of the state, according to the proportion of suffrages. The provinces of the United Netherlands cannot follow this proportion; they must be directed by that of their power.

In Lycia the judges and town magistrates were elected by the common council, and according to the proportion already mentioned. In the republic of Holland they are not chosen by the common council, but each town names its magistrates. Were I to give a model of an excellent confederate republic, I should pitch upon that of Lycia.

---

6. The Lycian Confederation, existing between 200 and 43 b.c.e., was a league of twenty-three Greek city-states situated along the southern coast of Anatolia, or modern-day Turkey. It is referenced by several of the delegates to the Constitutional Convention.

BOOK XI.1–6

1. I make a distinction between the laws that establish political liberty, as it relates to the constitution, and those by which it is established, as it relates to the citizen. The former shall be the subject of this book; the latter I shall examine in the next.

2. There is no word that admits of more various significations, and has made more varied impressions on the human mind, than that of Liberty. Some have taken it as a means of deposing a person on whom they had conferred a tyrannical authority; others for the power of choosing a superior whom they are obliged to obey; others for the right of bearing arms, and of being thereby enabled to use violence; others, in fine, for the privilege of being governed by a native of their own country, or by their own laws. A certain nation for a long time thought liberty consisted in the privilege of wearing a long beard. Some have annexed this name to one form of government exclusive of others: those who had a republican taste applied it to this species of polity; those who liked a monarchical state gave it to monarchy. Thus they have all applied the name of liberty to the government most suitable to their own customs and inclinations; and as in republics the people have not so constant and so present a view of the causes of their misery, and as the magistrates seem to act only in conformity to the laws, hence liberty is generally said to reside in republics, and to be banished from monarchies. In fine, as in democracies, the people seem to act almost as they please, this sort of government has been deemed the most free, and the power of the people has been confounded with their liberty.

3. It is true that in democracies the people seem to act as they please; but political liberty does not consist in an unlimited freedom. In governments—that is, in societies directed by laws—liberty can consist only in the power of doing what we ought to will, and in not being constrained to do what we ought not to will.

We must have continually present to our minds the difference between independence and liberty. Liberty is a right of doing whatever the laws permit, and if a citizen could do what they forbid he would be no longer possessed of liberty, because all his fellow-citizens would have the same power.

While liberty may mean many things, the one true meaning is government under law, which exists where there are constitutional safeguards against the abuse of power.

4. Democratic and aristocratic states are not in their own nature free. Political liberty is to be found only in moderate governments; and even in these it is not always found. It is there only when there is no abuse of power. But constant experience shows us that every man invested with power is apt to abuse it, and to carry his authority as far as it will go. Is it not strange, though true, to say that virtue itself has need of limits?

To prevent this abuse, it is necessary from the very nature of things that power should be a check to power. A government may be so constituted as no man shall be compelled to do things to which the law does not oblige him, nor forced to abstain from things which the law permits.

PART 5: CORE TEXTS

5. Though all governments have the same general end, which is that of preservation, yet each has another particular object. Increase of dominion was the object of Rome; war, that of Sparta; religion, that of the Jewish laws; commerce, that of Marseilles; public tranquility, that of the laws of China; navigation, that of the laws of Rhodes; natural liberty, that of the policy of the savages; in general, the pleasures of the prince, that of despotic states; that of monarchies, the prince's and the kingdom's glory; the independence of individuals is the end aimed at by the laws of Poland, thence results the oppression of the whole.

One nation there is also in the world that has for the direct end of its constitution political liberty.[7] We shall presently examine the principles on which this liberty is founded; if they are sound, liberty will appear in its highest perfection.

To discover political liberty in a constitution, no great labor is requisite. If we are capable of seeing it where it exists, it is soon found, and we need not go far in search of it.

6. (1)[8] In every government there are three sorts of power: the legislative; the executive in respect to things dependent on the law of nations [foreign affairs]; and the executive in regard to matters that depend on the civil law [adjudication].

Montesquieu is the first political theorist to separate the judiciary power from the executive power.

(2) By virtue of the first, the prince or magistrate enacts temporary or perpetual laws, and amends or abrogates those that have been already enacted. By the second, he makes peace or war, sends or receives embassies, establishes the public security, and provides against invasions. By the third he punishes criminals, or determines the disputes that arise between individuals. The latter we shall call the judiciary power, and the other simply the executive power of the state.

(3) The political liberty of the subject is a tranquility of mind arising from the opinion each person has of his safety. In order to have this liberty, it is requisite that the government be so constituted that one man need not be afraid of another.

(4) When the legislative and executive powers are united in the same person, or in the same body of magistrates, there can be no liberty, because apprehensions may arise lest the same monarch or senate should enact tyrannical laws, to execute them in a tyrannical manner.

(5) Again, there is no liberty if the judiciary power be not separated from the legislative and executive. Were it joined with the legislative, the life and liberty of the subject would be exposed to arbitrary control; for the judge would be then the legislator. Were it joined to the executive power, the judge might behave with violence and oppression.

(6) There would be an end of everything, were the same man or the same body, whether of the nobles or of the people, to exercise these three powers: that of enacting laws, that of executing the public resolutions, and of trying the causes of individuals.

---

7. This nation is England.

8. Paragraph numbering is added here to allow for more precise citation.

(7) Most kingdoms in Europe enjoy a moderate government because the prince who is invested with the first two powers leaves the third to his subjects. In Turkey, where these three powers are united in the Sultan's person, the subjects groan under the most dreadful oppression.[9] . . .

(8) The judiciary power ought not to be given to a standing senate; it should be exercised by persons taken from the body of the people at certain times of the year, and consistently with a form and manner prescribed by law, in order to erect a tribunal that should last only so long as necessity requires.

(9) By this method the judicial power, so terrible to mankind, not being annexed to any particular state or profession, becomes, as it were, invisible. People have not then the judges continually present to their view; they fear the office, but not the magistrate.

(10) In accusations of a deep and criminal nature, it is proper that the person accused should have the privilege of choosing, in some measure, his judges, in concurrence with the law; or at least he should have a right to except against so great a number that the remaining part may be deemed his own choice.

(11) The other two powers may be given rather to magistrates or permanent bodies, because they are not exercised on any private subject; one being no more than the general will of the state, and the other the execution of that general will.

(12) But though the tribunals ought not to be fixed, the judgments ought; and to such a degree as to be ever conformable to the letter of the law. Were they to be the private opinion of the judge, people would then live in society without exactly knowing the nature of their obligations.

(13) The judges ought likewise to be of the same rank as the accused, or, in other words, his peers; to the end that he may not imagine he is fallen into the hands of persons inclined to treat him with rigor.

(14) If the legislature leaves the executive power in possession of a right to imprison those subjects who can give security for their good behavior, there is an end of liberty; unless they are taken up, in order to answer without delay to a capital crime, in which case they are really free, being subject only to the power of the law.

(15) But should the legislature think itself in danger by some secret conspiracy against the state, or by a correspondence with a foreign enemy, it might authorize the executive power, for a short and limited time, to imprison suspected persons, who in that case would lose their liberty only for a while, to preserve it forever. . . .

---

9. Turkey in the eighteenth century was the seat of the Ottoman Empire. Mahmud I was sultan from 1730 to 1754.

(16) As in a country of liberty, every man who is supposed a free agent ought to be his own governor; the legislative power should reside in the whole body of the people. But since this is impossible in large states, and in small ones is subject to many inconveniences, it is fit that the people should transact by their representatives what they can not transact by themselves.

(17) The inhabitants of a particular town are much better acquainted with its wants and interests than with those of other places; and are better judges of the capacity of their neighbors than of that of the rest of their countrymen. The members, therefore, of the legislature should not be chosen from the general body of the nation; but it is proper that in every considerable place a representative should be elected by the inhabitants.

(18) The great advantage of representatives is their capacity of discussing public affairs. For this the people collectively are extremely unfit, which is one of the chief inconveniences of a democracy.

(19) It is not at all necessary that the representatives who have received a general instruction from their constituents should wait to be directed on each particular affair, as is practiced in the Diets of Germany.[10] True it is that by this way of proceeding the speeches of the deputies might with greater propriety be called the voice of the nation; but, on the other hand, this would occasion infinite delays; would give each deputy a power of controlling the assembly; and, on the most urgent and pressing occasions, the wheels of government might be stopped by the caprice of a single person.

(20) When the deputies, as Mr. Sidney[11] well observes, represent a body of people, as in Holland, they ought to be accountable to their constituents; but it is a different thing in England, where they are deputed by boroughs.

(21) All the inhabitants of the several districts ought to have a right of voting at the election of a representative, except such as are in so mean a situation as to be deemed to have no will of their own.

(22) One great fault there was in most of the ancient republics, that the people had a right to active resolutions, such as require some execution, a thing of which they are absolutely incapable. They ought to have no share in the government but for the choosing of representatives, which is within their reach; for though few can tell the exact degree of men's capacities, yet there are none but are capable of knowing in general whether the person they choose is better qualified than most of his neighbors.

Popular participation in a republic should be confined to the election of representatives.

(23) Neither ought the representative body to be chosen for the executive part of government, for which it is not so fit; but for the enacting of laws, or to see

10. The Diet was the parliament of the German Confederation.

11. Algernon Sidney (1622–1683) was the author of *Discourses Concerning Government* (1698). The reference is to chapter III, section 44 of the *Discourses.*

whether the laws in being are duly executed, a thing suited to their abilities, and which none indeed but themselves can properly perform.

(24) In such a state there are always persons distinguished by their birth, riches, or honors; but were they to be confounded with the common people, and to have only the weight of a single vote like the rest, the common liberty would be their slavery, and they would have no interest in supporting it, as most of the popular resolutions would be against them. The share they have, therefore, in the legislature ought to be proportioned to their other advantages in the state, which happens only when they form a body that has a right to check the licentiousness of the people, as the people have a right to oppose any encroachment of theirs.

(25) The legislative power is therefore committed to the body of the nobles, and to that which represents the people, each having their assemblies and deliberations apart, each their separate views and interests.

(26) Of the three powers above mentioned, the judiciary is in some measure next to nothing; there remain, therefore, only two, and as these have need of a regulating power to moderate them, the part of the legislative body composed of the nobility is extremely proper for this purpose.

(27) The body of the nobility ought to be hereditary. In the first place it is so in its own nature; and in the next there must be a considerable interest to preserve its privileges—privileges that in themselves are obnoxious to popular envy, and of course in a free state are always in danger.

(28) But as a hereditary power might be tempted to pursue its own particular interests, and forget those of the people, it is proper that where a singular advantage may be gained by corrupting the nobility, as in the laws relating to the supplies, they should have no other share in the legislation than the power of rejecting, and not that of resolving.

(29) By the power of resolving I mean the right of ordaining by their own authority, or of amending what has been ordained by others. By the power of rejecting I would be understood to mean the right of annulling a resolution taken by another, which was the power of the tribunes at Rome.[12] And though the person possessed of the privilege of rejecting may likewise have the right of approving, yet this approbation passes for no more than a declaration, that he intends to make no use of his privilege of rejecting, and is derived from that very privilege.

(30) The executive power ought to be in the hands of a monarch, because this branch of government, having need of dispatch, is better administered by one than by many; on the other hand, whatever depends on the legislative power is oftentimes better regulated by many than by a single person.

(31) But if there were no monarch, and the executive power should be committed to a certain number of persons selected from the legislative body, there would

---

12. Roman tribunes, in the early days of the republic, had the power to intervene, preventing the arrest of an individual or the implementation of a senate decree.

be an end then of liberty; by reason that the two powers would be united, as the same persons would sometimes possess, and would be always able to possess, a share in both.

(32) Were the legislative body to be a considerable time without meeting, this would likewise put an end to liberty. For of two things one would naturally follow: either that there would be no longer any legislative resolutions, and then the state would fall into anarchy; or that these resolutions would be taken by the executive power, which would render it absolute.

(33) It would be needless for the legislative body to continue always assembled. This would be troublesome to the representatives, and, moreover, would cut out too much work for the executive power, so as to take off its attention to its office, and oblige it to think only of defending its own prerogatives, and the right it has to execute.

(34) Again, were the legislative body to be always assembled, it might happen to be kept up only by filling the places of the deceased members with new representatives; and in that case, if the legislative body were once corrupted, the evil would be past all remedy. When different legislative bodies succeed one another, the people who have a bad opinion of that which is actually sitting may reasonably entertain some hopes of the next; but were it to be always the same body, the people upon seeing it once corrupted would no longer expect any good from its laws; and of course they would either become desperate or fall into a state of indolence.

(35) The legislative body should not meet of itself. For a body is supposed to have no will but when it is met; and besides, were it not to meet unanimously, it would be impossible to determine which was really the legislative body; the part assembled, or the other. And if it had a right to prorogue itself, it might happen never to be prorogued; which would be extremely dangerous, in case it should ever attempt to encroach on the executive power. Besides, there are seasons, some more proper than others, for assembling the legislative body; it is fit, therefore, that the executive power should regulate the time of meeting, as well as the duration of those assemblies, according to the circumstances and exigencies of a state known to itself.

(36) Were the executive power not to have a right of restraining the encroachments of the legislative body, the latter would become despotic; for as it might arrogate to itself what authority it pleased, it would soon destroy all the other powers.

(37) But it is not proper, on the other hand, that the legislative power should have a right to stay the executive; for as the execution has its natural limits, it is useless to confine it; besides, the executive power is generally employed in momentary operations. The power, therefore, of the Roman tribunes was faulty, as it put a stop not only to the legislation, but likewise to the executive part of government, which was attended with infinite mischief.

(38) But if the legislative power in a free state has no right to stay the executive, it has a right and ought to have the means of examining in what manner its

laws have been executed; an advantage which this government [England] has over that of Crete and Sparta, where the Cosmi and the Ephori gave no account of their administration.[13]

(39) But whatever may be the issue of that examination, the legislative body ought not to have a power of arraigning the person, nor, of course, the conduct, of him who is entrusted with the executive power. His person should be sacred, because as it is necessary for the good of the state to prevent the legislative body from rendering themselves arbitrary, the moment he is accused or tried there is an end of liberty.

(40) In this case the state would be no longer a monarchy, but a kind of republic, though not a free government. But as the person entrusted with the executive power can not abuse it without bad counselors, and such as have the laws as ministers, though the laws protect them as subjects, these men may be examined and punished. . . .

(41) Though, in general, the judiciary power ought not to be united with any part of the legislative, yet this is liable to three exceptions, founded on the particular interest of the party accused.

(42) The great are always obnoxious to popular envy; and were they to be judged by the people, they might be in danger from their judges, and would, moreover, be deprived of the privilege which the meanest subject is possessed of in a free state, of being tried by his peers. The nobility, for this reason, ought not to be cited before the ordinary courts of judicature, but before that part of the legislature which is composed of their own body.

(43) It is possible that the law, which is clear-sighted in one sense, and blind in another, might, in some cases, be too severe. But, as we have already observed, the national judges are no more than the mouth that pronounces the words of the law, mere passive beings, incapable of moderating either its force or rigor. That part, therefore, of the legislative body which we have just now observed to be a necessary tribunal on another occasion, is also a necessary tribunal in this; it belongs to its supreme authority to moderate the law in favor of the law itself, by mitigating the sentence.

(44) It might also happen that a subject entrusted with the administration of public affairs may infringe the rights of the people, and be guilty of crimes which the ordinary magistrates either could not or would not punish. But, in general, the legislative power can not try causes; and much less can it try this particular case, where it represents the party aggrieved, which is the people. It can only, therefore, impeach. But before what court shall it bring its impeachment? Must it go and demean itself before the ordinary tribunals, which are its inferiors, and, being

---

13. The Cretan constitution consisted of the cosmi (magistrates), the gerousia (council of elders), and the ecclesia (assembly of the people). The Spartan constitution was similarly organized.

composed, moreover, of men who are chosen from the people as well as itself, will naturally be swayed by the authority of so powerful an accuser? No; in order to preserve the dignity of the people, and the security of the subject, the legislative part which represents the people must bring in its charge before the legislative part which represents the nobility, who have neither the same interests nor the same passions.

(45) Here is an advantage which this government has over most of the ancient republics, where this abuse prevailed, that the people were at the same time both judge and accuser.

(46) The executive power, pursuant of what has been already said, ought to have a share in the legislature by the power of rejecting, otherwise it would soon be stripped of its prerogative. But should the legislative power usurp a share of the executive, the latter would be equally undone.

(47) If the prince were to have a part in the legislature by the power of resolving, liberty would be lost. But as it is necessary he should have a share in the legislature for the support of his own prerogative, this share must consist in the power of rejecting.

(48) The change of government at Rome was owing to this, that neither the senate, who had one part of the executive power, nor the magistrates, who were entrusted with the other, had the right of rejecting, which was entirely lodged in the people.[14]

Notice that the natural state of a government composed of divided powers is inaction, not action.

(49) Here, then, is the fundamental constitution of the government we are treating of [England]. The legislative body being composed of two parts, they check one another by the mutual privilege of rejecting. They are both restrained by the executive power, as the executive is by the legislative.

(50) These three powers should naturally form a state of repose or inaction. But as there is a necessity for movement in the course of human affairs, they are forced to move, but still in concert.

(51) As the executive power has no other part in the legislative than the privilege of rejecting, it can have no share in the public debates. It is not even necessary that it should propose, because as it may always disapprove of the resolutions that shall be taken, it may likewise reject the decisions on those proposals which were made against its will.

(52) In some ancient commonwealths, where public debates were carried on by the people in a body, it was natural for the executive power to propose and debate in conjunction with the people, otherwise their resolutions must have been attended with a strange confusion.

---

14. The change in the government of Rome was from the republic, founded in 509 B.C.E., to the empire under the Caesars. A century of civil wars preceded the change. Rome had multiple assemblies during its republican period, the most important being the assembly of tribes (*comitia tributa*). Its laws could not be rejected by the senate, representing the patrician class, or by the consuls, functioning as Rome's chief magistrates.

(53) Were the executive power to determine the raising of public money otherwise than by giving its consent, liberty would be at an end, because it would become legislative in the most important point of legislation.

(54) If the legislative power was to settle the subsidies, not from year to year, but forever, it would run the risk of losing its liberty, because the executive power would be no longer dependent; and when once it was possessed of such a perpetual right, it would be a matter of indifference whether it held it of itself or of another. The same may be said if it should come to a resolution of entrusting, not an annual but a perpetual command of the fleets and armies to the executive power.

(55) To prevent the executive power from being able to oppress, it is requisite that the armies with which it is entrusted should consist of the people, and have the same spirit as the people, as was the case at Rome till the time of Marius.[15] To obtain this end, there are only two ways: either that the persons employed in the army should have sufficient property to answer for their conduct to their fellow-subjects, and be enlisted only for a year, as was customary at Rome; or if there should be a standing army, composed chiefly of the most despicable part of the nation, the legislative power should have a right to disband them as soon as it pleased; the soldiers should live in common with the rest of the people; and no separate camp, barracks, or fortress should be suffered.

(56) When once an army is established, it ought not to depend immediately on the legislative but on the executive power; and this from the very nature of the thing, its business consisting more in action than in deliberation.

The English mixed government is modeled on the political practices of the German "barbarians" who fought and defeated the Romans.

(57) It is natural for mankind to set a higher value upon courage than timidity, on activity than prudence, on strength than counsel. Hence the army will ever despise a senate, and respect their own officers. They will naturally slight the orders sent them by a body of men whom they look upon as cowards, and therefore unworthy to command them. So that as soon as the troops depend entirely on the legislative body, it becomes a military government; and if the contrary has ever happened, it has been owing to some extraordinary circumstances. It is because the army was always kept divided; it is because it was composed of several bodies that depended each on a particular province; it is because the capital towns were strong places, defended by their natural situation, and not garrisoned with regular troops. Holland, for instance, is still safer than Venice; she might drown or starve the revolted troops, for as they are not quartered in towns capable of furnishing them with necessary subsistence, this subsistence is of course precarious.

---

15. Gaius Marius (157–86 B.C.E.), a seven-time consul of Rome, extended opportunity for military service to the landless masses. Previously, and from the time of the kings, soldiers were property-owning citizens, placed in a class, or century, and assigned duty according to the arms they personally could supply. Marius converted this citizen militia into a professional, standing army, composed mainly of the poor whose loyalty was to their general.

(58) In perusing the admirable treatise of Tacitus "On the Manners of the Germans,"[16] we find it is from that nation that the English have borrowed the idea of their political government. This beautiful system was invented first in the woods.

(59) As all human things have an end, the state we are speaking of will lose its liberty, will perish. Have not Rome, Sparta, and Carthage perished? It will perish when the legislative power shall be more corrupt than the executive.

(60) It is not my business to examine whether the English actually enjoy this liberty or not. Sufficient it is for my purpose to observe that it is established by their laws; and I inquire no further.

(61) Neither do I pretend by this to undervalue other governments, nor to say that this extreme political liberty ought to give uneasiness to those who have only a moderate share of it. How should I have any such design, I who think that even the highest refinement of reason is not always desirable, and that mankind generally find their account better in mediums than in extremes?

(62) Harrington, in his "Oceana," has also inquired into the utmost degree of liberty to which the constitution of a state may be carried. But of him, indeed, it may be said that for want of knowing the nature of real liberty he busied himself in pursuit of an imaginary one; and that he built a Chalcedon, though he had a Byzantium before his eyes.[17]

Study Guide Questions

1. Why does size matter? Why can there be no monarchy in a single town and no republic over an extended state?

2. What protects confederations from abuse and usurpation within? Might these wider protections suggest wider purposes than defense against foreign invaders?

3. What does Montesquieu think about instructed representatives as a means of expressing the voice of the people?

4. What function does bicameralism serve for Montesquieu?

---

16. Publius Cornelius Tacitus (56–117 c.e.) was a Roman historian writing during the early empire. His two major works, the Annals and the Histories, relate the lives of the emperors from Tiberius (42 b.c.e.–37 c.e.) to Domitian (51–96 c.e.) Montesquieu's reference is to *Germania*, an ethnographic work on the Germanic tribes outside the Roman Empire.

17. James Harrington (1611–1677) was the author of *The Commonwealth of Oceana and a System of Politics* (1656). Harrington's Oceana is an imaginary republic. Montesquieu is critiquing Harrington for creating an ideal constitution (Chalcedon on the Asian side of the Bosphorus) when he could have used the materials of the English constitution (Byzantium on the European side of the Bosphorus).

5. A refrain running through Montesquieu's Book XI is that such and such practice or institution will "bring an end to liberty." What are some of these liberty-killing constitutional arrangements?

6. What are the dangers of a legislative body too frequently in session, too permanently in session, and empowered to call itself into and out of session?

7. What power should the legislative branch have over the executive branch?

8. Does Montesquieu believe in judicial review?

9. What legislative power is appropriate for the executive to exercise?

10. What is Montesquieu's view of standing armies?

DAVID HUME

Essays Moral, Political, and Literary, 1758

Many Americans, realizing that popular government was bedeviled by parties, sects, and factions, thought it imperative to find ways of preventing their emergence or of minimizing their harm. The small republic, recommended by the ancients, was the solution of choice.

David Hume (1711–1776) was one of the early political philosophers to regard faction as indelibly stamped on human nature; he thus turned his attention from eliminating factions to managing their ill effects. James Madison agreed and built on Hume's insight that faction is better managed in large rather than in small republics.

SOURCE: *David Hume,* Essays Moral, Political, and Literary *(Indianapolis: Liberty Fund, 1987).*

"OF PARTIES IN GENERAL"

*O*f all men, that distinguish themselves by memorable achievements, the first place of honor seems due to LEGISLATORS and founders of states, who transmit a system of laws and institutions to secure the peace, happiness, and liberty of future generations. The influence of useful inventions in the arts and sciences may, perhaps, extend farther than that of wise laws, whose effects are limited both in time and place; but the benefit arising from the former, is not so sensible as that which results from the latter. Speculative sciences do, indeed, improve the mind; but this advantage reaches only to a few persons, who have leisure to apply themselves to them. And as to practical arts, which increase the commodities and enjoyments of life, it is well known, that men's happiness consists not so much in an abundance of these, as in the peace and security with which they possess them; and those blessings can only be derived from good government. Not to mention, that general virtue and good morals in a state, which are so requisite to happiness, can never arise from the most refined precepts of philosophy, or even the severest injunctions of religion; but must proceed entirely from the virtuous education of youth, the effect of wise laws and institutions. I must, therefore, presume to differ from LORD BACON[1] in this particular, and must regard antiquity as somewhat unjust in its distribution of honors, when it made gods of all the inventors of useful arts, such as CERES, BACCHUS, AESCULAPIUS;[2] and dignified legislators, such as ROMULUS and THESEUS,[3] only with the appellation of demigods and heroes.

As much as legislators and founders of states ought to be honored and respected among men, as much ought the founders of sects and factions to be detested and hated; because the influence of faction is directly contrary to that of laws. Factions subvert government, render laws impotent, and beget the fiercest animosities among men of the same nation, who ought to give mutual assistance and protection to each other. And what should render the founders of parties more odious is, the difficulty of extirpating these weeds, when once they have taken root in any state. They naturally propagate themselves for many centuries, and seldom end but by the total dissolution of that government, in which they are sown. They are, besides, plants which grow most plentifully in the richest soil; and though absolute governments be not entirely free from them, it must be confessed, that they rise more easily, and propagate themselves faster in free governments, where they always infect the legislature itself, which alone could be able, by the steady application of rewards and punishments, to eradicate them.

Political faction is an evil that occurs most commonly in free governments.

Factions may be divided into PERSONAL and REAL; that is, into factions, founded on personal friendship or animosity among such as compose the contending parties, and into those founded on some real difference of sentiment or interest. The

---

1. Francis Bacon (1561–1626), author of *The New Organon*, gives first prize to inventors, "for the benefits of discoveries may extend to the whole race of man, civil benefits only to particular places; the latter last not beyond a few ages, the former through all time. Moreover, the reformation of a state in civil matters is seldom brought in without violence and confusion; but discoveries carry blessings with them, and confer benefits without causing harm or sorrow to any" (Aphorism CXXIX).

2. All were Roman gods: Ceres the god of crops (cereal); Bacchus the god of wine; and Aesculapius the god of medicine.

3. Romulus, the legendary founder of Rome, was said to be the offspring of Mars, and Theseus, the legendary founder of Athens, was said to be the offspring of Poseidon.

reason of this distinction is obvious; though I must acknowledge, that parties are seldom found pure and unmixed, either of the one kind or the other. It is not often seen, that a government divides into factions, where there is no difference in the views of the constituent members, either real or apparent, trivial or material: And in those factions, which are founded on the most real and most material difference, there is always observed a great deal of personal animosity or affection. But notwithstanding this mixture, a party may be denominated either personal or real, according to that principle which is predominant, and is found to have the greatest influence.

Personal factions arise most easily in small republics. Every domestic quarrel, there, becomes an affair of state. Love, vanity, emulation, any passion, as well as ambition and resentment, begets public division. The NERI and BIANCHI of FLORENCE,[4] the FREGOSI and ADORNI of GENOA,[5] the COLONESI and ORSINI of modern ROME,[6] were parties of this kind.

Men have such a propensity to divide into personal factions, that the smallest appearance of real difference will produce them. What can be imagined more trivial than the difference between one color of livery and another in horse races? Yet this difference begat two most inveterate factions in the GREEK empire, the PRASINI and VENETI,[7] who never suspended their animosities, till they ruined that unhappy government.

We find in the ROMAN history a remarkable dissension between two tribes, the POLLIA and PAPIRIA,[8] which continued for the space of near three hundred years, and discovered itself in their suffrages at every election of magistrates. This faction was the more remarkable, as it could continue for so long a tract of time; even though it did not spread itself, nor draw any of the other tribes into a share of the quarrel. If mankind had not a strong propensity to such divisions, the indifference of the rest of the community must have suppressed this foolish animosity, that had not

---

4. The Neri (Blacks) and the Bianchi (Whites) were two factions within the Guelf party of Florence. The split occurred around 1300.

5. The Fregosi and the Adorni were prominent Genoese families who for a century and a half competed for the office of Doge. Their rivalry began around 1370.

6. Roman politics from the thirteenth century on divided between the Colonna family of the Guelf party and the Orsini family of the Ghibelline party.

7. The Prasini (Greens) and the Veneti (Blues) were teams of charioteers who competed in the hippodrome of Constantinople. They and their fans often engaged in bloody conflicts.

8. The Pollia and the Papiria were two of the thirty-five tribes of Rome. As reported by Livy in his *History of Rome* (VIII.37), the people of Tusculum, in 325 B.C.E., were put on trial for having given support to Rome's enemies. All the tribes voted for leniency, except the Pollia, which proposed killing the men and selling the women and children into slavery. The Tusculans were spared and later made part of the Papirian tribe. For three centuries thereafter, down to Livy's time, the Papiria, remembering the event, voted against political candidates from the Pollian tribe.

any aliment of new benefits and injuries, of general sympathy and antipathy, which never fail to take place, when the whole state is rent into two equal factions.

Nothing is more usual than to see parties, which have begun upon a real difference, continue even after that difference is lost. When men are once enlisted on opposite sides, they contract an affection to the persons with whom they are united, and an animosity against their antagonists: And these passions they often transmit to their posterity. The real difference between GUELF and GHIBBELLINE was long lost in ITALY, before these factions were extinguished. The GUELFs adhered to the pope, the GHIBBELLINEs to the emperor;[9] and yet the family of SFORZA, who were in alliance with the emperor, though they were GUELFs, being expelled [from] MILAN by the king of FRANCE, assisted by JACOMO TRIVULZIO and the GHIBBELLINES, the pope concurred with the latter, and they formed leagues with the pope against the emperor.[10]

The civil wars which arose some few years ago in MOROCCO, between the *blacks* and *whites*, merely on account of their complexion, are founded on a pleasant difference.[11] We laugh at them; but I believe, were things rightly examined, we afford much more occasion of ridicule to the MOORS. For, what are all the wars of religion, which have prevailed in this polite and knowing part of the world? They are certainly more absurd than the MOORISH civil wars. The difference of complexion is a sensible and a real difference: But the controversy about an article of faith, which is utterly absurd and unintelligible, is not a difference in sentiment, but in a few phrases and expressions, which one party accepts of, without understanding them; and the other refuses in the same manner.

Real factions may be divided into those from *interest*, from *principle*, from *affection*. Of all factions, the first are the most reasonable, and the most excusable. Where two orders of men, such as the nobles and people, have a distinct authority in a government, not very accurately balanced and modelled, they naturally follow a distinct interest; nor can we reasonably expect a different conduct, considering that degree of selfishness implanted in human nature. It requires great skill in a legislator to prevent such parties; and many philosophers are of opinion, that this secret, like the *grand elixir*, or *perpetual motion*,[12] may amuse men in theory, but can never

> *Eliminating real factions of interest may well exceed the capacity of legislators.*

---

9. The Guelf–Ghibelline division had its origins in the twelfth century when Holy Roman Emperor Frederick Barbarossa invaded Italy.

10. Duke Ludovico Sforza of Milan formed an alliance with Emperor Maximilian I to resist an invasion of Italy by the French king Louis XII (1499–1500). Ludovico's former commander, Gian Giacomo Trivulzio, led the French army. Pope Alexander VI was in league with the French.

11. The bodyguard of Sultan Moulay Ishmail (r. 1672–1727), called the Black Guard, was made up of descendants of sub-Saharan black slaves. After the sultan's death, a civil war broke out, with race as a factor.

12. The grand elixir is an alchemical potion thought to cure disease and restore youth. A perpetual motion machine is one that, once started, runs forever without additional fuel.

possibly be reduced to practice. In despotic governments, indeed, factions often do not appear; but they are not the less real; or rather, they are more real and more pernicious, upon that very account. The distinct orders of men, nobles and people, soldiers and merchants, have all a distinct interest; but the more powerful oppresses the weaker with impunity, and without resistance; which begets a seeming tranquillity in such governments.

There has been an attempt in ENGLAND to divide the landed and trading part of the nation; but without success. The interest of these two bodies are not really distinct, and never will be so, till our public debts increase to such a degree, as to become altogether oppressive and intolerable.

Parties from principle, especially abstract speculative principle, are known only to modern times, and are, perhaps, the most extraordinary and unaccountable phenomenon, that has yet appeared in human affairs. Where different principles beget a contrariety of conduct, which is the case with all different political principles, the matter may be more easily explained. A man, who esteems the true right of government to lie in one man, or one family, cannot easily agree with his fellow citizen, who thinks that another man or family is possessed of this right. Each naturally wishes that right may take place, according to his own notions of it. But where the difference of principle is attended with no contrariety of action, but every one may follow his own way, without interfering with his neighbor, as happens in all religious controversies; what madness, what fury can beget such unhappy and such fatal divisions?

Two men, travelling on the highway, the one east, the other west, can easily pass each other, if the way be broad enough: But two men, reasoning upon opposite principles of religion, cannot so easily pass, without shocking; though one should think, that the way were also, in that case, sufficiently broad, and that each might proceed, without interruption, in his own course. But such is the nature of the human mind, that it always lays hold on every mind that approaches it; and as it is wonderfully fortified by an unanimity of sentiments, so is it shocked and disturbed by any contrariety. Hence the eagerness, which most people discover in a dispute; and hence their impatience of opposition, even in the most speculative and indifferent opinions. . . .

I have mentioned parties from affection as a kind of real parties, beside those from interest and principle. By parties from affection, I understand those which are founded on the different attachments of men towards particular families and persons, whom they desire to rule over them. These factions are often very violent; though, I must own, it may seem unaccountable, that men should attach themselves so strongly to persons, with whom they are no wise acquainted, whom perhaps they never saw, and from whom they never received, nor can ever hope for any favor. Yet this we often find to be the case, and even with men, who, on other occasions, discover no great generosity of spirit, nor are found to be easily transported by friendship beyond their own interest. We are apt to think the relation

Lingering attachment to the Stuart line after the arrival of the Hanovers would be an example of real faction based on affection.

between us and our sovereign very close and intimate. The splendor of majesty and power bestows an importance on the fortunes even of a single person. And when a man's good-nature does not give him this imaginary interest, his ill-nature will, from spite and opposition to persons whose sentiments are different from his own.

"OF THE PARTIES OF GREAT BRITAIN"

*W*ere the BRITISH government proposed as a subject of speculation, one would immediately perceive in it a source of division and party, which it would be almost impossible for it, under any administration, to avoid. The just balance between the republican and monarchical part of our constitution is really, in itself, so extremely delicate and uncertain, that, when joined to men's passions and prejudices, it is impossible but different opinions must arise concerning it, even among persons of the best understanding. Those of mild tempers, who love peace and order, and detest sedition and civil wars, will always entertain more favorable sentiments of monarchy, than men of bold and generous spirits, who are passionate lovers of liberty, and think no evil comparable to subjection and slavery. And though all reasonable men agree in general to preserve our mixed government; yet, when they come to particulars, some will incline to trust larger powers to the crown, to bestow on it more influence, and to guard against its encroachments with less caution, than others who are terrified at the most distant approaches of tyranny and despotic power.

> *Human temperament is one cause of party, dividing those who prefer order from those who prefer liberty.*

Thus are there parties of PRINCIPLE involved in the very nature of our constitution, which may properly enough be denominated those of COURT and COUNTRY.[13] The strength and violence of each of these parties will much depend upon the particular administration. An administration may be so bad, as to throw a great majority into the opposition; as a good administration will reconcile to the court many of the most passionate lovers of liberty. But however the nation may fluctuate between them, the parties themselves will always subsist, so long as we are governed by a limited monarchy.

But, besides this difference of *Principle*, those parties are very much fomented by a difference of INTEREST, without which they could scarcely ever be dangerous or violent. The crown will naturally bestow all trust and power upon those, whose principles, real or pretended, are most favorable to monarchical government; and this temptation will naturally engage them to go to greater lengths than their principles would otherwise carry them. Their antagonists, who are disappointed in their ambitious aims, throw themselves into the party whose sentiments incline them to be most jealous of royal power, and naturally carry those sentiments to

---

13. These terms were defined earlier in the game book in the section "Republican Theory at the Time of the Founding."

a greater height than sound politics will justify. Thus *Court* and *Country*, which are the genuine offspring of the BRITISH government, are a kind of mixed parties, and are influenced both by principle and by interest. The heads of the factions are commonly most governed by the latter motive; the inferior members of them by the former. . . .

If we consider the first rise of parties in ENGLAND, during the great rebellion,[14] we shall find, that it was conformable to this general theory, and that the species of government gave birth to them, by a regular and infallible operation. The ENGLISH constitution, before that time, had lain in a kind of confusion; yet so, as that the subjects possessed many noble privileges, which, though not exactly bounded and secured by law, were universally deemed, from long possession, to belong to them as their birth-right. An ambitious, or rather a misguided, prince arose,[15] who deemed all these privileges to be concessions of his predecessors, revokeable at pleasure; and, in prosecution of this principle, he openly acted in violation of liberty, during the course of several years. Necessity, at last, constrained him to call a parliament; the spirit of liberty arose and spread itself; the prince, being without any support, was obliged to grant every thing required of him; and his enemies, jealous and implacable, set no bounds to their pretensions. Here then began those contests, in which it was no wonder, that men of that age were divided into different parties; since, even at this day, the impartial are at a loss to decide concerning the justice of the quarrel. The pretensions of the parliament, if yielded to, broke the balance of the constitution, by rendering the government almost entirely republican. If not yielded to, the nation was, perhaps, still in danger of absolute power, from the settled principles and inveterate habits of the king, which had plainly appeared in every concession that he had been constrained to make to his people. In this question, so delicate and uncertain, men naturally fell to the side which was most conformable to their usual principles; and the more passionate favorers of monarchy declared for the king, as the zealous friends of liberty sided with the parliament. The hopes of success being nearly equal on both sides, interest had no general influence in this contest: So that ROUND-HEAD and CAVALIER were merely parties of principle;[16] neither of which disowned either monarchy or liberty; but the former party inclined most to the republican part of our government, the latter to the monarchical. In this respect, they may be considered as court and country-party, inflamed into a civil war, by an unhappy concurrence of circumstances, and by the turbulent spirit of the age. The commonwealth's men, and the partisans of absolute power, lay concealed in both parties, and formed but an inconsiderable part of them. . . .

---

14. The English Civil Wars of 1642–51.

15. Charles I (r. 1625–49). Charles started the war when he organized an army to oppose Parliament. Parliament had previously extorted concessions in exchange for revenues to fight the Scots who had entered English territory.

16. Roundheads were the supporters of Parliament; Cavaliers, the supporters of the king.

Every one knows the event of this quarrel; fatal to the king first, to the parliament afterwards.[17] After many confusions and revolutions, the royal family was at last restored, and the ancient government re-established. CHARLES II was not made wiser by the example of his father; but prosecuted the same measures, though at first, with more secrecy and caution. New parties arose, under the appellation of *Whig* and *Tory*,[18] which have continued ever since to confound and distract our government. . . .

A TORY, therefore, since the *revolution*, may be defined in a few words, to be *a lover of monarchy, though without abandoning liberty; and a partisan of the family of* STUART. As a WHIG may be defined to be *a lover of liberty though without renouncing monarchy; and a friend to the settlement in the* PROTESTANT *line.*

These different views, with regard to the settlement of the crown, were accidental, but natural additions to the principles of the *court* and *country* parties, which are the genuine divisions in the BRITISH government. A passionate lover of monarchy is apt to be displeased at any change of the succession, as favoring too much of a commonwealth; a passionate lover of liberty is apt to think that every part of the government ought to be subordinate to the interests of liberty. . . .

"IDEA OF A PERFECT COMMONWEALTH"

. . . *W*e shall conclude this subject, with observing the falsehood of the common opinion, that no large state, such as FRANCE or BRITAIN, could ever be modeled into a commonwealth, but that such a form of government can only take place in a city or small territory. The contrary seems probable. Though it is more difficult to form a republican government in an extensive country than in a city; there is more facility, when once it is formed, of preserving it steady and uniform, without tumult and faction. It is not easy, for the distant parts of a large state to combine in any plan of free government; but they easily conspire in the esteem and reverence for a single person, who, by means of this popular favor, may seize the power, and forcing the more obstinate to submit, may establish a monarchical government. On the other hand, a city readily concurs in the same notions of government, the natural equality of property favors liberty, and the nearness of

Contrary to what Montesquieu claims, republics can be established in country-size states.

---

17. Charles I was executed in 1649. Parliament's heyday lasted only a decade. Not long after the death of Oliver Cromwell, lord protector, Charles's son, living in exile in France, was restored to the throne as Charles II (r. 1660–85). Thus began the period in English history known as the Restoration.

18. Whig, originally, was a Scottish-Gaelic term of abuse connoting thievery and rebellion. It was first used politically in the 1670s to denominate persons agitating to exclude the king's brother, James, from ascending to the throne. Tory, originally, was an Irish term of abuse connoting papist sympathizer. It was used to describe supporters of James, who was suspected of being a Catholic. (See "Republican Theory at the Time of the Founding," earlier in the game book.)

habitation enables the citizens mutually to assist each other. Even under absolute princes, the subordinate government of cities is commonly republican; while that of counties and provinces is monarchical. But these same circumstances, which facilitate the erection of commonwealths in cities, render their constitution more frail and uncertain. Democracies are turbulent. For however the people may be separated or divided into small parties, either in their votes or elections; their near habitation in a city will always make the force of popular tides and currents very sensible. Aristocracies are better adapted for peace and order, and accordingly were most admired by ancient writers; but they are jealous and oppressive. In a large government, which is modeled with masterly skill, there is compass and room enough to refine the democracy from the lower people, who may be admitted into the first elections or first concoction of the commonwealth, to the higher magistrates, who direct all the movements. At the same time, the parts are so distant and remote, that it is very difficult, either by intrigue, prejudice, or passion, to hurry them into any measures against the public interest.

It is needless to inquire, whether such a government would be immortal. I allow the justness of the poet's exclamation on the endless projects of human race, *Man and for ever!*[19] The world itself probably is not immortal. Such consuming plagues may arise as would leave even a perfect government a weak prey to its neighbors. We know not to what length enthusiasm, or other extraordinary movements of the human mind, may transport men, to the neglect of all order and public good. Where difference of interest is removed, whimsical and unaccountable factions often arise, from personal favor or enmity. Perhaps, rust may grow to the springs of the most accurate political machine, and disorder its motions. Lastly, extensive conquests, when pursued, must be the ruin of every free government; and of the more perfect governments sooner than of the imperfect; because of the very advantages which the former possess above the latter. And though such a state ought to establish a fundamental law against conquest; yet republics have ambition as well as individuals, and present interest makes men forgetful of their posterity. It is a sufficient incitement to human endeavors, that such a government would flourish for many ages; without pretending to bestow, on any work of man, that immortality, which the Almighty seems to have refused to his own productions.

Study Guide Questions

"Of Parties in General"

1. According to Hume, what types of factions exist in developed societies?

2. Give examples of factions derived from interest.

---

19. The poet is unknown, though Horace (Satires, II.8.62) and Lucretius (*The Nature of Things*, II.76) express similar sentiments about the impermanence of human creations.

"Of the Parties of Great Britain"

3. What are the contending principles and interests that cause Britain's mixed government to be divided by faction?

4. What was the origin of parties in seventeenth-century Britain? How does that division manifest itself in eighteenth-century Britain?

"Idea of a Perfect Commonwealth"

5. Although a republic can more easily be established in a small state than in a large state, a small state will more easily be destroyed by a republic. Why?

THOMAS PAINE

Common Sense, 1776

Thomas Paine (1737–1809), a recent immigrant to America, soon became the country's premier defender of the simple, or unitary, regime. He lived in Pennsylvania, whose constitution of 1776 most nearly approximated a simple regime.

The standard typology of regimes traces to Aristotle, who identified three simple regimes based on the number of persons exercising power: one, few, or many. Government by one is kingship (or monarchy), by a few is aristocracy, and by many is polity. Aristotle added that these simple regimes present in healthy and unhealthy forms, depending on whether they serve the common good or merely the good of the rulers. When the latter, government by one is tyranny, by a few is oligarchy, and by the many is democracy.

Today, and for the past two centuries, democracy has been used in a positive way to designate popular rule in service to the commonweal. Americans at the time of the founding, however, regarded democracy as did Aristotle, as government by the many, who are the poor, ruling solely for the sake of the poor (hence democracies were noted for such policies as cancellation of debts, redistribution of land, and emissions of paper money). Instead of Aristotle's polity, Americans used republic to denominate the good form of popular rule. But a republic was usually a mixed regime, combining popular and nonpopular elements. Paine denounces mixed regimes, and in particular the mixed regime of the English constitution, so widely admired in the Western world.

SOURCE: *Thomas Paine,* Common Sense *(New York: Penguin, 1986).*

ON THE ORIGIN AND DESIGN OF GOVERNMENT IN GENERAL, WITH CONCISE REMARKS ON THE ENGLISH CONSTITUTION

Some writers have so confounded society with government, as to leave little or no distinction between them; whereas they are not only different, but have different origins. Society is produced by our wants, and government by our wickedness; the former promotes our happiness positively by uniting our affections, the latter negatively by restraining our vices. The one encourages intercourse, the other creates distinctions. The first is a patron, the last a punisher.

Society in every state is a blessing, but government even in its best state is but a necessary evil; in its worst state an intolerable one; for when we suffer, or are exposed to the same miseries by a government, which we might expect in a country without government, our calamities are heightened by reflecting that we furnish the means by which we suffer. Government, like dress, is the badge of lost innocence; the palaces of kings are built on the ruins of the bowers of paradise. For were the impulses of conscience clear, uniform, and irresistibly obeyed, man would need no other lawgiver; but that not being the case, he finds it necessary to surrender up a part of his property to furnish means for the protection of the rest; and this he is induced to do by the same prudence which in every other case advises him out of two evils to choose the least. Wherefore, security being the true design and end of government, it unanswerably follows that whatever form thereof appears most likely to ensure it to us, with the least expense and greatest benefit, is preferable to all others.

In order to gain a clear and just idea of the design and end of government, let us suppose a small number of persons settled in some sequestered part of the earth, unconnected with the rest; they will then represent the first peopling of any country, or of the world. In this state of natural liberty, society will be their first thought. A thousand motives will excite them thereto, the strength of one man is so unequal to his wants, and his mind so unfitted for perpetual solitude, that he is soon obliged to seek assistance and relief of another, who in his turn requires the same. Four or five united would be able to raise a tolerable dwelling in the midst of a wilderness, but one man might labor out the common period of life without accomplishing anything; when he had felled his timber he could not remove it, nor erect it after it was removed; hunger in the mean time would urge him from his work, and every different want call him a different way. Disease, nay even misfortune, would be death, for though neither might be mortal, yet either would disable him from living, and reduce him to a state in which he might rather be said to perish than to die.

Thus necessity, like a gravitating power, would soon form our newly arrived emigrants into society, the reciprocal blessings of which, would supersede, and render the obligations of law and government unnecessary while they remained perfectly just to each other; but as nothing but heaven is impregnable to vice, it will unavoidably happen, that in proportion as they surmount the first difficulties of emigration, which bound them together in a common cause, they will begin to relax in their duty and attachment to each other; and this remissness, will point out the necessity of establishing some form of government to supply the defect of moral virtue.

Some convenient tree will afford them a State-House, under the branches of which the whole colony may assemble to deliberate on public matters. It is more than probable that their first laws will have the title only of REGULATIONS, and be enforced by no other penalty than public disesteem. In this first parliament every man, by natural right, will have a seat.

But as the colony increases, the public concerns will increase likewise, and the distance at which the members may be separated, will render it too inconvenient for all of them to meet on every occasion as at first, when their number was small, their habitations near, and the public concerns few and trifling. This will point out the convenience of their consenting to leave the legislative part to be managed by a select number chosen from the whole body, who are supposed to have the same concerns at stake which those have who appointed them, and who will act in the same manner as the whole body would act were they present. If the colony continue increasing, it will become necessary to augment the number of the representatives; and that the interest of every part of the colony may be attended to, it will be found best to divide the whole into convenient parts, each part sending its proper number; and that the *elected* might never form to themselves an interest separate from the *electors*, prudence will point out the propriety of having elections often; because as the *elected* might by that means return and mix again with the general body of the *electors* in a few months, their fidelity to the public will be secured by the prudent reflection of not making a rod for themselves. And as this frequent interchange will establish a common interest with every part of the community, they will mutually and naturally support each other, and on this (not on the unmeaning name of king) depends the *strength of government, and the happiness of the governed.*

Here then is the origin and rise of government; namely, a mode rendered necessary by the inability of moral virtue to govern the world; here too is the design and end of government, viz. [namely] freedom and security. And however our eyes may be dazzled with snow, or our ears deceived by sound; however prejudice may warp our wills, or interest darken our understanding, the simple voice of nature and of reason will say, it is right.

I draw my idea of the form of government from a principle in nature, which no art can overturn, viz. [namely] that the more simple anything is, the less liable it is to be disordered, and the easier repaired when disordered; and with this maxim in view, I offer a few remarks on the so much boasted constitution of

Simple government with elected representatives is less prone to corruption than mixed government with nobles and a king.

England. That it was noble for the dark and slavish times in which it was erected is granted. When the world was overrun with tyranny, the least remove therefrom was a glorious rescue. But that it is imperfect, subject to convulsions, and incapable of producing what it seems to promise, is easily demonstrated.

Absolute governments (though the disgrace of human nature) have this advantage with them, that they are simple; if the people suffer, they know the head from which their suffering springs, know likewise the remedy, and are not bewildered by a variety of causes and cures. But the constitution of England is so exceedingly complex, that the nation may suffer for years together without being able to discover in which part the fault lies; some will say in one and some in another, and every political physician will advise a different medicine.

I know it is difficult to get over local or long-standing prejudices, yet if we will suffer ourselves to examine the component parts of the English constitution, we shall find them to be the base remains of two ancient tyrannies, compounded with some new republican materials.

First. – The remains of monarchical tyranny in the person of the king.

Secondly. – The remains of aristocratical tyranny in the persons of the peers.

Thirdly. – The new republican materials, in the persons of the commons, on whose virtue depends the freedom of England.

The two first, by being hereditary, are independent of the people; wherefore in a *constitutional sense* they contribute nothing towards the freedom of the state.

To say that the constitution of England is a *union* of three powers, reciprocally *checking* each other, is farcical, either the words have no meaning, or they are flat contradictions.

To say that the commons is a check upon the king, presupposes two things.

First. – That the king is not to be trusted without being looked after, or in other words, that a thirst for absolute power is the natural disease of monarchy.

Secondly. – That the commons, by being appointed for that purpose, are either wiser or more worthy of confidence than the crown.

But as the same constitution which gives the commons a power to check the king by withholding the supplies, gives afterwards the king a power to check the commons, by empowering him to reject their other bills; it again supposes that the king is wiser than those whom it has already supposed to be wiser than he. A mere absurdity!

There is something exceedingly ridiculous in the composition of monarchy; it first excludes a man from the means of information, yet empowers him to act in cases where the highest judgment is required. The state of a king shuts him from the world, yet the business of a king requires him to know it thoroughly; wherefore the different parts, unnaturally opposing and destroying each other, prove the whole character to be absurd and useless.

Some writers have explained the English constitution thus: the king, say they, is one, the people another; the peers are an house in behalf of the king; the commons in behalf of the people; but this hath all the distinctions of an house divided against itself; and though the expressions be pleasantly arranged, yet when examined they appear idle and ambiguous; and it will always happen that the nicest construction that words are capable of, when applied to the description of something which either cannot exist, or is too incomprehensible to be within the compass of description, will be words of sound only, and though they may amuse the ear, they cannot inform the mind, for this explanation includes a previous question, viz. [namely] *How came the king by a power which the people are afraid to trust, and always obliged to check?* Such a power could not be the gift of a wise people, neither can any power, *which needs checking*, be from God; yet the provision, which the constitution makes, supposes such a power to exist.

But the provision is unequal to the task; the means either cannot or will not accomplish the end, and the whole affair is a *felo de se* [suicide]; for as the greater weight will always carry up the less, and as all the wheels of a machine are put in motion by one, it only remains to know which power in the constitution has the most weight, for that will govern; and though the others, or a part of them, may clog, or, as the phrase is, check the rapidity of its motion, yet so long as they cannot stop it, their endeavors will be ineffectual; the first moving power will at last have its way, and what it wants in speed is supplied by time.

That the crown is this overbearing part in the English constitution needs not be mentioned, and that it derives its whole consequence merely from being the giver of places and pensions is self-evident; wherefore, though we have been wise enough to shut and lock a door against absolute monarchy, we at the same time have been foolish enough to put the crown in possession of the key.

The prejudice of Englishmen, in favor of their own government by king, lords, and commons, arises as much or more from national pride than reason. Individuals are undoubtedly safer in England than in some other countries, but the *will* of the king is as much the *law* of the land in Britain as in France, with this difference, that instead of proceeding directly from his mouth, it is handed to the people under the most formidable shape of an act of parliament. For the fate of Charles the First, hath only made kings more subtle—not more just.

Wherefore, laying aside all national pride and prejudice in favor of modes and forms, the plain truth is, that *it is wholly owing to the constitution of the people, and not to the constitution of the government* that the crown is not as oppressive in England as in Turkey.

An inquiry into the *constitutional errors* in the English form of government is at this time highly necessary; for as we are never in a proper condition of doing justice to others, while we continue under the influence of some leading partiality, so neither are we capable of doing it to ourselves while we remain fettered by any obstinate prejudice. And as a man, who is attached to a prostitute, is unfitted to choose or judge of a wife, so any prepossession in favor of a rotten constitution of government will disable us from discerning a good one.

1. Why does Paine prefer simple regimes to mixed regimes—democracies to republics? The argument against simple regimes is that they corrupt easily. What is the argument in their favor?

2. What reasons does Paine give for why mixed regimes make no sense and are certain to fail?

THOMAS JEFFERSON

Notes on the State of Virginia, 1785

Thomas Jefferson (1743–1826) published only one full-length book in his lifetime, Notes on the State of Virginia. *The book consists of a set of answers to questions, or queries, posed by a secretary to the French legation in Philadelphia. Initially sent to the Continental Congress in late 1780, these queries came to Jefferson's notice by way of a Virginia delegate to the Congress. Jefferson at the time was governor of Virginia. A first draft of his answers was written in the summer and fall of 1781, as Jefferson was trying to elude capture by the British. Over the next few years, Jefferson revised and added to his* Notes, *which he had published in Paris upon his arrival there as ambassador in May 1785.*

Although a slaveholder himself, Jefferson, like many southerners of the late eighteenth century, agonized over the problem of slavery. Here Jefferson comments on the moral effects of slavery, worries that America has put itself outside of God's protection, and expresses the hope that the Revolution will hasten the day of emancipation. In a separate and earlier query, he outlines a plan for emancipation prepared by a committee charged with revising the colonial laws of the state.

On a different subject, the virtues of agrarian life, Jefferson voices the Country republican disdain for manufacturing and cities, both thought to be the cause of moral and political decay.

SOURCE: *Thomas Jefferson,* Notes on the State of Virginia *(New York: Harper, 1964).*

QUERY XVIII

 here must doubtless be an unhappy influence on the manners of our people produced by the existence of slavery among us. The whole commerce between master and slave is a perpetual exercise of the most boisterous passions, the most unremitting despotism on the one part, and degrading submissions on the other. Our children see this, and learn to imitate it; for man is an imitative animal. This quality is the germ of all education in him. From his cradle to his grave he is learning to do what he sees others do. If a parent could find no motive either in his philanthropy or his self-love, for restraining the intemperance of passion towards his slave, it should always be a sufficient one that his child is present. But generally it is not sufficient. The parent storms, the child looks on, catches the lineaments of wrath, puts on the same airs in the circle of smaller slaves, gives a loose to the worst of passions, and thus nursed, educated, and daily exercised in tyranny, cannot but be stamped by it with odious peculiarities. The man must be a prodigy who can retain his manners and morals undepraved by such circum-

Either America will emancipate its slaves, or America will suffer a revolt of its slaves.

stances. And with what execrations should the statesman be loaded, who permitting one-half the citizens thus to trample on the rights of the other, transforms those into despots, and these into enemies, destroys the morals of the one part, and the *amor patriae* of the other. For if a slave can have a country in this world, it must be any other in preference to that in which he is born to live and labor for another: in which he must lock up the faculties of his nature, contribute as far as depends on his individual endeavors to the evanishment of the human race, or entail his own miserable condition on the endless generations proceeding from him. With the morals of the people, their industry also is destroyed. For in a warm climate, no man will labor for himself who can make another labor for him. This is so true, that of the proprietors of slaves a very small proportion indeed are ever seen to labor. And can the liberties of a nation be thought secure when we have removed their only firm basis, a conviction in the minds of the people that these liberties are of the gift of God? That they are not to be violated but with his wrath? Indeed I tremble for my country when I reflect that God is just; that his justice cannot sleep forever; that considering numbers, nature, and natural means only, a revolution of the wheel of fortune, an exchange of situation, is among possible events; that it may become probable by supernatural interference! The Almighty has no attribute which can take side with us in such a contest. But it is impossible to be temperate and to pursue this subject through the various considerations of policy, of morals, of history natural and civil. We must be contented to hope they will force their way into every one's mind. I think a change already perceptible, since the origin of the present revolution. The spirit of the master is abating, that of the slave rising from the dust, his condition mollifying, the way I hope preparing, under the auspices of heaven, for a total emancipation, and that this is disposed, in the order of events, to be with the consent of the masters, rather than by their extirpation.

QUERY XIV

he bill as amended proposes that the slaves of Virginia] should continue with their parents to a certain age, then to be brought up, at the public expense, to tillage, arts, or sciences, according to their geniuses, till the females should be eighteen and the males twenty-one years of age, when they should be colonized to such place as the circumstances of the time should render most proper; sending them out with arms, implements of household and of handicraft arts, seeds, pairs of useful domestic animals, etc., to declare them a free and independent people and extend to them our alliance and protection, till they have acquired strength; and to send vessels at the same time to other parts of the world for an equal number of white inhabitants; to induce them to migrate hither, proper encouragements were to be proposed. It will probably be asked, Why not retain and incorporate the blacks into the State and thus save the expense of supplying by importation of white settlers the vacancies they will leave? Deep-rooted prejudices entertained by the whites; ten thousand recollections, by the blacks, of the injuries they have sustained; new provocations; the real distinctions which nature has made; and many other circumstances, will divide us into parties and produce convulsions, which will probably never end but in the extermination of one or the other race.

QUERY XIX

The political economists of Europe have established it as a principle, that every State should endeavor to manufacture for itself; and this principle, like many others, we transfer to America, without calculating the difference of circumstance which should often produce a difference of result. In Europe the lands are either cultivated, or locked up against the cultivator. Manufacture must therefore be resorted to of necessity not of choice, to support the surplus of their people. But we have an immensity of land courting the industry of the husbandman. Is it best then that all our citizens should be employed in its improvement, or that one half should be called off from that to exercise manufactures and handicraft arts for the other? Those who labor in the earth are the chosen people of God, if ever He had a chosen people, whose breast He has made His

A nation is healthy and fit for self-rule to the extent that its people live on farms and not in cities, till the soil and not manufacture goods.

peculiar deposit for substantial and genuine virtue. It is the focus in which he keeps alive that sacred fire, which otherwise might escape from the face of the earth. Corruption of morals in the mass of cultivators is a phenomenon of which no age nor nation has furnished an example. It is the mark set on those, who, not looking up to heaven, to their own soil and industry, as does the husbandman, for their subsistence, depend for it on casualties and caprice of customers. Dependence begets subservience and venality, suffocates the germ of virtue, and prepares fit tools for the designs of ambition. This, the natural progress and consequence of the arts, has sometimes perhaps been retarded by accidental circumstances; but, generally speaking, the proportion which the aggregate of the other classes of citizens bears in any State to that of its husbandmen, is the proportion of its unsound to its healthy parts, and is a good enough barometer whereby to measure its degree of corruption. While we have land to labor then, let us never wish to see our citizens occupied at a workbench, or twirling a distaff. Carpenters, masons, smiths are wanting in husbandry; but, for the general operations of manufacture, let our workshops remain in Europe. It is better to carry provisions and materials to workmen there, than bring them to the provisions and materials, and with them their manners and principles. The loss by the transportation of commodities across the Atlantic will be made up in happiness and permanence of government. The mobs of great cities add just so much to the support of pure government, as sores do to the strength of the human body. It is the manners and spirit of a people which preserve a republic in vigor. A degeneracy in these is a canker which soon eats to the heart of its laws and constitution.

Study Guide Questions

1. What antirepublican effects does slavery have on the children of masters and on the slaves who are oppressed?

2. Why would it not be possible, according to Jefferson, to emancipate the slaves and then employ them as free laborers?

3. To rub away regional diversities and achieve a more perfect union, should the South become more like the North by transitioning from an agrarian to a manufacturing economy?

JOHN ADAMS

A Defence of the Constitutions of Government of the United States of America, 1786, 1787

John Adams (1735–1826) was in Britain at the time of the Constitutional Convention, serving as American ambassador to the Court of St. James. In addition to his diplomatic duties, Adams occupied himself writing a three-volume book on government, titled A Defence of the Constitutions of Government of the United States of America. *He undertook the work in the fall of 1786 in response to a published letter, eight years earlier, by a French economist named Jacques Turgot to a British moral philosopher named Richard Price. Price had included the letter as an appendix to a book of his own on the American Revolution (1784). In the letter Turgot criticized the American state constitutions for imitating the British constitution—a mixed monarchy with a divided parliament—when what the states should have instituted were simple, unitary democracies with single-chambered legislatures. Fearing that this opinion was becoming popular in America and that senates, governors, and checks and balances would all be discountenanced and discarded, Adams hurriedly wrote his* Defense. *The complete work was finished by December 1787, but volume I was reprinted in Philadelphia as the convention met.*

The Defense *is a comparative study of past and present republics—democratic, aristocratic, and monarchical—and of authors who wrote on the same. The third volume is devoted mostly to a critique of the 1656 book (republished in 1767) by Marchamont Nedham, titled* The Excellency of a Free State. *As with Turgot, Nedham argued the case for unitary democracy.*

Adam's main theme is that liberty cannot be guarded and preserved unless power is divided. Democracy provides no cure for human selfishness. The people in power—meaning the majority, meaning the poor—are no less oppressive than princes and nobles. No individual is so virtuous and wise as to rule unchecked, and collectives, such as classes and parties, are vastly more dangerous.

SOURCE: *John Adams,* The Works of John Adams, *ed. Charles Francis Adams, vols. IV and VI (Boston: Little, Brown, 1851).*

VOLUME I

Preface

(1)[1] THE arts and sciences, in general, during the three or four last centuries, have had a regular course of progressive improvement. The inventions in mechanic arts, the discoveries in natural philosophy, navigation, and commerce, and the advancement of civilization and humanity, have occasioned changes in the condition of the world, and the human character, which would have astonished the most refined nations of antiquity. A continuation of similar exertions is every day rendering Europe more and more like one community, or single family. Even in the theory and practice of government, in all the simple monarchies, considerable improvements have been made. The checks and balances of republican governments have been in some degree adopted at the courts of princes. By the erection of various tribunals, to register the laws, and exercise the judicial power—by indulging the petitions and remonstrances of subjects, until by habit they are regarded as rights—a control has been established over ministers of state, and the royal councils, which, in some degree, approaches the spirit of republics. Property is generally secure, and personal liberty seldom invaded. The press has great influence, even where it is not expressly tolerated; and the public opinion must be respected by a minister, or his place becomes insecure. Commerce begins to thrive; and if religious

---

1. Paragraph numbering has been added to allow for more precise citation.

toleration were established, personal liberty a little more pro- tected, by giving an absolute right to demand a public trial in a certain reasonable time, and the states were invested with a few more privileges, or rather restored to some that have been taken away, these governments would be brought to as great a degree of perfection, they would approach as near to the charac- ter of governments of laws and not of men, as their nature will probably admit of. In so general a refinement, or more properly a reformation of manners and improvement in science, is it not unaccountable that the knowledge of the principles and construction of free governments, in which the happiness of life, and even the further progress of improvement in education and society, in knowledge and virtue, are so deeply interested, should have remained at a full stand for two or three thousand years?

While progress has occurred in the practice of government, with monarchies becoming more like republics, the science of government has seen little improvement over the centuries.

(2) According to a story in Herodotus, the nature of monarchy, aristocracy, and democracy, and the advantages and inconveniences of each, were as well understood at the time of the neighing of the horse of Darius, as they are at this hour.[2] A variety of mixtures of these simple species were conceived and attempted, with various success, by the Greeks and Romans. Representations, instead of collections, of the people; a total separation of the executive from the legislative power, and of the judicial from both; and a balance in the legislature, by three independent, equal branches, are perhaps the only three discoveries in the con- stitution of a free government, since the institution of Lycurgus. Even these have been so unfortunate, that they have never spread: the first has been given up by all the nations, excepting one [England], which had once adopted it; and the other two, reduced to practice, if not invented, by the English nation, have never been imitated by any other, except their own descendants in America.

(3) While it would be rash to say, that nothing further can be done to bring a free government, in all its parts, still nearer to perfection, the representations of the people are most obviously susceptible of improvement. The end to be aimed at, in the formation of a representative assembly, seems to be the sense of the people, the public voice. The perfection of the portrait consists in its like- ness. Numbers, or property, or both, should be the rule; and the proportions of electors and members an affair of calculation. The duration should not be so long that the deputy should have time to forget the opinions of his constituents. Corrup- tion in elections is the great enemy of freedom. Among the provisions to prevent

---

2. Herodotus (484–425 B.C.E.), in Book III of the *Histories*, tells the story of seven Persian nobles debating the best form of government. One recommends democracy; a second recommends aristocracy; and a third, Darius, recommends kingship. Darius wins the debate, and the nobles agree that the one among them whose horse is the first to neigh on the following morning will be crowned king. Through clever subterfuge Darius ensures that his horse is the first to neigh, and his colleagues name him king.

it, more frequent elections, and a more general privilege of voting, are not all that might be devised. Dividing the districts, diminishing the distance of travel, and confining the choice to residents, would be great advances towards the annihilation of corruption. The modern aristocracies of Holland, Venice, Bern, etc., have tempered themselves with innumerable checks, by which they have given a great degree of stability to that form of government; and though liberty and life can never be there enjoyed so well as in a free republic, none is perhaps more capable of profound sagacity. We shall learn to prize the checks and balances of a free government, and even those of the modern aristocracies, if we recollect the miseries of Greece, which arose from its ignorance of them. The only balance attempted against the ancient kings was a body of nobles; and the consequences were perpetual alternations of rebellion and tyranny, and the butchery of thousands upon every revolution from one to the other. When kings were abolished, aristocracies tyrannized; and then no balance was attempted but between aristocracy and democracy.[3] This, in the nature of things, could be no balance at all, and therefore the pendulum was forever on the swing.

(4) It is impossible to read in Thucydides, his account of the factions and confusions throughout all Greece, which were introduced by this want of an equilibrium, without horror. "During the few days that Eurymedon, with his troops, continued at Corcyra, the people of that city extended the massacre to all whom they judged their enemies. The crime alleged was, their attempt to overturn the democracy. Some perished merely through private enmity; some, by the hands of the borrower, on account of the money they had lent. Every kind of death, every dreadful act, was perpetrated. Fathers slew their children; some were dragged from altars, some were butchered at them; numbers, immured in temples, were starved. The contagion spread through the whole extent of Greece; factions raged in every city; the licentious many contending for the Athenians, and the aspiring few for the Lacedemonians. The consequence was, seditions in cities, with all their numerous and tragical incidents."[4]

(5) "Such things ever will be," says Thucydides, "so long as human nature continues the same." But if this nervous historian had known a balance of three powers, he would not have pronounced the distemper so incurable, but would have added—*so long as parties in cities remain unbalanced.* . . .

(6) Mr. Hume[5] has collected, from Diodorus Siculus[6] alone, a few massacres which happened in only sixty of the most polished years of Greece: "From Sybaris,

---

3. Adams is describing the Archaic Age of Greece (800–480 B.C.E.) and the early Classical Age (480–300 B.C.E.).

4. In the run-up to the Peloponnesian War (429–404 B.C.E.), Corcyra, an island-state off the northwest coast of Greece, fell into civil war. Thucydides (ca. 460–ca. 395 B.C.E.) narrates the event in his *History of the Peloponnesian War* (Book III.80–84).

5. The following quotation is from David Hume, "On the Populousness of Ancient Nations," in *Essays Moral, Political, and Literary.*

6. Diodorus Siculus was a Greek historian of the first century B.C.E. He wrote a forty-volume universal history titled *Bibliotheca Historica.*

500 nobles banished; of Chians, 600 citizens; at Ephesus, 340 killed, 1000 banished; of Cyrenians, 500 nobles killed, all the rest banished; the Corinthians killed 120, banished 500; Phnebidas banished 300 Boeotians. Upon the fall of the Lacedaemonians, democracies were restored in many cities, and severe vengeance taken of the nobles; the banished nobles returning, butchered their adversaries at Phialm, in Corinth, in Megara, in Phliasia, where they killed 300 of the people; but these again revolting, killed above 600 of the nobles, and banished the rest. In Arcadia, 1400 banished, besides many killed; the banished retired to Sparta and Pallantium; the latter were delivered up to their countrymen, and all killed. Of the banished from Argos and Thebes, there were 500 in the Spartan army. The people, before the usurpation of Agathocles,[7] had banished 600 nobles; afterwards that tyrant, in concurrence with the people, killed 4000 nobles, and banished 6000; and killed 4000 people at Gela; his brother banished 8000 from Syracuse. The inhabitants of Aegesta, to the number of 40,000, were killed, man, woman, and child, for the sake of their money; all the relations of the Libyan army, fathers, brothers, children, killed; 7000 exiles killed after capitulation. These numbers, compared with the population of those cities, are prodigious; yet Agathocles was a man of character, and not to be suspected of wanton cruelty, contrary to the maxims of his age."

(7) Such were the fashionable outrages of unbalanced parties. In the name of human and divine benevolence, is such a system as this to be recommended to Americans, in this age of the world? Human nature is as incapable now of going through revolutions with temper and sobriety, with patience and prudence, or without fury and madness, as it was among the Greeks so long ago. . . . Without three orders, and an effectual balance between them, in every American constitution, it must be destined to frequent unavoidable revolutions; though they are delayed a few years, they must come in time. . . .

(8) If there is one certain truth to be collected from the history of all ages, it is this; that the people's rights and liberties, and the democratical mixture in a constitution, can never be preserved without a strong executive, or, in other words, without separating the executive from the legislative power. If the executive power, or any considerable part of it, is left in the hands either of an aristocratical or a democratical assembly, it will corrupt the legislature as necessarily as rust corrupts iron, or as arsenic poisons the human body; and when the legislature is corrupted, the people are undone.

(9) The rich, the well-born, and the able, acquire an influence among the people that will soon be too much for simple honesty and plain sense, in a house of representatives. The most illustrious of them must, therefore, be separated from the mass, and placed by themselves in a senate; this is, to all honest and useful intents,

The wealthy, well-born, and able few should be segregated in a chamber of their own, lest they take control of the chamber of the people.

---

7. Agathocles (361–289 B.C.E), born a potter's son, rose to become the tyrant of Syracuse in 304.

an ostracism. A member of a senate, of immense wealth, the most respected birth, and transcendent abilities, has no influence in the nation, in comparison of what he would have in a single representative assembly. When a senate exists, the most powerful man in the state may be safely admitted into the house of representatives, because the people have it in their power to remove him into the senate as soon as his influence becomes dangerous. The senate becomes the great object of ambition; and the richest and the most sagacious wish to merit an advancement to it by services to the public in the house. When he has obtained the object of his wishes, you may still hope for the benefits of his exertions, without dreading his passions; for the executive power being in other hands, he has lost much of his influence with the people, and can govern very few votes more than his own among the senators. . . .

Preliminary Observations

(10) THREE writers in Europe of great abilities, reputation, and learning, M. Turgot, the Abbe de Mably, and Dr. Price,[8] have turned their attention to the constitutions of government in the United States of America, and have written and published their criticisms and advice. . . .

Adams is referring to the states of Pennsylvania and Georgia and perhaps to the territory of Vermont.

(11) M. Turgot, in his letter to Dr. Price, confesses, "that he is not satisfied with the constitutions which have hitherto been formed for the different states of America." He observes, "that by most of them the customs of England are imitated, without any particular motive. Instead of collecting all authority into one center, that of the nation, they have established different bodies, a body of representatives, a council, and a governor, because there is in England a house of commons, a house of lords, and a king. They endeavor to balance these different powers, as if this equilibrium, which in England may be a necessary check to the enormous influence of royalty, could be of any use in republics founded upon the equality of all the citizens, and as if establishing different orders of men was not a source of divisions and disputes."

(12) There has been, from the beginning of the revolution in America, a party in every state, who have entertained sentiments similar to these of M. Turgot. Two or three of them have established governments upon his principle; and, by advices from Boston, certain committees of counties have been held, and other conventions proposed in the Massachusetts, with the express purpose of deposing the governor and senate as useless and expensive branches of the constitution; and as it is probable that the publication of M. Turgot's opinion has contributed to excite such

---

8. Anne-Robert-Jacques Turgot, Baron de Laune (1727–1781) was a reform-minded economist and minister of the navy. Gabriel Bonnot de Mably (1709–1785) was a radical intellectual fiercely critical of the French aristocracy. Richard Price (1723–1791) was a dissenting minister and political pamphleteer who wrote in defense of the American Revolution and then of the French Revolution.

discontents among the people, it becomes necessary to examine it, and, if it can be shown to be an error, whatever veneration the Americans very justly entertain for his memory, it is to be hoped they will not be misled by his authority.

(13) M. Turgot is offended, because the customs of England are imitated in most of the new constitutions in America, without any particular motive. . . . What English customs [have they] retained which may with any propriety be called evil? M. Turgot has instanced only one—namely, "that a body of representatives, a council, and a governor, have been established, because there is in England a house of commons, a house of lords, and a king." It was not so much because the legislature in England consisted of three branches, that such a division of power was adopted by the states, as because their own assemblies had ever been so constituted. It was not so much from attachment by habit to such a plan of power that it was continued, as from conviction that it was founded in nature and reason.

(14) M. Turgot seems to be of a different opinion, and is for "collecting all authority into one center, the nation." It is easily understood how all authority may be collected into "one center" in a despot or monarch; but how it can be done when the center is to be the nation, is more difficult to comprehend. Before we attempt to discuss the notions of an author, we should be careful to ascertain his meaning. . . .

(15) Shall we suppose, then, that M. Turgot intended that an assembly of representatives should be chosen by the nation, and vested with all the powers of government; and that this assembly should be the center which all the authority was to be collected, and should be virtually deemed the nation? After long reflection, I have not been able to discover any other sense in his words, and this was probably his real meaning. . . .

Recapitulation

(16) As we have taken a cursory view of those countries in Europe where the government may be called, in any reasonable construction of the word, republican, let us now pause a few moments, and reflect upon what we have seen.

(17) Among every people, and in every species of republics, we have constantly found a first magistrate, a head, a chief, under various denominations, indeed, and with different degrees of authority, with the title of stadtholder, burgomaster, avoyer, doge, gonfaloniero, president, syndic, mayor, alcalde, capitaneo, governor, or king; in every nation we have met with a distinguished officer. If there is no example, then, in any free government, any more than in those which are not free, of a society without a principal personage, we may fairly conclude that the body politic cannot subsist, any more than the animal body, without a head. If M. Turgot had made any discovery which had escaped the penetration of all the legislators and philosophers who have lived before him, he ought at least to have communicated it to the world for their improvement; but as he has never hinted at any such invention, we may safely conclude that he had none; and, therefore, that the Americans are not justly liable to censure for instituting governors.

(18) In every form of government we have seen a senate, or little council, a composition, generally, of those officers of state who have the most experience and power, and of a few other members selected from the highest ranks and most illustrious reputations. On these lesser councils, with the first magistrate at their head, generally rests the principal burden of administration, a share in the legislative, as well as executive and judicial authority of government. The admission of such senates to a participation of these three kinds of power, has been generally observed to produce in the minds of their members an ardent aristocratical ambition, grasping equally at the prerogatives of the first magistrate, and the privileges of the people, and ending in the nobility of a few families, and a tyrannical oligarchy. But in those states, where the senates have been debarred from all executive power, and confined to the legislative, they have been observed to be firm barriers against the encroachments of the crown, and often great supporters of the liberties of the people. The Americans, then, who have carefully confined their senates to the legislative power, have done wisely in adopting them.

Research shows that nearly all republican governments consist of an executive, however described, and of a bicameral legislature, however composed. State governments in America have adopted this model and are improvements upon it.

(19) We have seen, in every instance, another and a larger assembly, composed of the body of the people, in some little states; of representatives chosen by the people, in others; of members appointed by the senate, and supposed to represent the people, in a third sort; and of persons appointed by themselves or the senate, in certain aristocracies, to prevent them from becoming oligarchies. The Americans, then, whose assemblies are the most adequate, proportional, and equitable representations of the people, that are known in the world, will not be thought mistaken in appointing houses of representatives.

(20) In every republic—in the smallest and most popular, in the larger and more aristocratical, as well as in the largest and most monarchical—we have observed a multitude of curious and ingenious inventions to balance, in their turn, all those powers, to check the passions peculiar to them, and to control them from rushing into those exorbitancies to which they are most addicted. The Americans will then be no longer censured for endeavoring to introduce an equilibrium, which is much more profoundly meditated, and much more effectual for the protection of the laws, than any we have seen, except in England. We may even question whether that is an exception.

(21) In every country we have found a variety of *orders*, with very great distinctions. In America, there are different orders of *offices*, but none of *men*. Out of office, all men are of the same species, and of one blood; there is neither a greater nor a lesser nobility.[9] Why, then, are the Americans accused of establishing different

---

9. France had a greater nobility of the sword (ancient families with a history of military service) and a lesser nobility of the robe (newly wealthy families who had bought their titles and offices).

orders of men? To our inexpressible mortification, we must have observed, that the people have preserved a share of power, or an existence in the government, in no country out of England, except upon the tops of a few inaccessible mountains, among rocks and precipices, in territories so narrow that you may span them with a hand's breadth, where, living unenvied, in extreme poverty, chiefly upon pasturage, destitute of manufactures and commerce, they still exhibit the most charming picture of life, and the most dignified character of human nature.

(22) Wherever we have seen a territory somewhat larger, arts and sciences more cultivated, commerce flourishing, or even agriculture improved to any great degree, an aristocracy has risen up in a course of time, consisting of a few rich and honorable families, who have united with each other against both the people and the first magistrate; who have wrested from the former, by art and by force, all their participation in the government; and have even inspired them with so mean an esteem of themselves, and so deep a veneration and strong attachment to their rulers, as to believe and confess them a superior order of beings.

(23) We have seen these noble families, although necessitated to have a head, extremely jealous of his influence, anxious to reduce his power, and to constrain him to as near a level as possible with themselves; always endeavoring to establish a rotation, by which they may all equally be entitled in turn to the preeminence, and likewise anxious to preserve to themselves as large a share as possible of power in the executive and judicial, as well as the legislative departments of the state.

(24) These patrician families have also appeared in every instance to be equally jealous of each other, and to have contrived, by blending lot and choice, by mixing various bodies in the elections to the same offices, and even by a resort to the horrors of an inquisition, to guard against the sin that so easily besets them, of being wholly influenced and governed by a junto or oligarchy of a few among themselves.

(25) We have seen no one government in which is a distinct separation of the legislative from the executive power, and of the judicial from both, or in which any attempt has been made to balance these powers with one another, or to form an equilibrium between the one, the few, and the many, for the purpose of enacting and executing equal laws, by common consent, for the general interest, excepting in England.

A nobility of sorts grows up in any developed society, and it will surely seize power unless constitutional barriers are placed in its way. England provides the model of how this is done.

(26) Shall we conclude, from these melancholy observations, that human nature is incapable of liberty, that no honest equality can be preserved in society, and that such forcible causes are always at work as must reduce all men to a submission to despotism, monarchy, oligarchy, or aristocracy?

(27) By no means. We have seen one of the first nations in Europe, possessed of ample and fertile territories at home and extensive dominions abroad, of a commerce with the whole world, immense wealth, and the greatest naval power which ever belonged to any nation, which has still preserved the power of the people by the equilibrium we are contending for, by the trial by jury, and by constantly

refusing a standing army. The people of England alone, by preserving their share in the legislature, at the expense of the blood of heroes and patriots, have enabled their king to curb the nobility, without giving him a standing army. . . .

Opinions of Philosophers

Dr. Franklin

(28) Let us now return to M. Turgot's idea of a government consisting in a single assembly. He tells us our republics are "founded on the equality of all the citizens, and, therefore, 'orders' and 'equilibriums' are unnecessary, and occasion disputes." But what are we to understand here by equality? Are the citizens to be all of the same age, sex, size, strength, stature, activity, courage, hardiness, industry, patience, ingenuity, wealth, knowledge, fame, wit, temperance, constancy, and wisdom? Was there, or will there ever be, a nation, whose individuals were all equal, in natural and acquired qualities, in virtues, talents, and riches? The answer of all mankind must be in the negative. It must then be acknowledged, that in every state, in the Massachusetts, for example, there are inequalities which God and nature have planted there, and which no human legislator ever can eradicate. . . .

(29) In this society of Massachusettensians then, there is, it is true, a moral and political equality of rights and duties among all the individuals, and as yet no appearance of artificial inequalities of condition, such as hereditary dignities, titles, magistracies, or legal distinctions; and no established marks, as stars, garters, crosses, or ribbons; there are, nevertheless, inequalities of great moment in the consideration of a legislator, because they have a natural and inevitable influence in society. Let us enumerate some of them: 1. There is an inequality of wealth; some individuals, whether by descent from their ancestors, or from greater skill, industry, and success in business, have estates both in lands and goods of great value; others have no property at all; and of all the rest of society, much the greater number are possessed of wealth, in all the variety of degrees between these extremes. . . . 2. Birth. Let no man be surprised that this species of inequality is introduced here. Let the page in history be quoted, where any nation, ancient or modern, civilized or savage, is mentioned, among whom no difference was made between the citizens, on account of their extraction. The truth is, that more influence is allowed to this advantage in free republics than in despotic governments, or than would be allowed to it in simple monarchies, if severe laws had not been made from age to age to secure it. The children of illustrious families have generally greater advantages of education, and earlier opportunities to be acquainted with public characters, and informed of public affairs, than those of meaner ones, or even than those in middle life; and what is more than all, an habitual national veneration for their names, and the characters of their ancestors described in history, or coming down by tradition, removes them farther from vulgar jealousy and popular envy, and secures them in some degree the favor, the affection, and respect of the public. . . .

(30) We cannot presume that a man is good or bad, merely because his father was one or the other; and we should always inform ourselves first, whether the virtues and talents are inherited, before we yield our confidence. Wise men beget fools, and honest men knaves; but these instances, although they may be frequent, are not general. If there is often a likeness in feature and figure, there is generally more in mind and heart, because education contributes to the formation of these as well as nature. The influence of example is very great, and almost universal, especially that of parents over their children. . . .

(31) It will be readily admitted, there are great inequalities of merit, or talents, virtues, services, and what is of more moment, very often of reputation. Some, in a long course of service in an army, have devoted their time, health, and fortunes, signalized their courage and address, exposed themselves to hardships and dangers, lost their limbs, and shed their blood, for the people. Others have displayed their wisdom, learning, and eloquence in council, and in various other ways acquired the confidence and affection of their fellow-citizens to such a degree, that the public have settled into a kind of habit of following their example and taking their advice.

(32) There are a few, in whom all these advantages of birth, fortune, and fame are united.

(33) These sources of inequality, which are common to every people, and can never be altered by any, because they are founded in the constitution of nature; this natural aristocracy among mankind, has been dilated on, because it is a fact essential to be considered in the institution of a government. It forms a body of men which contains the greatest collection of virtues and abilities in a free government, is the brightest ornament and glory of the nation, and may always be made the greatest blessing of society, if it be judiciously managed in the constitution. But if this be not done, it is always the most dangerous; nay, it may be added, it never fails to be the destruction of the commonwealth.

> *Every society possesses a "natural aristocracy" of the best and the brightest, which can either be a blessing or a curse, depending on how it is constitutionally managed.*

(34) What shall be done to guard against it? Shall they be all massacred? This experiment has been more than once attempted, and once at least executed. Guy Faux attempted it in England;[10] and a king of Denmark, aided by a popular party, effected it once in Sweden; but it answered no good end.[11] The moment they were

---

10. Guy Faux (Fawkes) (1570–1606) was the ringleader of the Gunpowder Plot (1605), an attempt by Catholic dissidents to kill King James I by blowing up the House of Lords. The plot was discovered, and Fawkes was executed.

11. King Christian II (1481–1559) is probably intended. He was the elected monarch of Denmark and Norway (1513–23). After conquering Sweden in 1520 and assuming the kingship there, he proceeded to slaughter the Swedish nobility in an event known as the Stockholm Bloodbath. A rebellion the following year removed him from power.

dead another aristocracy instantly arose, with equal art and influence, with less delicacy and discretion, if not principle, and behaved more intolerably than the former. The country, for centuries, never recovered from the ruinous consequences of a deed so horrible, that one would think it only to be met with in the history of the kingdom of darkness.

(35) There is but one expedient yet discovered, to avail the society of all the benefits from this body of men, which they are capable of affording, and at the same time, to prevent them from undermining or invading the public liberty; and that is, to throw them all, or at least the most remarkable of them, into one assembly together, in the legislature; to keep all the executive power entirely out of their hands as a body; to erect a first magistrate over them, invested with the whole executive authority; to make them dependent on that executive magistrate for all public executive employments; to give that first magistrate a negative on the legislature, by which he may defend both himself and the people from all their enterprises in the legislature; and to erect on the other side an impregnable barrier against them, in a house of commons, fairly, fully, and adequately representing the people, who shall have the power both of negativing all their attempts at encroachment in the legislature, and of withholding from them and from the crown all supplies, by which they may be paid for their services in executive offices, or even the public service may be carried on to the detriment of the nation.

(36) We have seen, both by reasoning and in experience, what kind of equality is to be found or expected in the simplest people in the world. There is not a city nor a village, any more than a kingdom or a commonwealth, in Europe or America; not a horde, clan, or tribe, among the negroes of Africa, or the savages of North or South America; nor a private club in the world, in which inequalities are not more or less visible. There is, then, a certain degree of weight, which property, family, and merit, will have in the public opinion and deliberations. If M. Turgot had discovered a mode of ascertaining the quantity which they ought to have, and had revealed it to mankind, so that it might be known to every citizen, he would have deserved more of gratitude than is due to all the inventions of philosophers. But, as long as human nature shall have passions and imagination, there is too much reason to fear that these advantages, in many instances, will have more influence than reason and equity can justify.

The natural inequalities among elected officials will cause a unicameral, or single-chambered, legislature to divide into three parts.

(37) Let us then reflect, how the single assembly in the Massachusetts, in which our great statesman wishes all authority concentrated, will be composed. There being no senate nor council, all the rich, the honorable, and meritorious will stand candidates for seats in the house of representatives, and nineteen in twenty of them will obtain elections. The house will be found to have all the inequalities in it that prevailed among the people at large. Such an assembly will be naturally divided into three parts. The first is, some great genius—some one masterly spirit, who unites in himself all the qualities which constitute the natural foundations of

authority, such as benevolence, wisdom, and power; and all the adventitious attractions of respect, such as riches, ancestry, and personal merit. All eyes are turned upon him for president or speaker. The second division comprehends a third, or a quarter, or, if you will, a sixth or an eighth of the whole; and consists of those who have the most to boast of resembling their head. In the third class are all the rest, who are nearly on a level in understanding and in all things. Such an assembly has in it, not only all the persons of the nation, who are most eminent for parts and virtues, but all those who are most inflamed with ambition and avarice, and who are most vain of their descent. These latter will, of course, constantly endeavor to increase their own influence, by exaggerating all the attributes they possess, and by augmenting them in every way they can think of; and will have friends, whose only chance of rising into public view will be under their protection, who will be even more active and zealous in their service than themselves. Notwithstanding all the equality that can ever be hoped for among men, it is easy to see that the third class will, in general be but humble imitators and followers of the second. Every man in the second class will have constantly about him a circle of members of the third, who will be his admirers, perhaps afraid of his influence in the districts they represent, or related to him by blood, or connected with him in trade, or dependent upon him for favors. There will be much envy, too, among individuals of the second class, against the speaker, although a sincere veneration is shown him by the majority, and great external respect by all. I said there would be envy; because there will be among the second class several whose fortunes, families, and merits, in the acknowledged judgment of all, approach near to the first; and, from the ordinary illusions of self-love and self-interest, they and their friends will be much disposed to claim the first place as their own right. This will introduce controversy and debate, as well as emulation; and those who wish for the first place, and cannot obtain it, will of course endeavor to keep down the speaker as near upon a level with themselves as possible, by paring away the dignity and importance of his office, as we saw was the case in Venice, Poland, and, indeed, everywhere else.[12]

(38) A single assembly thus constituted, without any counterpoise, balance, or equilibrium, is to have all authority, legislative, executive, and judicial, concentrated in it. It is to make a constitution and laws by its own will, execute those laws at its own pleasure, and adjudge all controversies that arise concerning the meaning and application of them, at its own discretion. What is there to restrain it from making tyrannical laws, in order to execute them in a tyrannical manner? Will it be pretended, that the jealousy and vigilance of the people, and their power to discard

It is unrealistic to expect the electorate to provide a check on the legislature.

---

12. Adams examines the constitutions of Venice and Poland and of twenty-four other modern states, in volume I of the *Defence*.

them at the next election, will restrain them? Even this idea supposes a balance, an equilibrium, which M. Turgot holds in so much contempt; it supposes the people at large to be a check and control over the representative assembly. But this would be found a mere delusion. A jealousy between the electors and the elected neither ought to exist, nor is it possible to exist. It is a contradiction to suppose that a body of electors should have at one moment a warm affection and entire confidence in a man, so as to intrust him with authority, limited or unlimited, over their lives and fortunes; and the next moment after his election, to commence a suspicion of him, that shall prompt them to watch all his words, actions, and motions, and dispose them to renounce and punish him. They choose him, indeed, because they think he knows more, and is better disposed than the generality, and very often even than themselves. Indeed, the best use of a representative assembly, arises from the cordial affection and unreserved confidence which subsists between it and the collective body of the people. It is by such kind and candid intercourse alone, that the wants and desires of the people can be made known, on the one hand, or the necessities of the public communicated or reconciled to them, on the other. In what did such a confidence in one assembly end, in Venice, Geneva, Biscay, Poland, but in an aristocracy and an oligarchy? There is no special providence for Americans, and their nature is the same with that of others. . . .

Conclusion [to Volume I]

(39) By the authorities and examples already recited, you will be convinced that three branches of power have an unalterable foundation in nature; that they exist in every society natural and artificial; and that if all of them are not acknowledged in any constitution of government, it will be found to be imperfect, unstable, and soon enslaved; that the legislative and executive authorities are naturally distinct; and that liberty and the laws depend entirely on a separation of them in the frame of government; that the legislative power is naturally and necessarily sovereign and supreme over the executive; and, therefore, that the latter must be made an essential branch of the former, even with a negative, or it will not be able to defend itself, but will be soon invaded, undermined, attacked, or in some way or other totally ruined and annihilated by the former. This is applicable to every state in America, in its individual capacity; but is it equally applicable to the United States in their federal capacity?

(40) The people of America and their delegates in congress were of opinion, that a single assembly was every way adequate to the management of all their federal concerns; and with very good reason, because congress is not a legislative assembly, nor a representative assembly, but only a diplomatic assembly. A single council has been found to answer the purposes of confederacies very well. But in all such cases the deputies are responsible to the states; their authority is clearly ascertained; and the states, in their separate capacities, are the checks. These are able to form an effectual balance, and at all times to control their delegates. The

security against the dangers of this kind of government will depend upon the accuracy and decision with which the governments of the separate states have their own orders arranged and balanced. . . .

(41) In the present state of society and manners in America, with a people living chiefly by agriculture, in small numbers, sprinkled over large tracts of land, they are not subject to those panics and transports, those contagions of madness and folly, which are seen in countries where large numbers live in small places, in daily fear of perishing for want. We know, therefore, that the people can live and increase under almost any kind of government, or without any government at all. But it is of great importance to begin well; misarrangements now made, will have great, extensive, and distant consequences; and we are now employed, how little soever we may think of it, in making establishments which will affect the happiness of a hundred millions of inhabitants at a time, in a period not very distant. All nations, under all governments, must have parties; the great secret is to control them. There are but two ways, either by a monarchy and standing army, or by a balance in the constitution. Where the people have a voice, and there is no balance, there will be everlasting fluctuations, revolutions, and horrors, until a standing army, with a general at its head, commands the peace, or the necessity of an equilibrium is made to appear to all, and is adopted by all. . . .

VOLUME III

The Right Constitution of a Commonwealth, Examined

(42) Marchamont Nedham[13] lays it down as a fundamental principle and an undeniable rule, "that the people, (that is, such as shall be successively chosen to represent the people,) are the best keepers of their own liberties, and that for many reasons. First, because they never think of usurping over other men's rights, but mind which way to preserve their own."

(43) Our first attention should be turned to the proposition itself—"The people are the best keepers of their own liberties."

(44) But who are the people? . . .

(45) If it is meant by *the people*, as our author explains himself, a representative assembly, "such as shall be successively chosen to represent the people," still they are not the best keepers of the people's liberties or their own, if you give them all the power, legislative, executive, and judicial. They would invade the liberties of the people, at least the majority of them would invade the liberties of the minority, sooner and oftener than an absolute monarchy, such as that of France, Spain, or Russia, or than a well-checked aristocracy, like Venice, Bern, or Holland.

---

13. Marchamont Nedham (1620–1678), author of *The Excellence of a Free State* (1756), was a journalist, publisher, and political pamphleteer during the English Civil Wars, the Protectorate of Oliver Cromwell, and the Restoration of King Charles II.

(46) An excellent writer has said, somewhat incautiously, that "a people will never oppress themselves, or invade their own rights."[14] This compliment, if applied to human nature, or to mankind, or to any nation or people in being or in memory, is more than has been merited. If it should be admitted that a people will not unanimously agree to oppress themselves, it is as much as is ever, and more than is always, true. All kinds of experience show, that great numbers of individuals do oppress great numbers of other individuals; that parties often, if not always, oppress other parties; and majorities almost universally minorities. All that this observation can mean then, consistently with any color of fact, is, that the people will never unanimously agree to oppress themselves. But if one party agrees to oppress another, or the majority the minority, the people still oppress themselves, for one part of them oppress another.

(47) "The people never think of usurping over other men's rights."

(48) What can this mean? Does it mean that the people never *unanimously* think of usurping over other men's rights? This would be trifling; for there would, by the supposition, be no other men's rights to usurp. But if the people never, jointly nor severally, think of usurping the rights of others, what occasion can there be for any government at all? Are there no robberies, burglaries, murders, adulteries, thefts, nor cheats? Is not every crime a usurpation over other men's rights? Is not a great part, I will not say the greatest part, of men detected every day in some disposition or other, stronger or weaker, more or less, to usurp over other men's rights? . . . Now, grant but this truth, and the question is decided. If a majority are capable of preferring their own private interest, or that of their families, counties, and party, to that of the nation collectively, some provision must be made in the constitution, in favor of justice, to compel all to respect the common right, the public good, the universal law, in preference to all private and partial considerations.

Contrary to Nedham's claim that the people will never usurp the rights of other men, the poor, if allowed, will certainly usurp the property rights of the rich.

(49) The proposition of our author, then, should be reversed, and it should have been said, that they mind so much their own, that they never think enough of others. Suppose a nation, rich and poor, high and low, ten millions in number, all assembled together; not more than one or two millions will have lands, houses, or any personal property; if we take into the account the women and children, or even if we leave them out of the question, a great majority of every nation is wholly destitute of property, except a small quantity of clothes, and a few trifles of other movables. Would Mr. Nedham be responsible that, if all were to be decided by a vote of the majority, the eight or nine millions who have no property, would not think of usurping over the rights of the one

---

14. Richard Price, *Additional Observations on the Nature and Value of Civil Liberty, and the War with America* (1777).

or two millions who have? Property is surely a right of mankind as really as liberty. Perhaps, at first, prejudice, habit, shame or fear, principle or religion, would restrain the poor from attacking the rich, and the idle from usurping on the industrious; but the time would not be long before courage and enterprise would come, and pretexts be invented by degrees, to countenance the majority in dividing all the property among them, or at least, in sharing it equally with its present possessors. Debts would be abolished first; taxes laid heavy on the rich, and not at all on the others; and at last a downright equal division of every thing be demanded, and voted. What would be the consequence of this? The idle, the vicious, the intemperate, would rush into the utmost extravagance of debauchery, sell and spend all their share, and then demand a new division of those who purchased from them. The moment the idea is admitted into society, that property is not as sacred as the laws of God, and that there is not a force of law and public justice to protect it, anarchy and tyranny commence. If "Thou shalt not covet," and "Thou shalt not steal," were not commandments of Heaven, they must be made inviolable precepts in every society, before it can be civilized or made free.

(50) If the first part of the proposition, namely, that "the people never think of usurping over other men's rights," cannot be admitted, is the second, namely, "they mind which way to preserve their own," better founded?

(51) There is in every nation and people under heaven a large proportion of persons who take no rational and prudent precautions to preserve what they have, much less to acquire more. Indolence is the natural character of man, to such a degree that nothing but the necessities of hunger, thirst, and other wants equally pressing, can stimulate him to action, until education is introduced in civilized societies, and the strongest motives of ambition to excel in arts, trades, and professions, are established in the minds of all men. Until this emulation is introduced, the lazy savage holds property in too little estimation to give himself trouble for the preservation or acquisition of it. In societies the most cultivated and polished, vanity, fashion, and folly prevail over every thought of ways to preserve their own. They seem rather to study what means of luxury, dissipation, and extravagance they can invent to get rid of it. . . .

(52) To expect self-denial from men, when they have a majority in their favor, and consequently power to gratify themselves, is to disbelieve all history and universal experience; it is to disbelieve Revelation and the Word of God, which informs us, the heart is deceitful above all things, and desperately wicked. There have been examples of self-denial, and will be again; but such exalted virtue never yet existed in any large body of men, and lasted long; and our author's argument requires it to be proved, not only that individuals, but that nations and majorities of nations, are capable, not only of a single act, or a few acts, of disinterested justice and exalted self-denial, but of a course of such heroic virtue for ages and generations; and not only that they are capable of this, but that it is probable they will practice it. There is no man so blind as not to see, that to talk of founding a government upon a

supposition that nations and great bodies of men, left to themselves, will practice a course of self-denial, is either to babble like a new-born infant, or to deceive like an unprincipled impostor. . . .

(53) It is pretended by some, that a sovereignty in a single assembly, annually elected, is the only one in which there is any responsibility for the exercise of power. In the mixed government we contend for, the ministers, at least of the executive power, are responsible for every instance of the exercise of it; and if they dispose of a single commission by corruption, they are responsible to a house of representatives, who may, by impeachment, make them responsible before a senate, where they may be accused, tried, condemned, and punished by independent judges. But in a single sovereign assembly, each member, at the end of his year, is only responsible to his constituents; and the majority of members who have been of one party, and carried all before them, are to be responsible only to their constituents, not to the constituents of the minority who have been overborne, injured, and plundered. And who are these constituents to whom the majority are accountable? Those very persons, to gratify whom they have prostituted the honors, rewards, wealth, and justice of the state. These, instead of punishing, will applaud; instead of discarding, will reelect, with still greater eclat, and a more numerous majority; for the losing cause will be deserted by numbers. And this will be done in hopes of having still more injustice done, still more honors and profits divided among themselves, to the exclusion and mortification of the minority. It is then astonishing that such a simple government should be preferred to a mixed one, by any rational creature, on the score of responsibility.

In a simple government without a divided legislature, only a minority veto can defend the rights of minorities; and even minorities of one may require such a veto.

(54) There is, in short, no possible way of defending the minority, in such a government, from the tyranny of the majority, but by giving the former a negative on the latter—the most absurd institution that ever took place among men. As the major may bear all possible relations of proportion to the minor part, it may be fifty-one against forty-nine in an assembly of a hundred, or it may be ninety-nine against one only. It becomes therefore necessary to give the negative to the minority, in all cases, though it be ever so small. Every member must possess it, or he can never be secure that himself and his constituents shall not be sacrificed by all the rest. This is the true ground and original of the *liberum veto* in Poland;[15] but the consequence has been ruin to that noble but ill-constituted republic. One fool, or one knave, one member of the diet, which is a single sovereign assembly, bribed by an intriguing ambassador of some foreign power, has prevented measures the most essential to the defense, safety, and existence of the nation. Hence humiliations and partitions! . . . Having no sufficient checks in their uncouth constitution,

---

15. Meaning "free vote" in Latin, the *liberum veto* permitted Polish noblemen, each one deemed a sovereign equal, to suspend the session of the legislature and to nullify all legislation passed by it.

nor any mediating power possessed of the whole executive, they have been driven to demand unanimity instead of a balance. And this must be done in every government of a single assembly, or the majority will instantly oppress the minority. But what kind of government would that be in the United States of America, or any one of them, that should require unanimity, or allow of the *liberum veto*? It is sufficient to ask the question, for every man will answer it alike. . . .

(55) It is agreed that the people are the best keepers of their own liberties, and the only keepers who can be always trusted; and, therefore, the people's fair, full, and honest consent, to every law, by their representatives, must be made an essential part of the constitution; but it is denied that they are the best keepers, or any keepers at all, of their own liberties, when they hold collectively, or by representation, the executive and judicial power, or the whole and uncontrolled legislative; on the contrary, the experience of all ages has proved, that they instantly give away their liberties into the hand of grandees, or kings, idols of their own creation. The management of the executive and judicial powers together always corrupts them, and throws the whole power into the hands of the most profligate and abandoned among themselves. The honest men are generally nearly equally divided in sentiment, and, therefore, the vicious and unprincipled, by joining one party, carry the majority; and the vicious and unprincipled always follow the most profligate leader, him who bribes the highest, and sets all decency and shame at defiance. It becomes more profitable, and reputable too, except with a very few, to be a party man than a public-spirited one. . . .

(56) In every society where property exists, there will ever be a struggle between rich and poor. Mixed in one assembly, equal laws can never be expected. They will either be made by numbers, to plunder the few who are rich, or by influence, to fleece the many who are poor. Both rich and poor, then, must be made independent, that equal justice may be done, and equal liberty enjoyed by all. To expect that in a single sovereign assembly no load shall be laid upon any but what is common to all, nor to gratify the passions of any, but only to supply the necessities of their country, is altogether chimerical. Such an assembly, under an awkward, unwieldy form, becomes at once a simple monarchy in effect. Some one overgrown genius, fortune, or reputation, becomes a despot, who rules the state at his pleasure, while the deluded nation, or rather a deluded majority, thinks itself free; and in every resolve, law, and act of government, you see the interest, fame, and power of that single individual attended to more than the general good. . . .

Conclusion [to Volume III]

(57) IT should have been before observed, that the Western [Roman] Empire fell in the fifth century, and the Eastern in the fifteenth. . . . The interval between the fall of these two empires, making a period of about a thousand years, is called THE Middle AGE. During this term, republics without number

Adams may intend here a criticism of Montesquieu, who argues in The Spirit of the Laws *that climate, like size, affects the choice of a regime (XIV–XVII).*

arose in Italy; whirled upon their axles or single centers; foamed, raged, and burst, like so many water-spouts upon the ocean. They were all alike ill-constituted; all alike miserable; and all ended in similar disgrace and despotism. . . .

(58) The world has been too long abused with notions, that climate and soil decide the characters and political institutions of nations. The laws of Solon and the despotism of Mahomet have,[16] at different times, prevailed at Athens; consuls, emperors, and pontiffs have ruled at Rome. Can there be desired a stronger proof, that policy and education are able to triumph over every disadvantage of climate? Mankind have been still more injured by insinuations, that a certain celestial virtue, more than human, has been necessary to preserve liberty. Happiness, whether in despotism or democracy, whether in slavery or liberty, can never be found without virtue. The best republics will be virtuous, and have been so; but we may hazard a conjecture, that the virtues have been the effect of the well-ordered constitution, rather than the cause. And, perhaps, it would be impossible to prove that a republic cannot exist even among highwaymen, by setting one rogue to watch another; and the knaves themselves may in time be made honest men by the struggle.

Study Guide Questions

1. What is the effect on legislative power when executive power is not separated from it?

2. M. Turgot contends that republics are "founded on the equality of all the citizens." What is Adams's assessment of the role of equality in a republican society?

3. If separation of powers is an essential element of constitutional government, why was it not employed in the construction of the Continental Congress?

4. Parties, which according to Adams are inevitable in developed societies, are controlled by either of two means. What are they?

5. Adams disputes Marchamont Nedham's claim that "the people are the best keepers of their own liberties." Why is this claim not true?

6. What is Adams's general view of human nature?

---

16. Solon (638–558 B.C.E.) was the poet-lawgiver of Athens in the late Archaic Age. Mahomet refers probably to Sultan Mehmed II (1432–1481), who conquered Constantinople in 1453. Greece fell under Ottoman rule at about the same time and remained a subject state until 1821.

JAMES MADISON

Federalist Papers, 1787–1788

Monarchical government was the norm in the eighteenth century (and for many centuries prior) because popular government had shown itself so vulnerable to the violence and injustice of faction. James Madison (1751–1836) understood that some remedy had to be devised if republicanism was to have a third chance at life. The failure of the ancient republics, and of their Renaissance imitators, had provided the enemies of liberty with convincing historical evidence of the superiority of monarchical rule; and Britain's slow evolution toward constitutionalism had further demonstrated monarchy's capacity for reform protective of liberty. Madison built his case on two innovations of practice and theory: representation and enlargement of the state.

In both papers, Madison is seeking "a republican remedy for the diseases most incident to republican government." In Federalist #10 *the disease is majority tyranny, and the remedy, principally, is the larger size of the extended republic. The majority, even though factious and partial, is effectively prevented from abusing its power when the republic is big. In* Federalist #51 *the disease is twofold: majority tyranny again, but more as the faction which captures the legislative power; and the government's oppression of the people. For the first disease, the remedy is separation of powers, called an "auxiliary precaution"; for the second, it is elections; and for both, it is federalism, representation, and the extended sphere.*

SOURCE: *Alexander Hamilton, John Jay, and James Madison,* The Federalist *(Indianapolis: Liberty Fund, 2001).*

FEDERALIST #10

*A*mong the numerous advantages promised by a well constructed union, none deserves to be more accurately developed, than its tendency to break and control the violence of faction. The friend of popular governments, never finds himself so much alarmed for their character and fate, as when he contemplates their propensity to this dangerous vice. He will not fail, therefore, to set a due value on any plan which, without violating the principles to which he is attached, provides a proper cure for it. The instability, injustice, and confusion, introduced into the public councils, have, in truth, been the mortal diseases under which popular governments have every where perished; as they continue to be the favorite and fruitful topics from which the adversaries to liberty derive their most specious declamations. The valuable improvements made by the American constitutions on the popular models, both ancient and modern, cannot certainly be too much admired; but it would be an unwarrantable partiality, to contend that they have as effectually obviated the danger on this side, as was wished and expected. Complaints are every where heard from our most considerate and virtuous citizens, equally the friends of public and private faith, and of public and personal liberty, that our governments are too unstable; that the public good is disregarded in the conflicts of rival parties; and that measures are too often decided, not according to the rules of justice, and the rights of the minor party, but by the superior force of an interested and overbearing majority. However anxiously we may wish that these complaints had no foundation, the evidence of known facts will not permit us to deny that they are in some degree true. It will be found, indeed, on a candid review of our situation, that some of the distresses under which we labor, have been erroneously charged on the operation of our governments; but it will be found, at the same time, that other causes will not alone account for many of our heaviest misfortunes; and, particularly, for that prevailing and increasing distrust of public engagements, and alarm for private rights, which are echoed from one end of the continent to the other. These must be chiefly, if not wholly, effects of the unsteadiness and injustice, with which a factious spirit has tainted our public administrations.

By a faction, I understand a number of citizens, whether amounting to a majority or minority of the whole, who are united and actuated by some common impulse of passion, or of interest, adverse to the rights of other citizens, or to the permanent and aggregate interests of the community.

There are two methods of curing the mischiefs of faction: The one, by removing its causes; the other, by controlling its effects.

There are again two methods of removing the causes of faction: The one, by destroying the liberty which is essential to its existence; the other, by giving to every citizen the same opinions, the same passions, and the same interests.

It could never be more truly said, than of the first remedy, that it is worse than the disease. Liberty is to faction, what air is to fire, an aliment, without which it instantly expires. But it could not be a less folly to abolish liberty, which is essential to political life, because it nourishes faction, than it would be to wish the annihilation of air, which is essential to animal life, because it imparts to fire its destructive agency.

Rousseau is someone who thinks that a uniformity of opinions, passions, and interests—called the general will—is a realistic possibility, so long as certain conditions are met, including the equalization of political rights. He likely is included among the "theoretic politicians" referred to later.

The second expedient is as impracticable, as the first would be unwise. As long as the reason of man continues fallible, and he is at liberty to exercise it, different opinions will be formed. As long as the connection subsists between his reason and his self-love, his opinions and his passions will have a reciprocal influence on each other; and the former will be objects to which the latter will attach themselves.

The diversity in the faculties of men, from which the rights of property originate, is not less an insuperable obstacle to an uniformity of interests. The protection of these faculties, is the first object of government. From the protection of different and unequal faculties of acquiring property, the possession of different degrees and kinds of property immediately results; and from the influence of these on the sentiments and views of the respective proprietors, ensues a division of the society into different interests and parties.

The latent causes of faction are thus sown in the nature of man; and we see them every where brought into different degrees of activity, according to the different circumstances of civil society.

Faction cannot be eliminated; it can only be managed.

A zeal for different opinions concerning religion, concerning government, and many other points, as well of speculation as of practice; an attachment to different leaders, ambitiously contending for pre-eminence and power; or to persons of other descriptions, whose fortunes have been interesting to the human passions, have, in turn, divided mankind into parties, inflamed them with mutual animosity, and rendered them much more disposed to vex and oppress each other, than to co-operate for their common good. So strong is this propensity of mankind, to fall into mutual animosities, that where no substantial occasion presents itself, the most frivolous and fanciful distinctions have been sufficient to kindle their unfriendly passions, and excite their most violent conflicts. But the most common and durable source of factions, has been the various and unequal distribution of property. Those who hold, and those who are without property, have ever formed distinct interests in society. Those who are creditors, and those who are debtors, fall under a like discrimination. A landed interest, a manufacturing interest, a mercantile interest, a moneyed interest, with many lesser interests, grow up of necessity in civilized nations, and divide them into different classes, actuated by different sentiments and views. The regulation of these various and interfering interests, forms the principal task of modern legislation, and involves the spirit of party and faction in the necessary and ordinary operations of government.

No man is allowed to be a judge in his own cause; because his interest would certainly bias his judgment, and, not improbably, corrupt his integrity. With equal, nay, with greater reason, a body of men are unfit to be both judges and parties, at the same time; yet, what are many of the most important acts of legislation, but so many judicial determinations, not indeed concerning the rights of single persons, but concerning the rights of large bodies of citizens? and what are the different classes of legislators, but advocates and parties to the causes which they determine? Is a law proposed concerning private debts? It is a question to which the creditors are parties on one side, and the debtors on the other. Justice ought to hold the balance between them. Yet the parties are, and must be, themselves the judges; and the most numerous party, or, in other words, the most powerful faction, must be expected to prevail. Shall domestic manufactures be encouraged, and in what degree, by restrictions on foreign manufactures? are questions which would be differently decided by the landed and the manufacturing classes; and probably by neither with a sole regard to justice and the public good. The apportionment of taxes, on the various descriptions of property, is an act which seems to require the most exact impartiality; yet there is, perhaps, no legislative act in which greater opportunity and temptation are given to a predominant party, to trample on the rules of justice. Every shilling with which they over-burden the inferior number, is a shilling saved to their own pockets.

It is in vain to say, that enlightened statesmen will be able to adjust these clashing interests, and render them all subservient to the public good. Enlightened statesmen will not always be at the helm: nor, in many cases, can such an adjustment be made at all, without taking into view indirect and remote considerations, which will rarely prevail over the immediate interest which one party may find in disregarding the rights of another, or the good of the whole.

The inference to which we are brought, is, that the *causes* of faction cannot be removed; and that relief is only to be sought in the means of controlling its *effects*.

The core question is this: How to prevent majority tyranny without abandoning popular government.

If a faction consists of less than a majority, relief is supplied by the republican principle, which enables the majority to defeat its sinister views, by regular vote. It may clog the administration, it may convulse the society; but it will be unable to execute and mask its violence under the forms of the constitution. When a majority is included in a faction, the form of popular government, on the other hand, enables it to sacrifice to its ruling passion or interest, both the public good and the rights of other citizens. To secure the public good, and private rights, against the danger of such a faction, and at the same time to preserve the spirit and the form of popular government, is then the great object to which our inquiries are directed. Let me add, that it is the great desideratum, by which alone this form of government can be rescued from the opprobrium under which it has so long labored, and be recommended to the esteem and adoption of mankind.

By what means is this object attainable? Evidently by one of two only. Either the existence of the same passion or interest in a majority, at the same time, must be prevented; or the majority, having such co-existent passion or interest, must be rendered, by their number and local situation, unable to concert and carry into effect schemes of oppression. If the impulse and the opportunity be suffered to coincide, we well know, that neither moral nor religious motives can be relied on as an adequate control. They are not found to be such on the injustice and violence of individuals, and lose their efficacy in proportion to the number combined together; that is, in proportion as their efficacy becomes needful.

From this view of the subject, it may be concluded, that a pure democracy, by which I mean, a society consisting of a small number of citizens, who assemble and administer the government in person, can admit of no cure for the mischiefs of faction. A common passion or interest will, in almost every case, be felt by a majority of the whole; a communication and concert, results from the form of government itself; and there is nothing to check the inducements to sacrifice the weaker party, or an obnoxious individual. Hence it is, that such democracies have ever been spectacles of turbulence and contention; have ever been found incompatible with personal security, or the rights of property; and have, in general, been as short in their lives, as they have been violent in their deaths. Theoretic politicians, who have patronized this species of government, have erroneously supposed, that, by reducing mankind to a perfect equality in their political rights, they would, at the same time, be perfectly equalized and assimilated in their possessions, their opinions, and their passions.

A republic, by which I mean a government in which the scheme of representation takes place, opens a different prospect, and promises the cure for which we are seeking. Let us examine the points in which it varies from pure democracy, and we shall comprehend both the nature of the cure and the efficacy which it must derive from the union.

The two great points of difference, between a democracy and a republic, are, first, the delegation of the government, in the latter, to a small number of citizens elected by the rest; secondly, the greater number of citizens, and greater sphere of country, over which the latter may be extended.

Madison, writing as Publius, subscribes to the "trustee" theory of representation.

The effect of the first difference is, on the one hand, to refine and enlarge the public views, by passing them through the medium of a chosen body of citizens, whose wisdom may best discern the true interest of their country, and whose patriotism and love of justice, will be least likely to sacrifice it to temporary or partial considerations. Under such a regulation, it may well happen, that the public voice, pronounced by the representatives of the people, will be more consonant to the public good, than if pronounced by the people themselves, convened for the purpose. On the other hand, the effect may be inverted. Men of factious tempers, of local prejudices, or of sinister designs, may by intrigue, by corruption, or by other means, first obtain the suffrages, and then betray the interests of the people. The question resulting is, whether small or extensive

Whether elected officials are better than the electorate they represent depends on the size and diversity of the country.

republics are most favorable to the election of proper guardians of the public weal; and it is clearly decided in favor of the latter by two obvious considerations.

In the first place, it is to be remarked, that however small the republic may be, the representatives must be raised to a certain number, in order to guard against the cabals of a few; and that, however large it may be, they must be limited to a certain number, in order to guard against the confusion of a multitude. Hence, the number of representatives in the two cases not being in proportion to that of the constituents, and being proportionally greatest in the small republic, it follows, that if the proportion of fit characters be not less in the large than in the small republic, the former will present a greater option, and consequently a greater probability of a fit choice.

In the next place, as each representative will be chosen by a greater number of citizens in the large than in the small republic, it will be more difficult for unworthy candidates to practice with success the vicious arts, by which elections are too often carried; and the suffrages of the people being more free, will be more likely to center in men who possess the most attractive merit, and the most diffusive and established characters.

It must be confessed, that in this, as in most other cases, there is a mean, on both sides of which inconveniences will be found to lie. By enlarging too much the number of electors, you render the representative too little acquainted with all their local circumstances and lesser interests; as by reducing it too much, you render him unduly attached to these, and too little fit to comprehend and pursue great and national objects. . . .

The other point of difference is, the greater number of citizens, and extent of territory, which may be brought within the compass of republican, than of democratic government; and it is this circumstance principally which renders factious combinations less to be dreaded in the former, than in the latter. The smaller the society, the fewer probably will be the distinct parties and interests composing it; the fewer the distinct parties and interests, the more frequently will a majority be found of the same party; and the smaller the number of individuals composing a majority, and the smaller the compass within which they are placed, the more easily will they concert and execute their plans of oppression. Extend the sphere, and you take in a greater variety of parties and interests; you make it less probable that a majority of the whole will have a common motive to invade the rights of other citizens; or if such a common motive exists, it will be more difficult for all who feel it to discover their own strength, and to act in unison with each other. Besides other impediments, it may be remarked, that where there is a consciousness of unjust or dishonorable purposes, communication is always checked by distrust, in proportion to the number whose concurrence is necessary.

Hence it clearly appears, that the same advantage, which a republic has over a democracy, in controlling the effects of faction, is enjoyed by a large over a small republic . . . is enjoyed by the union over the states composing it. Does this advantage consist in the substitution of representatives, whose enlightened views and virtuous sentiments render them superior to local prejudices, and to schemes of injustice? It will not be denied, that the representation of the union will be most likely to possess these requisite endowments. Does it consist in the greater security afforded by a greater variety of parties, against the event of any one party being able to outnumber and oppress the rest? In an equal degree does the increased variety of parties, comprised within the union, increase this security? Does it, in fine, consist in the greater obstacles opposed to the concert and accomplishment of the secret wishes of an unjust and interested majority? Here, again, the extent of the union gives it the most palpable advantage.

The influence of factious leaders may kindle a flame within their particular states, but will be unable to spread a general conflagration through the other states: a religious sect may degenerate into a political faction in a part of the confederacy;

but the variety of sects dispersed over the entire face of it, must secure the national councils against any danger from that source: a rage for paper money, for an abolition of debts, for an equal division of property, or for any other improper or wicked project, will be less apt to pervade the whole body of the union, than a particular member of it; in the same proportion as such a malady is more likely to taint a particular county or district, than an entire state.

In the extent and proper structure of the union, therefore, we behold a republican remedy for the diseases most incident to republican government. And according to the degree of pleasure and pride we feel in being republicans, ought to be our zeal in cherishing the spirit, and supporting the character of federalists.

FEDERALIST #51

To what expedient then shall we finally resort, for maintaining in practice the necessary partition of power among the several departments, as laid down in the constitution? The only answer that can be given is, that as all these exterior provisions are found to be inadequate, the defect must be supplied, by so contriving the interior structure of the government, as that its several constituent parts may, by their mutual relations, be the means of keeping each other in their proper places. Without presuming to undertake a full development of this important idea, I will hazard a few general observations, which may perhaps place it in a clearer light, and enable us to form a more correct judgment of the principles and structure of the government planned by the convention.

In order to lay a due foundation for that separate and distinct exercise of the different powers of government, which, to a certain extent, is admitted on all hands to be essential to the preservation of liberty, it is evident that each department should have a will of its own; and consequently should be so constituted, that the members of each should have as little agency as possible in the appointment of the members of the others. Were this principle rigorously adhered to, it would require that all the appointments for the supreme executive, legislative, and judiciary magistracies, should be drawn from the same fountain of authority, the people, through channels having no communication whatever with one another. Perhaps such a plan of constructing the several departments, would be less difficult in practice, than it may in contemplation appear. Some difficulties, however, and some additional expense, would attend the execution of it. Some deviations, therefore, from the principle must be admitted. In the constitution of the judiciary department in particular, it might be inexpedient to insist rigorously on the principle; first, because peculiar qualifications being essential in the members, the primary consideration ought to be to select that mode of choice which best secures these qualifications; secondly, because the permanent tenure by which the appointments are held in that department, must soon destroy all sense of dependence on the authority conferring them.

One example of relying on "rival interests" rather than on "better motives"—on vice rather than on virtue—is the adversarial system at work in courts of law. The jury is expected to deliver a just verdict in a situation in which the principals are not themselves responsible for justice: for the prosecutor is trying for a conviction, the defense attorney for an acquittal, and the judge for an impartial application of rules.

It is equally evident, that the members of each department should be as little dependent as possible on those of the others, for the emoluments annexed to their offices. Were the executive magistrate, or the judges, not independent of the legislature in this particular, their independence in every other, would be merely nominal.

But the great security against a gradual concentration of the several powers in the same department, consists in giving to those who administer each department, the necessary constitutional means, and personal motives, to resist encroachments of the others. The provision for defense must in this, as in all other cases, be made commensurate to the danger of attack. Ambition must be made to counteract ambition. The interest of the man, must be connected with the constitutional rights of the place. It may be a reflection on human nature, that such devices should be necessary to control the abuses of government. But what is government itself, but the greatest of all reflections on human nature? If men were angels, no government would be necessary. If angels were to govern men, neither external nor internal controls on government would be necessary. In framing a government which is to be administered by men over men, the great difficulty lies in this: you must first enable the government to control the governed; and in the next place oblige it to control itself. A dependence on the people is, no doubt, the primary control on the government; but experience has taught mankind the necessity of auxiliary precautions.

This policy of supplying, by opposite and rival interests, the defect of better motives, might be traced through the whole system of human affairs, private as well as public. We see it particularly displayed in all the subordinate distributions of power; where the constant aim is, to divide and arrange the several offices in such a manner as that each may be a check on the other; that the private interest of every individual may be a sentinel over the public rights. These inventions of prudence cannot be less requisite in the distribution of the supreme powers of the state.

But it is not possible to give to each department an equal power of self-defense. In republican government, the legislative authority necessarily predominates. The remedy for this inconveniency is, to divide the legislature into different branches; and to render them, by different modes of election, and different principles of action, as little connected with each other, as the nature of their common functions, and their common dependence on the society, will admit. It may even be necessary to guard against dangerous encroachments by still further precautions. As the weight of the legislative authority requires that it should be thus divided, the weakness of the executive may require, on the other hand, that it should be fortified. An absolute negative on the legislature, appears, at first view, to be the natural defense with which the executive magistrate should be armed.

A qualified veto requiring a supermajority to override will better protect the executive than an absolute veto because a qualified veto aligns the executive with the minority in the legislative branch.

But perhaps it would be neither altogether safe, nor alone sufficient. On ordinary occasions, it might not be exerted with the requisite firmness; and on extraordinary occasions, it might be perfidiously abused. May not this defect of an absolute negative be supplied by some qualified connection between this weaker department, and the weaker branch of the stronger department, by which the latter may be led to support the constitutional rights of the former, without being too much detached from the rights of its own department?

If the principles on which these observations are founded be just, as I persuade myself they are, and they be applied as a criterion to the several state constitutions, and to the federal constitution, it will be found, that if the latter does not perfectly correspond with them, the former are infinitely less able to bear such a test.

There are moreover two considerations particularly applicable to the federal system of America, which place that system in a very interesting point of view.

First. In a single republic, all the power surrendered by the people, is submitted to the administration of a single government; and the usurpations are guarded against, by a division of the government into distinct and separate departments. In the compound republic of America, the power surrendered by the people, is first divided between two distinct governments, and then the portion allotted to each subdivided among distinct and separate departments. Hence a double security arises to the rights of the people. The different governments will control each other; at the same time that each will be controlled by itself.

Second. It is of great importance in a republic, not only to guard the society against the oppression of its rulers; but to guard one part of the society against the injustice of the other part. Different interests necessarily exist in different classes of citizens. If a majority be united by a common interest, the rights of the minority will be insecure. There are but two methods of providing against this evil: the one, by creating a will in the community independent of the majority, that is, of the society itself; the other, by comprehending in the society so many separate descriptions of citizens, as will render an unjust combination of a majority of the whole very improbable, if not impracticable. The first method prevails in all governments possessing an hereditary or self-appointed authority. This, at best, is but a precarious security; because a power independent of the society may as well espouse the unjust views of the major, as the rightful interests of the minor party, and may possibly be turned against both parties. The second method will be exemplified in the federal republic of the United States. Whilst all authority in it will be derived from, and dependent on the society, the society itself will be broken into so many parts, interests, and classes of citizens, that the rights of individuals, or of the minority, will be in little danger from interested combinations of the majority. In a free government, the security for civil rights must be the same as that for religious rights. It consists in the one case in the multiplicity of interests, and in the other, in the multiplicity of sects. The degree of security in both cases

Civil liberties are protected by the multiplication of interests, just as religious liberties are protected by the multiplication of sects.

will depend on the number of interests and sects; and this may be presumed to depend on the extent of country and number of people comprehended under the same government. This view of the subject must particularly recommend a proper federal system to all the sincere and considerate friends of republican government: since it shows, that in exact proportion as the territory of the union may be formed into more circumscribed confederacies, or states, oppressive combinations of a majority will be facilitated; the best security under the republican form, for the rights of every class of citizens, will be diminished; and consequently, the stability and independence of some member of the government, the only other security, must be proportionally increased. Justice is the end of government. It is the end of civil society. It ever has been, and ever will be, pursued, until it be obtained, or until liberty be lost in the pursuit. In a society, under the forms of which the stronger faction can readily unite and oppress the weaker, anarchy may as truly be said to reign, as in a state of nature, where the weaker individual is not secured against the violence of the stronger: and as, in the latter state, even the stronger individuals are prompted, by the uncertainty of their condition, to submit to a government which may protect the weak, as well as themselves; so, in the former state, will the more powerful factions or parties be gradually induced, by a like motive, to wish for a government which will protect all parties, the weaker as well as the more powerful. It can be little doubted, that if the state of Rhode Island was separated from the confederacy, and left to itself, the insecurity of rights under the popular form of government within such narrow limits, would be displayed by such reiterated oppressions of factious majorities, that some power altogether independent of the people, would soon be called for by the voice of the very factions whose misrule had proved the necessity of it. In the extended republic of the United States, and among the great variety of interests, parties, and sects, which it embraces, a coalition of a majority of the whole society could seldom take place upon any other principles, than those of justice and the general good: whilst there being thus less danger to a minor from the will of the major party, there must be less pretext also, to provide for the security of the former, by introducing into the government a will not dependent on the latter; or, in other words, a will independent of the society itself. It is no less certain than it is important, notwithstanding the contrary opinions which have been entertained, that the larger the society, provided it lie within a practicable sphere, the more duly capable it will be of self-government. And happily for the *republican cause*, the practicable sphere may be carried to a very great extent, by a judicious modification and mixture of the *federal* principle.

Study Guide Questions

Federalist #10

1. One means of eliminating the causes of faction is to eliminate the liberty of the people. What forms would that take?

2. Why is it quite impossible to give to all peoples the same opinions, passions, and interests?

3. Explain how majority rule (i.e., democracy) is but an instance of judging in one's own case, which is a near-certain cause of injustice.

4. If faction cannot be prevented, then its deleterious effects must be controlled. Why is a large republic better able than a small republic to provide this control?

5. Why will there be better representatives in a large than in a small republic?

Federalist #51

6. "Ambition must be made to counteract ambition," says Madison. Why does Madison ascribe importance to the selfish desires of officeholders?

7. What explanation of bicameralism does Madison offer in *Federalist #51*?

8. Madison acknowledges only two ways of guarding against majority tyranny. One is to diversify the interests existing in society, the other is to create "a will in the community independent of the majority"—that is, a hereditary monarch in a mixed regime. Why is such a solution unacceptable?

BRUTUS

Essay #1, 1787

The sixteen essays written under the pseudonym "Brutus" are usually attributed to Robert Yates (1738–1801), to his uncle Abraham Yates (1724–1796), or to Melancton Smith (1744–1798), all of New York.[1] Whoever was the author, he provided in the first of his essays the most succinct statement of Country republican theory as it pertains to issues of size, representation, standing armies, and public officers.

SOURCE: The Complete Anti-Federalist, *ed. Herbert J. Storing, vol. II (Chicago: University of Chicago Press, 1981).*

1. For a discussion of authorship, see Michael Zuckert and Derek Webb, eds., *The Anti-Federalist Writings of the Melancton Smith Circle* (Indianapolis: Liberty Fund, 2009), pp. xxi–xxvii.

OCTOBER 18, 1787

. . . *L*et us now proceed to enquire, as I at first proposed, whether it be best the thirteen United States should be reduced to one great republic, or not? It is here taken for granted, that all agree in this, that whatever government we adopt, it ought to be a free one; that it should be so framed as to secure the liberty of the citizens of America, and such an one as to admit of a full, fair, and equal representation of the people. The question then will be, whether a government thus constituted, and founded on such principles, is practicable, and can be exercised over the whole United States, reduced into one state?

If respect is to be paid to the opinion of the greatest and wisest men who have ever thought or wrote on the science of government, we shall be constrained to conclude, that a free republic cannot succeed over a country of such immense extent, containing such a number of inhabitants, and these encreasing in such rapid progression as that of the whole United States. Among the many illustrious authorities which might be produced to this point, I shall content myself with quoting only two. The one is the baron de Montesquieu, *Spirit of Laws*, chap. xvi. vol. I [book VIII]. "It is natural to a republic to have only a small territory, otherwise it cannot long subsist. In a large republic there are men of large fortunes, and consequently of less moderation; there are trusts too great to be placed in any single subject; he has interest of his own; he soon begins to think that he may be happy, great and glorious, by oppressing his fellow citizens; and that he may raise himself to grandeur on the ruins of his country. In a large republic, the public good is sacrificed to a thousand views; it is subordinate to exceptions, and depends on accidents. In a small one, the interest of the public is easier perceived, better understood, and more within the reach of every citizen; abuses are of less extent, and of course are less protected." Of the same opinion is the marquis Beccarari.

History furnishes no example of a free republic, any thing like the extent of the United States. The Grecian republics were of small extent; so also was that of the Romans. Both of these, it is true, in process of time, extended their conquests over large territories of country; and the consequence was, that their governments were changed from that of free governments to those of the most tyrannical that ever existed in the world.

Not only the opinion of the greatest men, and the experience of mankind, are against the idea of an extensive republic, but a variety of reasons may be drawn from the reason and nature of things, against it. In every government, the will of the sovereign is the law. In despotic governments, the supreme authority being lodged in one, his will is law, and can be as easily expressed to a large extensive territory as to a small one. In a pure democracy the people are the sovereign, and their will is declared by themselves; for this purpose they must all come together to deliberate, and decide. This kind of government cannot be exercised, therefore, over a country of any considerable extent; it must be confined to a single city, or at least limited to such bounds as that the people can conveniently assemble, be able to debate, understand the subject submitted to them, and declare their opinion concerning it.

In a free republic, although all laws are derived from the consent of the people, yet the people do not declare their consent by themselves in person, but by representatives, chosen by them, who are supposed to know the minds of their constituents, and to be possessed of integrity to declare this mind.

In every free government, the people must give their assent to the laws by which they are governed. This is the true criterion between a free government and an arbitrary one. The former are ruled by the will of the whole, expressed in any manner they may agree upon; the latter by the will of one, or a few. If the people are to give their assent to the laws, by persons chosen and appointed by them, the manner of the choice and the number chosen, must be such, as to possess, be disposed, and consequently qualified to declare the sentiments of the people; for if they do not know, or are not disposed to speak the sentiments of the people, the people do not govern, but the sovereignty is in a few. Now, in a large extended country, it is impossible to have a representation, possessing the sentiments, and of integrity, to declare the minds of the people, without having it so numerous and unwieldly, as to be subject in great measure to the inconveniency of a democratic government.

Unless the laws made by representatives are the same laws as the people would make, it cannot be said that the people are self-governing.

Brutus subscribes to the "agent" theory of representation.

The territory of the United States is of vast extent; it now contains near three millions of souls, and is capable of containing much more than ten times that number. Is it practicable for a country, so large and so numerous as they will soon become, to elect a representation, that will speak their sentiments, without their becoming so numerous as to be incapable of transacting public business? It certainly is not.

In a republic, the manners, sentiments, and interests of the people should be similar. If this be not the case, there will be a constant clashing of opinions; and the representatives of one part will be continually striving against those of the other. This will retard the operations of government, and prevent such conclusions as will promote the public good. If we apply this remark to the condition of the United States, we shall be convinced that it forbids that we should be one government. The United States includes a variety of climates. The productions of the different parts of the union are very variant, and their interests, of consequence, diverse. Their manners and habits differ as much as their climates and productions; and their sentiments are by no means coincident. The laws and customs of the several states are, in many respects, very diverse, and in some opposite; each would be in favor of its own interests and customs, and, of consequence, a legislature, formed of representatives from the respective parts, would not only be too numerous to act with any care or decision, but would be composed of such heterogenous and discordant principles, as would constantly be contending with each other.

The laws cannot be executed in a republic, of an extent equal to that of the United States, with promptitude.

The magistrates in every government must be supported in the execution of the laws, either by an armed force, maintained at the public expense for that purpose; or by the people turning out to aid the magistrate upon his command, in case of resistance.

In despotic governments, as well as in all the monarchies of Europe, standing armies are kept up to execute the commands of the prince or the magistrate, and are employed for this purpose when occasion requires: But they have always proved the destruction of liberty, and [are] abhorrent to the spirit of a free republic. In England, where they depend upon the parliament for their annual support, they have always been complained of as oppressive and unconstitutional, and are seldom employed in executing of the laws; never except on extraordinary occasions, and then under the direction of a civil magistrate.

A free republic will never keep a standing army to execute its laws. It must depend upon the support of its citizens. But when a government is to receive its support from the aid of the citizens, it must be so constructed as to have the confidence, respect, and affection of the people. Men who, upon the call of the magistrate, offer themselves to execute the laws, are influenced to do it either by affection to the government, or from fear; where a standing army is at hand to punish offenders, every man is actuated by the latter principle, and therefore, when the magistrate calls, will obey: but, where this is not the case, the government must rest for its support upon the confidence and respect which the people have for their government and laws. The body of the people being attached, the government will always be sufficient to support and execute its laws, and to operate upon the fears of any faction which may be opposed to it, not only to prevent an opposition to the execution of the laws themselves, but also to compel the most of them to aid the magistrate; but the people will not be likely to have such confidence in their rulers, in a republic so extensive as the United States, as necessary for these purposes. The confidence which the people have in their rulers, in a free republic, arises from their knowing them, from their being responsible to them for their conduct, and from the power they have of displacing them when they misbehave: but in a republic of the extent of this continent, the people in general would be acquainted with very few of their rulers: the people at large would know little of their proceedings, and it would be extremely difficult to change them. The people in Georgia and New Hampshire would not know one another's mind, and therefore could not act in concert to enable them to effect a general change of representatives. The different parts of so extensive a country could not possibly be made acquainted with the conduct of their representatives, nor be informed of the reasons upon which measures were founded. The consequence will be, they will have no confidence in their legislature, suspect them of ambitious views, be jealous of every measure they adopt, and will not support the laws they pass. Hence the government will be nerveless and inefficient, and no way will be left to render it otherwise, but by establishing an armed force to execute the laws at the point of the bayonet—a government of all others the most to be dreaded.

In a republic of such vast extent as the United-States, the legislature cannot attend to the various concerns and wants of its different parts. It cannot be sufficiently numerous to be acquainted with the local condition and wants of the different districts, and if it could, it is impossible it should have sufficient time to attend to and provide for all the variety of cases of this nature, that would be continually arising.

In so extensive a republic, the great officers of government would soon become above the control of the people, and abuse their power to the purpose of aggrandizing themselves, and oppressing them. The trust committed to the executive offices, in a country of the extent of the United States, must be various and of magnitude. The command of all the troops and navy of the republic, the appointment of officers, the power of pardoning offenses, the collecting of all the public revenues, and the power of expending them, with a number of other powers, must be lodged and exercised in every state, in the hands of a few. When these are attended with great honor and emolument, as they always will be in large states, so as greatly to interest men to pursue them, and to be proper objects for ambitious and designing men, such men will be ever restless in their pursuit after them. They will use the power, when they have acquired it, to the purposes of gratifying their own interest and ambition, and it is scarcely possible, in a very large republic, to call them to account for their misconduct, or to prevent their abuse of power.

These are some of the reasons by which it appears, that a free republic cannot long subsist over a country of the great extent of these states. If then this new constitution is calculated to consolidate the thirteen states into one, as it evidently is, it ought not to be adopted. . . .

Study Guide Questions

1. What historically happened to small republics when they grew large?

2. What is the difference between a democracy and a republic?

3. What conclusion does Brutus draw from the size and diversity of the country?

4. By what logic does a large country require a standing army to enforce its laws?

5. What happens to the character of political officers in a large state?

ALEXIS DE TOCQUEVILLE

Democracy in America, 1835, 1840

Alexis de Tocqueville (1805–1859) visited America for nine months in 1831–32. His observations and reflections resulted in a two-volume book titled Democracy in America. *In the selection reprinted here, Tocqueville seems to straddle the fence between Nationalist and Confederalist opinion, appreciating the advantages of consolidation and size, while admitting that liberty's natural home is the small republic. In the end, though (and looking back almost half a century since the Constitutional Convention), he concludes that a system partly national and partly confederal is superior to either consolidation or confederation alone.*

SOURCE: *Alexis de Tocqueville,* Democracy in America, *trans. Henry Reeve, vol. I* (New York: Colonial Press, 1899).

VOLUME I, PART ONE, CHAPTER VIII

Advantages of the Federal System in General, and Its Special Utility in America

. . . Small nations have therefore ever been the cradle of political liberty; and the fact that many of them have lost their immunities by extending their dominion shows that the freedom they enjoyed was more a consequence of the inferior size than of the character of the people.

The history of the world affords no instance of a great nation retaining the form of republican government for a long series of years, and this has led to the conclusion that such a state of things is impracticable. For my own part, I cannot but censure the imprudence of attempting to limit the possible and to judge the future on the part of a being who is hourly deceived by the most palpable realities of life, and who is constantly taken by surprise in the circumstances with which he is most familiar. But it may be advanced with confidence that the existence of a great republic will always be exposed to far greater perils than that of a small one.

Republics depend on the virtue of their citizens. But that virtue diminishes as the size of the state increases.

All the passions which are most fatal to republican institutions spread with an increasing territory, whilst the virtues which maintain their dignity do not augment in the same proportion. The ambition of the citizens increases with the power of the state; the strength of parties with the importance of the ends they have in view; but that devotion to the common weal which is the surest check on destructive passions is not stronger in a large than in a small republic. It might, indeed, be proved without difficulty that it is less powerful and less sincere. The arrogance of wealth and the dejection of wretchedness, capital cities of unwonted extent, a lax morality, a vulgar egotism, and a great confusion of interests, are the dangers which almost invariably arise from the magnitude of states. But several of these evils are scarcely prejudicial to a monarchy, and some of them contribute to maintain its existence. In monarchical states the strength of the government is its own; it may use, but it does not depend on, the community, and the authority of the prince is proportioned to the prosperity of the nation; but the only security which a republican government possesses against these evils lies in the support of the majority. This support is not, however, proportionably greater in a large republic than it is in a small one; and thus, whilst the means of attack perpetually increase both in number and in influence, the power of resistance remains the same, or it may rather be said to diminish, since the propensities and interests of the people are diversified by the increase of the population, and the difficulty of forming a compact majority is constantly augmented. It has been observed, moreover, that the intensity of human passions is heightened, not only by the importance of the end which they propose to attain, but by the multitude of individuals who are animated by them at the same time. Every one has had occasion to remark that his emotions in the midst of a sympathizing crowd are far greater than those which he would have felt in solitude. In great republics the impetus of political passion is irresistible, not only because it aims at gigantic purposes, but because it is felt and shared by millions of men at the same time.

It may therefore be asserted as a general proposition that nothing is more opposed to the well-being and the freedom of man than vast empires. Nevertheless it is important to acknowledge the peculiar advantages of great states. For the very reason which renders the desire of power more intense in these communities than amongst ordinary men, the love of glory is also more prominent in the hearts of a class of citizens, who regard the applause of a great people as a reward worthy of their exertions, and an elevating encouragement to man. If we would learn why it is that great nations contribute more powerfully to the spread of human improvement than small states, we shall discover an adequate cause in the rapid and energetic circulation of ideas, and in those great cities which are the intellectual centers where all the rays of human genius are reflected and combined. To this it may be added that most important discoveries demand a display of national power which the government of a small state is unable to make; in great nations the government entertains a greater number of general notions, and is more completely disengaged from the routine of precedent and the egotism of local prejudice; its designs are conceived with more talent, and executed with more boldness.

In time of peace the well-being of small nations is undoubtedly more general and more complete, but they are apt to suffer more acutely from the calamities of war than those great empires whose distant frontiers may for ages avert the presence of the danger from the mass of the people, which is therefore more frequently afflicted than ruined by the evil.

But in this matter, as in many others, the argument derived from the necessity of the case predominates over all others. If none but small nations existed, I do not doubt that mankind would be more happy and more free; but the existence of great nations is unavoidable.

This consideration introduces the element of physical strength as a condition of national prosperity. It profits a people but little to be affluent and free if it is perpetually exposed to be pillaged or subjugated; the number of its manufactures and the extent of its commerce are of small advantage if another nation has the empire of the seas and gives the law in all the markets of the globe. Small nations are often impoverished, not because they are small, but because they are weak; the great empires prosper less because they are great than because they are strong. Physical strength is therefore one of the first conditions of the happiness and even of the existence of nations. Hence it occurs that, unless very peculiar circumstances intervene, small nations are always united to large empires in the end, either by force or by their own consent: yet I am unacquainted with a more deplorable spectacle than that of a people unable either to defend or to maintain its independence.

The Federal system was created with the intention of combining the different advantages which result from the greater and the lesser extent of nations; and a single glance over the United States of America suffices to discover the advantages which they have derived from its adoption.

In great centralized nations the legislator is obliged to impart a character of uniformity to the laws which does not always suit the diversity of customs and of districts; as he takes no cognizance of special cases, he can only proceed upon general principles; and the population is obliged to conform to the exigencies of the legislation, since the legislation cannot adapt itself to the exigencies and the customs of the population, which is the cause of endless trouble and misery. This disadvantage does not exist in confederations. Congress regulates the principal measures of the national government, and all the details of the administration are reserved to the provincial legislatures. It is impossible to imagine how much this division of sovereignty contributes to the well-being of each of the states which compose the Union. In these small communities, which are never agitated by the desire of aggrandizement or the cares of self-defence, all public authority and private energy is employed in internal amelioration. The central government of each state, which is in immediate juxtaposition to the citizens, is daily apprised of the wants which arise in society; and new projects are proposed every year, which are discussed either at town meetings or by the legislature of the state, and which are transmitted by the press to stimulate the zeal and to excite the interest of the citizens. This spirit of amelioration is constantly alive in the American republics,

The federal system of America assigns great objects to the national government and small objects to the state governments.

without compromising their tranquility; the ambition of power yields to the less refined and less dangerous love of comfort. It is generally believed in America that the existence and the permanence of the republican form of government in the New World depend upon the existence and the permanence of the Federal system; and it is not unusual to attribute a large share of the misfortunes which have befallen the new states of South America to the injudicious erection of great republics, instead of a divided and confederate sovereignty.

It is incontestably true that the love and the habits of republican government in the United States were engendered in the townships and in the provincial assemblies. In a small state, like that of Connecticut for instance, where cutting a canal or laying down a road is a momentous political question, where the state has no army to pay and no wars to carry on, and where much wealth and much honor cannot be bestowed upon the chief citizens, no form of government can be more natural or more appropriate than that of a republic. But it is this same republican spirit, it is these manners and customs of a free people, which are engendered and nurtured in the different states, to be afterwards applied to the country at large. The public spirit of the Union is, so to speak, nothing more than an abstract of the patriotic zeal of the provinces. Every citizen of the United States transfuses his attachment to his little republic in the common store of American patriotism. In defending the Union he defends the increasing prosperity of his own district, the right of conducting its affairs, and the hope of causing measures of improvement to be adopted which may be favorable to his own interest; and these are motives which are wont to stir men more readily than the general interests of the country and the glory of the nation.

On the other hand, if the temper and the manners of the inhabitants especially fitted them to promote the welfare of a great republic, the Federal system smoothed the obstacles which they might have encountered. The confederation of all the American states presents none of the ordinary disadvantages resulting from great agglomerations of men. The Union is a great republic in extent, but the paucity of objects for which its government provides assimilates it to a small state. Its acts are important, but they are rare. As the sovereignty of the Union is limited and incomplete, its exercise is not incompatible with liberty; for it does not excite those insatiable desires of fame and power which have proved so fatal to great republics. As there is no common center to the country, vast capital cities, colossal wealth, abject poverty, and sudden revolutions are alike unknown; and political passion, instead of spreading over the land like a torrent of desolation, spends its strength against the interests and the individual passions of every state.

Nevertheless, all commodities and ideas circulate throughout the Union as freely as in a country inhabited by one people. Nothing checks the spirit of enterprise. Government avails itself of the assistance of all who have talents or knowledge to serve it. Within the frontiers of the Union the profoundest peace prevails, as within the heart of some great empire; abroad, it ranks with the most powerful nations of the earth; two thousand miles of coast are open to the commerce of the world; and as it possesses the keys of the globe, its flag is respected in the most remote seas. The Union is as happy and as free as a small people, and as glorious and as strong as a great nation.

Study Guide Questions

1. Taking notice of human passions and virtues, Tocqueville contends that the difficulties of maintaining republican government increase with the size of the state. Why? (Hume thinks that the difficulties lie only in the establishment not in the maintenance.)

2. While small republics may be the home of freedom, great states have much to recommend them too. What, according to Tocqueville, are the advantages of size?

3. Tocqueville sees some value in both smallness and largeness; but he finds maximum value in the combination of the two. What are the advantages of a federal republic, such as was created by the Constitution?

APPENDIX A: THE GAME (EXPANDED VERSIONS)

SETTING: STATE HOUSE, PHILADELPHIA

The date is summer 1787, or late May to mid-September. The place is Philadelphia, Pennsylvania, the largest city in America at the time (forty thousand). The building in which you gather, where the Declaration of Independence was written and signed, is the State House, known later as Independence Hall. You sit as members of state delegations convened to write a new constitution for the United States of America, replacing the Articles of Confederation, which has been in effect since 1781. Or—a point of great contention—you sit to revise the Articles while retaining the confederal form of government. Twelve of the thirteen states are represented, the exception being the ever-exceptional Rhode Island.

You may meet additionally in taverns, coffeehouses, and over dinners. Such out-of-class sessions may be convivial or serve as venues in which convention business is discussed and committee work is accomplished.

FRAMING A CONSTITUTION

Your job is to create *a* constitution, not to re-create *the* Constitution. Whether you depart from the original—and the extent to which you do depart—is entirely for you to decide. But you must address the same structural problems and respond to the same historical contingencies as confronted the delegates in Philadelphia. Thus your freedom of action is bounded.

Before you are questions of constitutional architecture: the branches of government (legislative, executive, judicial); their respective compositions, modes of selection, tenures in office, jurisdictions, and powers; the relationship of national to state governments and the limitations on each; and the rights retained by the people. Many of these elements are interconnected, and so it may happen that adjustments made to one have consequences for several others. Framing a constitution, you likely will discover, is a challenge similar to solving a Rubik's Cube puzzle. Meanwhile, above these problems of structure and powers are the rival theories of republican government, each striving to have its precepts reflected in the final charter.

The historical environment in which you operate is complicated by numerous factional divides: Nationalists versus Confederalists, large states versus small states, states with western domains versus states without, commercial versus agricultural interests, coastal towns versus backcountry settlements, democracy versus aristocracy, freedom versus slavery, North versus South, Anglophiles versus Anglophobes, and so on. But the main division is Nationalist and Confederalist, with moderate versions of each (described in Appendix B).

COUNTERFACTUALS

Once the Constitution was drafted, in September 1787, and sent to the states for their consideration and approval, a second round of debates immediately ensued. The full story of the making of the American Constitution includes the debates occurring at both stages of the contest, and books on the subject typically carry the narrative into the summer of 1788.

The game will do something of the same, incorporating elements from the ratification debates into the debates of the convention proper. The consequence should be a more principled debate around battle lines more clearly drawn. Serious opponents of the constitutional effort stayed away from Philadelphia, holding their fire for the state ratifying conventions to follow. Patrick Henry was one. He "smelt a rat" and refused his seat on the Virginia delegation. These opponents have a presence in the game, in the form of fictitious, composite characters, who will give voice to the Antifederalist position, or in the form of historical characters specially instructed to employ arguments from the ratification debates.

Some delegates from different states, while retaining their state identities, are combined into a single delegation for purposes of voting (see "Rules and Procedures" later in this appendix and "Delegates" in Appendix B). All delegates are present and seated for the entire convention, even though historically many arrived late and left early. Other minor alterations are noted under "Rules and Procedures."

MAJOR ISSUES FOR DEBATE

Most of the issues discussed are matters of political theory; a few are matters of political practice, eventuating in constitutional provisions voted on by the convention. Of the latter group, those that appear only in the Full-Size version of the game are identified by an asterisk.

Regime

It is said that Americans have a "genius" for republican government. It is certain that Americans have no tolerance for kings. It follows then that America will be a republic, whatever that might mean, and that America will not be a monarchy, whatever its intrinsic merits might be. Nor will America accept a republic presided over by a monarch. But how will this republic, which you are charged with creating, be defined, and how far in the direction of democracy are you prepared to go? What estimate have you of the common man's character and capacity for self-rule? What has the Revolution revealed about the people, and what new conditions obtain now that the Revolution has brought the people to the fore?

From the other side, how much of aristocracy are you prepared to import? America has no titled aristocrats, but might their equivalent be somehow included, and has government a chance of succeeding without use of their talents? Should the British model of mixed government, universally applauded, serve as a point of reference, or should it be disparaged and discounted because of that government's reckless behavior in the recent past?

Strength of Government

Drawing on republican theory: Is government to be thought of as a necessary but dangerous master, distrusted and kept strictly limited in its responsibilities and powers, or is it the people's protector and an instrument of human achievement when properly constructed? Will you want to hamper government or invigorate it?

Union

Nearly all delegates to the Constitutional Convention want to retain the union of thirteen states in some form or another. The question before you is the nature of that form: a confederation of semi-sovereign states as under the Articles, but with essential improvements; a consolidated nation with a single central government; or a hybrid federation never before seen. Both theory and practice warn against multiple sovereigns occupying the same territory; *imperium in imperio* it is called, and an absurdity it is commonly thought to be. Thus, how plausible will any hybrid prove to be?

States

Not unrelated to the issue just discussed: What will be the role of the states in this new union? They inherited the history and affection of colonial Americans. It is almost impossible, therefore (though not completely impossible), to imagine an America without states. But going forward, should they be viewed as parties to a compact, each one a sovereign equal, or as administrative units enabling the central government to extend its power to all parts of the country? Should the worry be that these states endanger the central government or that the central government, over time, will swallow up the states?

State Representation

What is fair? That people be represented according to their number or that states be represented in respect of their equality? Large states want equal representation of persons—hence unequal representation of states, based on population size. Small states want equal representation of states because, as colonies, they preexisted the union and because, as sovereign bodies, they are now in the process of creating the union—hence unequal representation of persons or no notice taken of them at all. How will you resolve this fundamental difference in outlook and interest?

Property

Aside from persons and states, does wealth enter into the equation? Should not those who carry the heavier tax burden be permitted the greater say over the raising and spending of taxes? Surely you have heard the saying, "He who pays the piper calls the tune." Should that not apply here? And how are property rights to be protected if subject

to the will of envious multitudes? What is there to prevent majority rule from degenerating into majority tyranny?

Slavery

What will you do about slavery, a moral abomination and flagrant affront to republican principles? Just that, you say—acknowledge the evil and abolish the institution. Or something more practical—blame the British and defer to present realities. Those realities include the opposition of the southern states whose plantation economies depend on slave labor. Will you sacrifice union with the South to have a union that is wholly free? Or, the question now put to the southern side: Will you risk your own republican liberty by acting the part of a tyrant toward others?

A second complicating factor is representation of the slaves (which does not mean giving slaves a voice in government). Should they count in the state's population, even though the states do not count them as citizens? They constitute a sizable portion of the South's wealth; and if wealth is a factor in determining a state's representation, then how in fairness can this species of wealth be ignored without the Constitution taking on a regional bias?

Yet a third factor is the slave trade. Every problem associated with slavery worsens with the importation of new slaves. Cannot this practice at least be stopped? But then states in need of slave labor will pay more for it, putting them at a disadvantage with states possessing a surplus of slaves.

Regions

The country is divided between the commercial North and the agrarian South. Policies favoring the interests of one region very often injure the interests of the other. In light of this dilemma, should a region's vital interests (e.g., tariffs for the protection of native manufacturing or open markets for the sale of cash crops) be placed beyond the reach of legislative majorities? But if that remedy is adopted, would not the need for supermajorities render the new government as crippled and ineffectual as the current government is thought to be?

This North–South problem is compounded by the impending entrance of a third party—the West. Should these newcomers (not all of which are in the west—Vermont and Maine) be admitted on equal terms with the charter members? Should they then be accorded the same rights and privileges and be granted the same voting power as the Atlantic states, no matter the sparseness of their populations or the backwardness of their manners? Or have the original thirteen states earned pride of place by virtue of their sacrifice and suffering during the resistance and war years? And are they entitled to protect themselves from the threat of depopulation by imposing discriminations on the West?

Social Condition

Do you believe that personal liberty is the outgrowth of independence and self-reliance and that the agrarian way of life, supposedly productive of these qualities, deserves protection and promotion? Is your ideal a modest, quiet, egalitarian community of farmers, made strong by tradition and faith—a community attached loosely to larger communities that are likewise happy to be free and content not to be great? And will commerce and so-called progress be the ruin of all that?

Or do you believe, contrarily, that the agrarian ideal is a golden-age myth, descriptive of an America that probably never existed and certainly cannot be preserved? Is liberty too a dream, contradicted by human nature? Or with wise institutions can flawed human beings live free? Should the constitution you are framing create and implement these institutions, or should it set up barriers against the tide of corruption—for example, sumptuary laws proscribing luxury and annual elections to tie untrustworthy officials to the people they serve?

Senate

Any talk about institutional correctives will eventually come to focus on the senate as a second chamber of the legislative power. The Old World reason for having a senate, or its equivalent, was to give representation to a permanent class of society—namely the nobility, an order separate from the commons. But the closest America comes to having nobles and commoners is the division between rich and poor, whose status is fluid, to a degree, and certainly not prescribed by law. Is a senate, therefore, needed?

Seen from another angle, is a senate even possible? In the Old World, fixed social orders defended their interests against advances from the other side, checking and balancing one another to the end of securing the liberty of each. But how can an American senate, without roots in society, accomplish the same moderating task? Will the amorphous rich have a class interest in fighting the more numerous poor, when from the poor they at some point came and to the poor they might well return? Here's an irony for you: America might have to create a body of aristocrats in order to have a republican government!

Separation of Powers

The division of government into three distinct branches—legislative, executive, and judicial—is called the separation of powers. Separation is part of a larger system of checks and balances designed to prevent power from becoming oppressive by locating all in one place.

One question is whether government should be divided into three equal branches or whether the legislative branch, as the people's representative, should be supreme relative to the other two. By this understanding, the executive is an agent of the legislature commissioned to carry out its will. If tyranny is the paramount concern, then you might not want a strong executive capable of influencing the legislature by vetoing its laws or appointing its members to executive positions.

But if your chief worry is the folly and inconstancy of the legislature (and also the chance of legislative tyranny), then an independent executive and judiciary are indeed desirable, and the question becomes how to create and maintain them in their independence. Here the mode of election/selection is important, along with other elements of structure and organization.

Standing Army*

Is liberty secure if government has a permanent and professional army at its beck and call? With the means of coercion so near at hand, will not rule by consent give way to rule by command? History is replete with examples of republican governments overthrown by enterprising generals and their devoted followers—for example, Rome by Julius Caesar, England by Oliver Cromwell. It would seem to follow, therefore, that a standing army, at least in times of peace, should be discouraged, even proscribed, and that responsibility for defense should lie with the populace, armed and organized locally as citizen militias.

But are citizen militias reliable and effective? They tend to be ill-trained, ill-disciplined, and poorly led; averse to fighting outside their home territories and inclined to abandon the fight the moment their enlistments are up. Further, they are no match for seasoned regulars, as proven by their disappointing and sometimes disastrous performance during the Revolutionary War. With English and Spanish forces poised to attack, can the country entrust its defense to amateurs?

Bill of Rights*

A bill of rights in republican theory is a means by which the people can curtail the power of government, otherwise absolute. Into those "fenced-off" areas where people have rights—to property, for instance—government may not enter. But is a bill of rights necessary in instances in which the government is thought to be the creature of another (whether of the people or of the states), having only those powers given to it? Is not a bill of rights, therefore, incompatible with the very idea of limited government (except insofar as the rights themselves impose limits)?

Legality

Are you aware that the work you are about to undertake, that of framing a constitution, is arguably illegal? You were sent to Philadelphia for "the sole and express purpose of revising the Articles of Confederation" (letter of authorization from the Continental Congress), and you have little warrant for doing anything else. Furthermore, the Articles stipulate that unanimity is required for the ratification of amendments. Ignore that requirement and the enterprise becomes invalid, does it not? How will you escape from this restriction of law? Perhaps you do not care to escape, but to have it enforced.

GAME LAYOUT

The game lays out in two parts. During the first part, the class will review the constitutional provisions of the Virginia Plan, consider an alternative plan of government put forward by New Jersey, and grapple with the vexing question of states' rights in the new union, especially the representation of states in the upper house. Here will occur broad-brush discussions of republican theory and of the constitution's basic form.

During the second part of the game, the class will be responding to reports from committees charged with resolving delayed matters and with rewriting the original language. A Committee of Detail will complete work on the branches of government (Full-Size version only); and a Committee of Style and Arrangement will put the constitution in its finished form. In between these committee reports, new issues will arise, possibly calling for the formation of additional, ad hoc committees.

PLANS OF GOVERNMENT

The debates in Philadelphia revolved around a plan of government submitted by the Virginia delegation under the nominal headship of Governor Edmund Randolph. Consisting of fifteen resolutions, the Virginia Plan occupied the convention's time for most of the months of June and July. It was debated, beginning to end, from May 29, when first presented, to June 5; then, from June 5 to June 13, selected provisions were revisited and postponed matters were addressed. That same day, June 13, the Committee of the Whole (see "Organization" later in this appendix), in existence since May 30, submitted a revised Virginia Plan, now expanded to nineteen resolutions. The convention (after first considering an alternate plan from New Jersey) proceeded to debate these nineteen resolutions until finishing a second, complete review on July 23, with further debate (chiefly on the presidency) continuing until July 26. At that point a revised-revised Virginia Plan, consisting of twenty-three resolutions, was referred to a five-member Committee of Detail charged with preparing a report on matters heretofore discussed. The convention then recessed for ten days to await the committee's report (August 6).

Virginia Plan

Once through (May 29–June 5; June 5–13)

Twice through (June 19–July 23; July 23–26)

Recess

Work by Committee of Detail (July 27–August 5)

A shortened and edited version of the revised Virginia Plan of June 13 (including one carryover from the original) will serve as the game's starting point. Most of the important debates came after June 13 because in the convention's first review of the plan, several initial suggestions were quickly discarded, while some key proposals were provisionally accepted with little or no discussion, or they were put off until a later time.

Virginia Plan [abbreviated from June 13]

1. Resolved that as a union merely confederal has proven itself inadequate to the needs of the country, a national government ought to be established consisting of a supreme legislative, executive, and judiciary.

2. Resolved that the National Legislature ought to consist of two chambers.

3. Resolved that members of the first chamber ought to be elected by the people of each state for a term of three years; to receive fixed stipends for their services, paid out by the national treasury; and to be ineligible for any office of the United States established during their term of service and for the space of one year thereafter.

4. Resolved that members of the second chamber of the National Legislature ought to be chosen by the state legislatures; to serve for a term of seven years; to receive fixed stipends for their services, paid out by the national treasury; and to be ineligible for any office of the United States established during their term of service and for the space of one year thereafter.

5. Resolved that the National Legislature ought to enjoy the legislative rights now vested in the Congress by the Confederation; to legislate in all cases to which the separate states are incompetent, or in which the harmony of the United States may be interrupted by

the exercise of individual legislation; and to negative all laws passed by the several states, contravening in the opinion of the National Legislature the articles of union or any treaties subsisting under the union.

6. Resolved that voting in the National Legislature ought to be in proportion to the whole number of free inhabitants, of every age, sex, and condition, including those bound to servitude for a term of years, and three-fifths of all other persons, not comprehended in the foregoing description, except Indians not paying taxes in each state.

7. Resolved that a National Executive ought to be instituted, enjoying the executive rights now vested in Congress by the Confederation; that the executive ought to consist of a single person, chosen by the National Legislature, for a term of seven years, with power to carry into execution the national laws and to appoint to offices in cases not otherwise provided for; to be ineligible for reelection; to be removable on impeachment and conviction of malpractices or neglect of duty; and to receive a fixed compensation paid out by the national treasury.

8. Resolved that the National Executive ought to have a right to negative any legislative act which shall not be afterwards passed unless by two-thirds of each chamber of the National Legislature; and that the National Judiciary, or a convenient number of its members, ought to compose with the National Executive a Council of revision, for the purpose of reviewing and vetoing acts of the National Legislature.

9. Resolved that a National Judiciary ought to be established, consisting of one supreme tribunal; that the judges

of this tribunal ought to be appointed by the second chamber of the National Legislature, to hold their offices during good behavior, and to receive a compensation paid out by the national treasury in which no diminution shall be made.

10. Resolved that the National Legislature ought to be empowered to create inferior tribunals.

11. Resolved that provision ought to be made for the admission of new states with the consent of a number of voices in the National Legislature less than the whole.

12. Resolved that provision ought to be made for the amendment of these articles of union whensoever it shall seem necessary.

13. Resolved that these articles of union ought to be submitted, for purpose of ratification, to assemblies chosen by the people.

Consideration of the Virginia Plan was interrupted for a time as the convention turned its attention to a rival plan presented by a delegate from New Jersey.

New Jersey Plan

Presentation and debate (June 15–19)

The New Jersey Plan, shortened and edited for game use, will also be debated in class.

New Jersey Plan [abbreviated from June 15]

1. Resolved that the Articles of Confederation ought to be so revised, corrected, and enlarged as to render the federal constitution adequate to the exigencies of government and the preservation of the union.

2. Resolved that the United States in Congress, in addition to its present powers, ought to be authorized to raise revenue by levying duties on all imports of foreign goods and on postage on letters or parcels passing through the general post-office; and that the Congress ought to be empowered to pass acts for the regulation of trade and commerce, both with foreign nations and among the confederated states.

3. Resolved that requisitions of funds ought to be in proportion to the whole number of free citizens of every age, sex, and condition, including those bound to service for a term of years and three-fifths of all other persons not comprehended in the foregoing description, except Indians not paying taxes; and that if such requisitions be not complied with, the United States in Congress ought to have power to pass acts directing and authorizing the collection of the same, provided that none of these acts and none of the powers elsewhere vested in Congress shall be exercised without the consent of at least _____ states, and in that proportion if the number of confederated states should hereafter be increased or diminished.

4. Resolved that the United States in Congress ought to be authorized to elect a federal Executive, to consist of _____ persons, to continue in office for a term of _____ years, to receive a fixed compensation paid out of the federal treasury; to be ineligible for reelection and removable by Congress on application by a majority of the executives of the several states; that the Executives, besides their general authority to execute the federal acts, ought to appoint all federal officers and direct all military operations, provided that none of the persons composing the federal Executive shall take command of any troops so as personally to conduct any enterprise as General or in other capacity.

5. Resolved that a federal Judiciary ought to be established, consisting of one supreme tribunal, the judges of which to be appointed by the Executive and to hold their offices during good behavior and to receive a fixed compensation for their services, paid out of the federal treasury;

6. Resolved that all acts of the United States in Congress and all treaties made and ratified under the authority of the United States shall be the supreme law of the respective states, and that the judiciary of the several states shall be bound thereby in their decisions, anything in the respective laws of the individual states to the contrary notwithstanding; and that if any state, or any body of men in any state, shall oppose or prevent the carrying into execution such acts or treaties, the federal Executive shall be authorized to call forth the power of the confederated states, or so much thereof as may be necessary to enforce and compel an obedience to such acts, or an observance of such treaties.

The presentation of the New Jersey Plan will provide the occasion for Country republican theory and Antifederalist opinion to come into the game; thus the New Jersey Plan will receive considerably more attention in the game than it received at the convention.

RULES AND PROCEDURES

Organization

To control the number of students and to ensure that all students work within groups, some of the twelve state delegations are combined. These are

New Hampshire and Massachusetts; New Jersey, Delaware, and Maryland; and North Carolina and Georgia. Thus there are eight delegations or delegation groups seated at the convention.

The convention will have three officers: a president, a secretary, and a president pro tempore. The president is George Washington, delegate from Virginia. The secretary and the president pro tempore are any delegates chosen by the convention to serve in these offices. Interested parties nominate themselves and offer brief speeches in support of their candidacies. In case of ties, run-off elections are conducted. The votes are by individual ballot, not group ballot.

The president determines the order in which speeches are presented and, to a limited degree, the convention's agenda. The president also calls on people in debate and makes necessary rulings (discussed later in the appendix).

The secretary records all motions and all votes.

The president pro tempore serves as acting president in the event of the president's absence. (At the Philadelphia convention, the president pro tempore presided when the assembly converted itself into a Committee of the Whole for purposes of preliminary debate and provisional voting. It did this only once. Because of time constraints, the game does not include the option of a Committee of the Whole, so the president pro tempore is included simply as a backup to the president.)

Committees

Two committees are built into the game (one in the Mid-Size version): the Committee of Detail and the Committee of Style and Arrangement. Besides these two, several other ad hoc committees may be formed to help resolve particularly difficult issues.

The general rule is that the convention first hears speeches introducing new agenda items, debates the merits of the proposals made, and then votes on particular resolutions, one by one. But if the voting fails to deliver positive results, the president has the option of calling for a committee.

These committees will consist either of three members (for maximum efficiency), five members (for wider participation), or seven members (for full representation—one member per delegation/group required, minus one to prevent tie voting). The president will determine the committee's size, though an exception is made in the case of the Committee of Detail (seven members) and a partial exception in the case of the Committee of Style and Arrangement (five or seven members, for reasons peculiar to it). Interested delegates nominate themselves, and election is by individual, not group, balloting. (If delegates cast weighted votes, the ballot is more likely to deliver clear results.) The three, five, or seven highest vote getters (depending on the committee's size) are elected; the first on the list is the chairman or, if preferred, the committee can choose its own chair. The president will decide whether caucusing is permitted in advance of an election.

If a committee is united, a presumption exists in favor of its work. Altering or rejecting its proposal(s) can be done only with the vote of a **double-majority (a majority of delegations that is also a majority of delegates**—a device once proposed by Roger Sherman and once by James Madison), **or a two-thirds supermajority in small classes in which delegation voting is not employed**. If a committee is divided, it will present the convention with a majority and a minority report. No changes are allowed, nor may both reports be rejected. The convention adopts whichever of the two garners more votes, even if neither obtains a majority. This fail-safe device is meant to prevent the convention from coming to a full stop. It is particularly necessary in cases of multifaceted issues, such as the presidency or slavery. Here, committees, if formed, are likely to report back complicated packages of interconnected proposals that cannot be opened for amendment without risk of the entire plan coming apart. If necessary, more than one minority report is allowed from a committee, but with the same rules in operation: no changes on the floor, take-it-or-leave-it votes on all plans, and the largest plurality prevails.

The Committee of Style and Arrangement operates somewhat differently. It submits a near-final draft of the constitution, having chosen between two competing drafts written by committee members. No minority report is allowed. Nor may the committee alter the convention's work; it may, though, fill in gaps in the game agenda left by the convention (e.g., impeachment). With the president's approval, clear mistakes or omissions can be corrected on the floor by simple majority voting. Whether substantive changes can also be made by simple majorities—or whether double-majorities/supermajorities are required—is a matter determined by a **die role** taken before the proposing of amendments. The purpose of the die roll is to discourage issue-by-issue voting done in the belief that until the last class the convention's work is merely provisional and easily changed.

Voting

State delegations, or delegation groups, will vote following a north-to-south geographical order: (1) New Hampshire–Massachusetts, (2) Connecticut, (3) New York, (4) Pennsylvania, (5) New Jersey–Delaware–Maryland, (6) Virginia, (7) North Carolina–Georgia, and (8) South Carolina.

Delegations cast as many votes as there are states composing them. Most therefore cast one vote, but New Hampshire–Massachusetts and North Carolina–Georgia each cast two, and New Jersey–Delaware–Maryland casts three.

Voting is done by individuals but counted by delegations (except in small classes). Each delegate has a vote card showing "Aye" on one side, and "Nay"

on the other. At the point of voting, delegation members decide individually how to cast their votes, and the convention secretary records these individual votes, plus whether the delegation's total represents a majority in favor of or in opposition to the measure, or whether the tally is even and the delegation votes divided.

Delegations vary in size, ordinarily from two to four members. But regardless of size, the delegation together casts a single group vote, or rather, one vote per state composing the delegation (thus one, two, or three). Abstentions are permitted, whether by individuals or by delegations; if the latter the effect is the same as a divided vote.

The delegation abstains if a quorum is not present. A quorum is half or more of the members assigned to the delegation. If, for example, a delegation of three is missing two, the remaining one can only abstain. If a delegation of four is missing two, the remaining two, if they agree, can vote aye or nay; otherwise they cancel each other out, and the delegation votes "divided." **Absent students, therefore, cannot ask others to serve as proxies and cast their votes for them.** (Historically, the quorum rule was determined by state governments. Half of the states required that half or more of their delegates be present in order to cast the state's vote; while half of the states allowed voting by less than half, or even by one. In the game the same quorum rule applies to all delegations.)

If the votes cast by state delegations and delegation groups divide evenly, the measure is defeated. That tie could be six affirmative votes against six negative votes, or it could be any number less because of votes lost to division or failure to make a quorum.

A majority quorum of five of eight states/groups is needed for positive action. It is not expected, however, that the convention would ever be brought to a standstill by four delegations unable to make a quorum. Divided votes count toward the quorum. Conceivably, a measure could pass with one affirmative vote and eleven divided votes.

Proposals require a second and on request may be broken into parts, so long as the president agrees. The president rules on any motion to amend, unless the motion is acceptable to the person who made the proposal. A "friendly" amendment, so called, must be offered before debate has begun and should at once be incorporated into the text of the original proposal. An "unfriendly" amendment, if allowed by the president, is considered after the original proposal and only in the event of its defeat. The president rules also on seconded motions to table (i.e., suspend consideration) or to call the question (i.e., have a vote).

If this simple procedure does not work—because in the course of debate a flurry of unfriendly amendments and rival proposals comes pouring forth—the president is free to decide the order of consideration. For efficiency sake, it is recommended that the president consider first the proposal most likely to command a majority and consider last the proposal least likely to command a majority. To determine degrees of popularity, the president can take a quick series of hand votes, counting only individuals, not delegations.

Revoting

Any measure may be revisited, but only with the approval of the president and with **a double-majority (or supermajority) to amend or over-turn**. The clock is ticking, and the president is responsible for ensuring that the work of the convention is completed on time.

Tie-Breaker/Tie-Maker Voting

Three tie-breaker/tie-maker vote cards will be distributed to the student (or students) winning the fill-in-the-blank quiz administered before the start of the game (discussed later in this appendix).

Because some students might find themselves in divided delegations, these tie-breaker/tie-maker cards could prove quite valuable. They also can be bartered away. They are to be played, not when the delegation votes and the outcome is uncertain, but at the end of the voting when the outcome is known and the importance of the card is plain. No card can be used more than once, nor can a card be used for the game's final vote to approve or reject the constitution.

Extra Votes, Lost Votes

Delegates to the Constitutional Convention did not arrive all at once and did not leave all at the same time. They drifted in over days and weeks and drifted away before the proceedings had concluded. To replicate the effects of these chance comings and goings, the Gamemaster, on several occasions, will draw the names of a few delegates from a bag. Those selected will, for that session only, cast an extra vote or cast no vote, depending on the roll of a die (fifty–fifty odds). Unlike the tie-breaker/tie-maker vote, this voting must be done at the time in the rotation when the affected delegates normally vote.

Final Vote

The constitution needs about two-thirds, **70 percent**, of the aye or nay delegation votes cast to be approved. The reason is that a bare majority would throw suspicion on the product, rendering nil its chances for ratification. Put differently, the reason is to oblige convention delegates to think prospectively about the reception their constitution is likely to receive. Votes are rounded up or down, and divided votes are not counted in the total. In the case in which only five votes are counted, rounding does not work, so a die roll will determine whether three votes (60 percent) or four votes (80 percent) are needed for approval. Otherwise the numbers are as follows:

VOTES COUNTED	VOTES REQUIRED
12	8
11	8
10	7
9	6
8	6
7	5
6	4
5	3 or 4
4	3
3	2
2	1
1	1

VOTES COUNTED	VOTES REQUIRED (75 PERCENT)	VOTES REQUIRED (80 PERCENT)
12	9	10
11	8	9
10	7 or 8	8
9	7	7
8	6	6
7	5	6
6	4 or 5	5
5	5	4
4	3	3
3	2	2
2	1 or 2	2
1	1	1

Two actions, should they occur during the course of the convention, would raise the required percentage by 5 percent—to **75 percent** if one does, to **80 percent** if both do, again with rounding up or down. These actions are a breach (or breaches) of the secrecy rule and a walk-out of the convention (both explained later in this appendix). It is again the case that in some instances rounding does not work, and so recourse will be had to the die roll.

Convention Walk-Out

A walk-out of the convention is accomplished if three of a possible five, predetermined but publicly unidentified, players decide that the emerging constitution, with respect to the question of state suffrage—**and this question only**—is better defeated than passed. They do not actually leave the convention; instead, by declaring their intention to walk out, they change the percentage needed for approval—from 70 percent to 75 percent (discussed in the previous section). This 5 percent change is reversed if the walk-out delegates (three of five) finally reconcile to the constitution, which they show themselves to have done by telling the Gamemaster and the president, or possibly the whole convention, and by arguing for Nationalist modes of amending and ratifying the constitution. Action is proof of intent.

Convention President's Powers

1. Setting the order of speeches and calling on delegates

2. Establishing committees and determining their size

3. Ruling on requests to caucus before votes and elections

4. Ruling on motions to break proposals into parts

5. Ruling on unfriendly amendments

6. Ruling on motions to table and to call the question

7. Ruling on requests to revisit decisions

8. Determining other rules, such as due times for website postings of papers and of anonymous leaks, but with the convention's approval

The president may not make or second a proposal, and the president does not serve on committees. The president does, however, vote.

Secrecy

The convention adopts a secrecy rule, forbidding members from revealing convention business to the outside world. Public commentary, most suppose, would be harmful to the success of the proceedings.

Because harm is the expected result, if word does get out, the percentage needed for final approval increases by 5 percent (as discussed earlier). If the culprit is identified, he is denied voting privileges for two whole sessions and must desist from further leaking. The quorum rule in this case is suspended, allowing the remaining member(s) of the delegation to vote.

A leak occurs if an anonymous posting on the class website communicating convention business and addressed to a newspaper, a private correspondent, or a state legislature goes undetected and unremarked by delegates at the start of their next session. The person responsible will privately notify the Gamemaster of the leak, and the Gamemaster will inform the convention and explain the consequences to the game.

A leak also occurs if a printed flyer, containing the same sort of information, is posted in a public place. The leak is prevented if a convention delegate discovers the flyer and presents it at the start of the next session. The president, with the convention's approval, will determine the location(s) where this copy might be placed as well as the time by which it must be posted.

Yet a third way to accomplish a leak is to have a story about the convention's deliberations published in the campus newspaper—or in any alternative, weekly publication open to the student body. The expected harm done by publicity can be neutralized, however, if friends of the constitution succeed in having a retraction published in the next issue. If this route is selected, there must remain enough time in the game for a retraction to appear.

Behavior

Proper decorum is expected of all members. Side conversations and note passing while another is speaking at the podium are impolite behaviors and may bring reprimands from any of the delegates, but especially from the president. Still, side conversations and note passing are regular features of Reacting games; so it remains to be seen what will be tolerated and what can be gotten away with.

Even your most detested enemy is to be addressed with respect. "The Right Honorable Mr. . . ." will do.

You are advised to remember that a Reacting game is only a game and that resistance, attack, and betrayal are not to be taken personally because game opponents are merely doing as their roles direct.

VICTORY

Individuals, not groups, win or lose in this game. Students win by achieving a majority of the victory points assigned to their roles (information provided to the Gamemaster but withheld from the students). They lose if they fall short of a majority.

ASSIGNMENTS AND GRADING

Game Quiz and Study Guide Questions

The instructor may distribute a fill-in-the-blank quiz in the first of the game's setup sessions. Serving less as a test than as a study guide, the quiz should be answered as you read through the assigned material. To play the game well, you need to absorb as much factual information about the period as you can, and you need to do so quickly. The quiz is intended to assist with the work of absorption and retention. If distributed, the quiz, or a portion of it, will then be taken by the class in the last of the setup sessions before the game proper begins. As an incentive to do well, the winner, or winners, will receive between one and three tie-breaker/tie-maker vote cards (discussed earlier). The instructor may choose to treat the quiz as a test, by assigning to it some small percentage of the course grade.

Separate from the quiz are the Study Guide Questions provided at the end of each of the core texts. You are advised to read the questions before, or as, you read the text and to write down the answers as you come across them. These questions may be used to structure the class discussions about the texts. In addition, the instructor may decide to include some of these questions on the quiz.

Fun-Facts Competition

Before the opening of every convention session, the Gamemaster will pose a multiple-choice question. During the course of the game, you are obliged to answer one such question correctly or suffer the loss of a victory point at the game's end. No penalty is incurred for wrong answers. Those succeeding early and protecting themselves from loss can gain a victory point by answering a second question correctly, and by answering a third they can gain one more. Two positive points are the maximum allowed. But in the pursuit of positive points, wrong answers do matter, causing those seeking a first point to return to the start where a correct answer is needed just to prevent a loss, and causing those seeking a second point to forfeit the one point already earned. Furthermore, you must commit to the contest before hearing the question.

As an inducement to compete, students who have committed to answering a question (and these students only), may consult the Internet using any electronic device in their possession. Students have about one minute to answer unless the Gamemaster changes the time limit.

Papers

Role descriptions provide directions regarding the topics and timing of student papers. Some paper topics are required, whereas others are merely suggested. Students are to write ten or more pages for the game (instructor's choice), but they will spread those pages over a varying and perhaps undetermined number of papers. Thus one of you may write three papers, each three or four pages in length; another of you may write five papers two pages in length. Some topics can be covered by oral remarks unsupported by papers.

To know when a paper is due, you should compare the "Assignments" section in your role descriptions with the game agenda and the course syllabus (distributed by the Gamemaster). When ambiguities occur (because the pace of debate has slowed or quickened or because a broad topic is spread over two or more class sessions), you should ask the Gamemaster and the convention president. It is always better, for obvious reasons, to be ready early than to be ready late.

Role descriptions refer you to secondary sources for use in writing your papers. Very often these sources are mentioned in no other role. When using this material, you effectively function as a teacher of the class and as such bear a special responsibility for conveying your research clearly and comprehensively, citing sources where appropriate. With each student learning parts of the founding and communicating the same to others, coverage is provided of the whole event.

Class Preparation

Once the game begins, you have no regular reading assignments other than the reading you do as research for your papers. But for each class there is work to be done. To prepare yourself for debate, you should reread the pertinent sections of your role description, looking up the references to Madison's *Notes* and all other references. Your role description provides you with "talking points," as it were, on most issues that will come before the convention. It is important that you articulate these points at the right moment because information contained in your role might not exist in any other. You should read the speeches your fellow delegates posted on the class website, for in this way you will be ready with supporting comments, queries, or rebuttals. And when appropriate you should meet or communicate with faction members in advance of class sessions.

Grades

Though the instructor is free to make adjustments, written work normally accounts for two-thirds of your grade and participation one-third—formal speeches from the podium (possibly graded higher if spoken and not read) and informal debate from the floor, plus caucusing, negotiating, and strategizing, to the extent that these activities are known to the instructor. It is the instructor's option whether to award a bonus for winning and impose a penalty for losing, as it is the instructor's option whether to factor in quiz performance as part of the course grade.

APPENDIX B: ROLES (EXPANDED VERSIONS)

FACTIONS

Although the game organizes players into state delegations, it is by republican principles that players are mainly identified, with some called Nationalists, some Moderate Nationalists, some Confederalists, and some Moderate Confederalists. These affiliations, depending on the issue, are disrupted by state size (large and small) and by region (North and South).

State Delegations

The one structural division in the game is the collecting of students into eight state delegations or delegation groups. To underscore this division, delegates will sit together, ideally at separate tables, but more likely in clusters of desks set apart in the room or as groups of students seated around a central table. When matters affecting a particular state (or region) are being discussed, the delegation(s) affected will often speak with one voice. But unified action should not always be expected because divisions may exist within the delegation—divisions of a political, philosophical, economic, or personal nature. The first challenge, therefore, is to establish a group identity strong enough to contain the predilections of individual members. Some delegations will have an easier time at this than will others.

Nationalists

Nationalists, or Court republicans, are united in the belief that state governments possess too much power, exercise it badly, and pose serious danger to the peace, prosperity, and continued unity of the country. Some even would do away with the states, except as administrative departments. They endorse the Virginia Plan and its vision of a national government composed of a supreme legislative, executive, and judiciary. They despair of solving the country's problems by patched-up reforms of the Articles of Confederation. At most points they work to invigorate the national government at the expense of the state governments. They particularly oppose use of state legislatures as electoral bodies for national offices. Other constitutional positions taken by them (or some of them) are a national veto over state laws, a complete national judiciary consisting of supreme and inferior tribunals, payment of national officials by the national treasury, national supervision of national elections, and control over state militias. They tend to favor a strong executive and the constitutional devices to bring it about; likewise the independence of the judiciary is a priority. Legislatures they regard less as the palladium of liberty than as hothouses of parochial selfishness.

In general, Nationalists take a realistic (i.e., low) view of human nature and are inclined to use corruption as much as guard against it. They appreciate the special talents of the political elite and spare no effort to draw them into national service; on the other hand, they sometimes support democratic institutions, and they always champion the rights of minorities (meaning, mainly, the wealthy few).

Moderate Nationalists

This milder variant of the Nationalist position holds that the Congress under the Articles of

Confederation is a proven failure, too strong in structure (e.g., a unicameral legislature) to be trusted with power and too lacking in power to accomplish national objectives (e.g., the regulation of trade). But Moderate Nationalists, unlike some of their Nationalist kin, value the states as a check and balance on the federal government. They therefore are open to constitutional provisions that include and protect the states. Their hope is that jurisdictional boundaries, properly delineated, will allow each level of government to be supreme within its own separate sphere.

Confederalists

Confederalists are Country republicans having all the small-republic reasons for defending the states. They therefore worry that the push to nationalize will end in despotism and the destruction of liberty. They agree that the Articles of Confederation falls short of expectation, and they welcome amendments to fix problems widely recognized. But the framework, they insist, should remain that of a confederation of states, not a consolidated union.

The law is on their side, they note, for it is under the authority of the Articles that the delegates have gathered in Philadelphia; and so it is by the procedures of the Articles that they are obliged to operate—meaning that any changes recommended by the Convention must secure the unanimous approval of the states. Anything less is illegal, as well as impolitic because recourse to irregular means will all but guarantee rejection of the final product.

Confederalists rally around the New Jersey Plan, which creates an executive office to enforce federal law and serve as commander-in-chief (although it is a plural executive, as a safeguard against tyranny), along with a permanent judiciary made (somewhat) independent by fixed salaries and specified jurisdictions. These branches complement the already existing unicameral Congress. The plan also invests the national government with new means for raising revenue and new power to regulate trade. Confederalists accept a national government competent within its sphere, so long as that sphere is kept strictly limited. They therefore will tolerate no encroachments on the states' "police power," an imprecise concept covering an assortment of responsibilities, including criminal justice, slave codes, militias, taxes, land ownership, manufacturing, transportation, education, religion, and marriage.

The great fear of Confederalists is that a single American nation under a centralized government may one day emerge to obliterate the identities of the states. Their goal, in reaction, is to defend the rights of states and to enhance their profile and importance within the union. Confederalists, accordingly, support such constitutional provisions as the payment of national legislators by state treasuries—the better to hold them bound; and to further ensure dependence, their terms of office should be kept short and unfixed. Confederalists also support voting in Congress by states; the election of the president, the senators, and even lower-house members by state assemblies; a federal judiciary confined to hearing cases on appeal; state permission required before federal authorities can suppress a rebellion or purchase land for the construction of forts; power to appoint militia officers; and the designation of state legislatures as the ratifying bodies for the revised constitution.

Confederalists evince some wariness of ambitious individuals talented enough and/or wealthy enough to operate on a national stage. Confederalists also seek constitutional protection of individual rights. These twin concerns mark them as democrats. But Confederalists, like Nationalists, hail from the wealthy elite, and most fancy themselves talented; plus their attachment to states outpaces their regard for the poor and the powerless. Hence their democratic bona fides are a little shaky, if not a thing of convenience.

Moderate Confederalists

Moderate Confederalists affirm most of what the Confederalists do, albeit moderately. They support the Country republican premise that the small republic is the place where people are freest and happiest, and they suppose that the thirteen states—notwithstanding the size of some—are a close approximation of small republics. Thus the states must be preserved. But they must also be reined in because they have behaved badly during the Confederation period and threaten the integrity of the union. Moderate Confederalists hope (they don't quite assert) that reforms to the Continental Congress will suffice to solve the problem.

Large States

The categories of state size (large versus small) overlap with the categories of republican theory (Nationalist versus Confederalist), which is to say that the large-state–small-state categories do not stand for wholly new factions.

The Nationalist position is more likely to be adopted by large-state delegates, while the Confederalist position is the more likely choice of small-state delegates. Even so, Nationalists and Confederalists can be found in both large and small states, and once state interests are secured, many delegates feel liberated to move in new directions.

Congressional representation is the main issue between states when distinguished by size. Large-state delegates make an equity argument in favor of proportional representation, noting the undeniable wrong of granting equal votes to states with unequal populations. Some large-state delegates worry about the fate of the constitution if made to rest on so gross an injustice. The senate is the focus here, whether to use it to house and protect the states as equal parties to a compact or to use it to further represent the people, to represent wealth,

or to secure sage counsel from the country's elite. Practical concerns also figure in: the extension of equal voting to new states with populations not surpassing the current smallest; the danger to small states from large states in the event of disunion; the corruption that invariably attends on malapportionment, with the "rotten boroughs" of England serving as the cautionary model (about which it is said that some pastures have more representation than some cities).

Small States

Small staters may have less of equity to support them, but they have more of tradition . . . and they have the law. The national government under the Articles of Confederation represents not people but states, which vote equally regardless of size. Likewise, voting at the convention is equal and by states. Large staters agreed to this procedure—and to the confederal structure to which it is appropriate—when they drafted and ratified the Articles. They continue to be bound.

By some counts the small states number ten, the large states only three (Massachusetts, Pennsylvania, Virginia). Is there not injustice as well, say small-state advocates, in subjecting the less populous ten to the rule of the more populous three by representing their numbers in both houses of congress? Furthermore, if it is a principle of republican government that powers be separated for the defense of distinct branches, does it not follow that the states too need a means of defense, which a senate, organized by equal suffrage, supplies? The small staters observe that of the many failings of the Continental Congress, none have been traced to equal-state voting. At bottom, though, the reason for representation of states in the senate is that states, as small republics, are the place where people are freest and happiest; thus for the public's well-being, the states must be given a strong voice in the new national government.

Northern States

The northern states have two commercial interests that they would like to see written into the constitution, or at least not put at risk by hostile provisions. They are navigation acts (i.e., commercial regulations) and export taxes. The northern economy depends on shipping and manufacturing; hence the northern delegates want protection for these enterprises and industries. That protection might take the form of legislation favoring American shippers over foreign competitors and tariffs on manufactured goods imported from abroad. They argue that a merchant fleet will produce the sailors needed by the navy, which in turn will provide protection for the southern states, currently vulnerable to naval attack.

Revenue is needed, and it will not be gotten through import taxes alone. Export taxes cannot be excluded, even though the country's main exports are the staple crops produced in the South. Revenue from direct taxation (population) is not to be counted on because it is little different from a requisition on the states.

Direct taxation is often tied to the representation of slaves—another objection of the northern delegates. If the time is not right for prohibiting slavery, at least the prohibition of slave trading can be achieved. But the practice of augmenting the represented population by three-fifths the number of slaves (permitted under the Virginia Plan and expected by the South) works to encourage slave trading, not eliminate it. This and other measures hospitable to slavery (e.g., the exclusion of imported slaves from import taxation) must not become part of a republican constitution. To the South's predictable complaint that slavery is an internal matter of concern to no one outside the region, the northerners reply that their constitutional obligation to defend the southern states against insurrection makes slavery (itself an incitement to insurrection) the North's business, too.

Southern States

The economic interests of the southern states are in diametric opposition to the interests of the North (or so most people believe). The South is agrarian, not commercial; it needs markets for its crops and relief from regulations that hinder trade. Thus the southern delegates (most of them) want a constitutional ban on navigation acts, or at a minimum a two-thirds majority requirement to secure their passage. They also want export taxes prohibited by law. The southern states of Maryland, Virginia, North Carolina, South Carolina, and Georgia are at present a minority faction within the union; if they are to join with the North, they expect some constitutional protections of their minority rights. By and large, they distrust majoritarian politics—until they become the majority themselves, which all suppose will happen sometime in the future.

Southern delegates do not attempt to defend the morality of slavery. They admit the evil of it, especially for republican societies, but they do not know how to remove it. Slavery is an interest, and interest more than morality determines behavior. Even the slave trade—a crime against humanity, as all would acknowledge—is nonetheless a matter of interest because without it slaves become prohibitively expensive, plantations fail, and the southern economy collapses. Slavery, they note, is practiced everywhere and from time immemorial, with one-half of mankind usually enslaved by the other half. Can America afford to be the lone exception? And don't ignore the hypocrisy of the North, whose merchants have grown fat off the slave trade and who bear responsibility, along with the British, for slavery's widespread presence in the South.

DELEGATES

Fifty-five men representing twelve states participated in the Constitutional Convention. Of these fifty-five, forty were present for most of the debates; and of these forty, perhaps twenty-five made significant contributions. Thirty-nine signed the final document.

There are only individualized roles in the Extended versions of the game, twenty-two in all. Most are historical figures; a few are composites, partly fictional to serve game needs. These are identified by an asterisk.

The public descriptions of the twenty-two included delegates are given in the table, along with the votes cast by state delegations or delegation groups (see "Organization" and "Voting" in this appendix).

New Hampshire– Massachusetts (2 votes)

Nicholas Langman* (NH)
Self-made man, now a wealthy merchant with political experience in the state legislature and national Congress; recent president of the state.

Elbridge Gerry (pronounced GARY) (MA)
Prominent merchant from a prominent family; experienced politician; signer of the Declaration of Independence and the Articles of Confederation.

Rufus King (MA)
Rising young man, married to the daughter of a wealthy New York merchant; has important friends, including John Hancock, governor of Massachusetts.

Connecticut (1 vote)

Roger Sherman
Elderly jack-of-all-trades with political experience tracing back to the First Continental Congress; signer of the Declaration of Independence and co-drafter of the Articles of Confederation.

Oliver Ellsworth
Businessman, lawyer, judge; former delegate to the Continental Congress; prolific consumer of snuff, given to talking to himself.

New York (1 vote)

Robert Yansing*
Wealthy landowner and justice of the state supreme court; follower of George Clinton, governor of New York.

Alexander Hamilton
Revolutionary War veteran on Washington's staff and hero of Yorktown; pamphleteer; organizer of the Annapolis Convention; gifted lawyer married into a prominent political family; not native born but from the Caribbean and an orphan.

Pennsylvania (1 vote)

Benjamin Franklin
Oldest delegate at age eighty-one; printer, scientist, inventor, diplomat; architect of the Albany Plan (early attempt at colonial union, 1754); signer of the Declaration of Independence; supporter of the Pennsylvania constitution; co-drafter of the Articles of Confederation; America's most famous citizen.

James Wilson
Scottish immigrant, arriving before the Revolution; important pamphleteer; lawyer-jurist; signer of the Declaration of Independence; opponent of the Pennsylvania constitution; land speculator and financier, sometimes in debt.

Gouverneur Morris
Transplanted New Yorker from an aristocratic family; young, talented lawyer with a wooden peg leg, the original lost under mysterious

circumstances; bon vivant; active in state government; master constitutional draftsman; Washington and Robert Morris his patrons.

New Jersey–Delaware–Maryland (3 votes)

William Paterson (NJ)
Lawyer and storekeeper; state legislator; owner of a confiscated loyalist estate.

John Dickinson (DE)
Important pamphleteer during the protest years; member of the Stamp Act Congress; member of the First and Second Continental Congresses, inclining toward reconciliation with Britain; co-drafter of the Articles of Confederation; war veteran; former president of Delaware and of Pennsylvania; lawyer married to an heiress.

Luther Martin (MD)
Attorney general of Maryland; a fill-in for the state's more prominent politicians who declined their appointments; alcoholic.

Virginia (1 vote)

George Washington
Virginia planter, surveyor, and soldier; commander of American forces during the Revolutionary War; unanimous choice for convention president, though a reluctant attendee.

George Mason
Planter-aristocrat but with democratic leanings; owner of many slaves but a supporter of abolition; author of the Fairfax Resolves (revolutionary tract, 1774); draftsman of the Virginia constitution of 1776 and of the Virginia Bill of Rights; out of politics for ten years before the convention; friends with Virginia's political elite.

James Madison
Son of a Virginia planter; Princeton graduate and student of John Witherspoon; state legislator; delegate to the Continental Congress; main author of the Virginia Plan and driving force behind the Virginia delegation, though young at age thirty-six.

Edmund Randolph
Ex officio head of the Virginia delegation, current governor of Virginia at the age of thirty-three and former attorney general; former delegate to the Continental Congress and to the Annapolis Convention; from a prominent Virginia family divided by politics.

North Carolina–Georgia (2 votes)

Hugh Williamson (NC)
Physician and scientist; state legislator; delegate to the Continental Congress and signer of the Northwest Ordinance of 1784; investor in western lands.

Herman Wylie★ (NC)
Backcountry populist and pamphleteer; propagandist for the Regulator Movement, a local protest movement of the late 1760s/early 1770s; colonial and state legislator; delegate to the Continental Congress.

Abraham Pierce Blunwin★ (GA)
Militia commander, state legislator, and delegate to the Continental Congress; investor in western lands.

South Carolina (1 vote)

John Rutledge
Planter-aristocrat, lawyer-judge; member of the Stamp Act Congress and the First and Second Continental Congresses; drafter of South Carolina

constitution; state legislator and governor; war hero whose estate the British confiscated; older cousin of Charles Pinckney; owner of twenty-six slaves.

Charles Pinckney

At twenty-nine, among the youngest of the delegates, and proud of the fact; war veteran; state legislator; delegate to the Continental Congress and opponent of the Jay-Gardoqui treaty; author of his own plan of government.

INDETERMINATES

Reacting games commonly assign a number of students to roles called "Indeterminate." Indeterminate roles are representative types unattached to any faction. They may have leanings and a task or two to perform, but their main function is to provide the game with a persuadable audience for arguments made by others.

No student in this game is an Indeterminate as such. All have individualized roles with positions to advance and objectives to achieve, and all belong to one of four ideological factions. The complexity of characters, the variety of issues, and the fluidity of factional alliances mean that indeterminacy is everywhere, to some degree, and so does not need to be the special responsibility of a few roles set aside for the purpose.

APPENDIX C: TERMS IN USE

Antifederal: Against a strong, central national government of a union tending toward consolidation; supportive of a confederated union or loose league of states resting on trust (e.g., requisitions), not on force (e.g., taxes).

Branch: The different elements (or branches) of governmental power—legislative, executive, and judicial, by contemporaries used sometimes interchangeably with *chamber*.

Chamber: A synonym for *house*, giving rise to *unicameral* (a one-chambered legislature) and *bicameral* (a two-chambered legislature).

Confederal: Pertaining to confederation; a term occasionally used in place of the more common *federal*, this the preferred term for game purposes because the latter word can have opposite meanings.

Confederalist: A delegate espousing confederal principles; a term invented for game use to identify delegates opposed to nationalism, known also as states-rights localist and a Country republican.

Congress: The national government under the Articles of Confederation; by scholarly convention sometimes called the Confederation Congress after ratification (1781) to distinguish it from the First and Second Continental Congresses before ratification (1774, 1775–81), not named "Confederation Congress" in the Articles, rather called "the United States in Congress assembled," abbreviated "Congress"; called Congress here, or Continental Congress.

Consolidation: A union more integrated than a league of states, with laws touching individuals as a distinguishing characteristic.

Council of advisers: A body of advisers attached to the executive; possibly a cabinet but usually a collective co-executive whose approval is needed for the president to act.

Council of revision: The union of the executive and judicial branches in exercising a veto over national laws (possibly also state laws).

Country republicanism: The political persuasion of eighteenth century English Whigs opposed to the monarchy and its centralizing policies and of their American counterparts opposed to consolidated union.

Court republicanism: The political persuasion of eighteenth century English Whigs supportive of the monarchy and patronized by it and of their American counterparts supportive of stronger central government.

Federal: Pertaining to the central government, but equally to the central government of a confederated union (e.g., the Continental Congress) or to the central government of a consolidated union (e.g., the U.S. government)—though never so consolidated as to eliminate the constituent parts (the states), sometimes a synonym for *national*, but not wrong when used as a synonym for *confederal*, derived from *fides*, Latin for "faith," thus applicable to associations based more on trust than on force—that is, *confederations*, meaning "with faith"; a confusing term open to misuse.
(In the immediate aftermath of the convention, Nationalists took the name Federalists, and so left their Confederalist adversaries to be called Antifederalists—even though the word *federal* was then largely synonymous with *confederal* or *confederated*, the adjectival forms of *confederation*. Thus the opponents of confederation shrewdly, and falsely, represented themselves as the friends of confederation.)

House: The chamber, or chambers, of the legislative branch, *upper house* and *lower house* used as synonyms for the *Senate* and the *House of Representatives*, respectively.

National: Pertaining to a larger union than individual states, one in which states are subordinate partners, central government of this union, sometimes called federal.

Nationalist: A delegate espousing national principles and wanting the country to move toward a more integrated union; a Court republican.

Negative: A power residing in the national legislature to veto state laws.

APPENDIX D: STATE HISTORIES AND STATE CONSTITUTIONS

NEW HAMPSHIRE

Population: *141,500 plus 150 slaves*[1]

New Hampshire was first settled in 1620 by English merchants seeking to profit from fur trading with native Indians; shortly after came colonists from Massachusetts, unhappy with the religion-inflected politics practiced there. The economy of New Hampshire relied on fishing, textiles, timber, shipbuilding, and river-powered mills. Three geographical regions emerged during colonial times: the coastal Piscataqua region; the central Merrimack region; and the western Connecticut River Valley region. The less populated and underrepresented west resented the more populated and overrepresented east, where government (both colonial and state) was located. Localist opinion was strong in all regions, but postwar recession and a farmers' uprising caused those in the east to acknowledge the need for outside assistance and stronger central government. Slavery arrived as early as 1648. New Hampshire laid no tax on imported slaves, and so Portsmouth became a vital center for the slave-trading business. Congregationalists made up the principal denomination; the rest were largely Presbyterians, Baptists, Episcopalians, and Quakers.

MASSACHUSETTS

Population: *379,000 with no slaves*

Massachusetts was founded by two groups of religious dissidents: the Pilgrims, who arrived in

1620 and settled in Plymouth Plantation, and the Puritans, who arrived ten years later and settled in Boston and its environs. The latter, organized under the Massachusetts Bay Company, soon predominated, and the theocratic democracy established there and spread by them was intolerant of other religious groups, who migrated to neighboring colonies. Some of these migrants, however, took with them the town hall system of local government developed by the Puritans. The economy of Massachusetts consisted of fishing, livestock, foodstuffs, shipbuilding, and timber. Boston was a major port city. Resistance to British rule began in Massachusetts, and the closing of the Boston port in 1774 (in reprisal for the Boston Tea Party) was the event that impelled the colonies toward independence. Fighting first broke out at Lexington and Concord the following year. After the war the state's economy suffered from debts and falling trade with the West Indies. Those difficulties, aggravated by Shays' Rebellion in the winter of 1786–87, convinced the merchant class that the Articles of Confederation had to be revised. Slavery had existed in Massachusetts since early colonial times. But several court rulings under the new constitution of 1780 brought the institution to an end.

RHODE ISLAND

Population: *68,000 plus 950 slaves*

Rhode Island was originally founded in 1636 by Roger Williams, a nonconforming minister exiled from Massachusetts. Other oppressed faiths soon flocked to the colony because of its reputation for religious tolerance. The small colony secured a charter from King Charles II in 1663 to protect

---

1. All population data in this appendix are from the 1790 census; figures are rounded up or down.

itself against land-grabbing by its larger neighbors. Under the charter, Rhode Island officials were either elected directly by eligible voters in town halls or indirectly by representatives elected annually. That much democracy brought Rhode Island the scorn of Massachusetts and New York. During colonial times the Rhode Island economy consisted chiefly of fishing, livestock, dairy, and lumber. Newport was a major port city at the start of the Revolution, but not at the close, because the British occupation of 1776–79 reduced the population by half—and the town never recovered. In keeping with its liberal values, Rhode Island emancipated slaves born after 1784, and it prohibited the slave trade in 1787. But in keeping with its radical politics (paper emissions, debt cancellations), it rarely cooperated with the Continental Congress, and it refused to send delegates to the Constitutional Convention.

CONNECTICUT

Population: *235,000 plus 3,000 slaves*

Puritan settlers came to Connecticut in the 1630s, seeking to make their fortunes and to escape what they perceived as objectionable leadership in the Massachusetts Bay Colony. Most were of the Congregationalist denomination, whose democratic structure affected the colony's politics as well. Also affecting local politics was the royal charter, granted in 1662, which allowed the colony an unusual degree of autonomy. Connecticut residents, in consequence, came to place a high value on self-government and personal liberty. Most inhabitants worked as farmers, growing wheat and corn, or as fisherman, trolling the waters of the Long Island Sound or Massachusetts's outer banks. Manufacturing developed because of a limited supply of land, with the colony becoming noted for its clocks, its iron works, and its shipbuilding. Connecticut had five midsize ports located in New Haven, Hartford, Middletown,

Norwich, and New London, but these faced fierce competition from rivals outside of the colony. During the eighteenth century, Connecticut merchants traded mainly with the West Indies and the other colonies, but not with Europe. Import and export duties imposed by other states were a bone of contention at the time of the convention. Connecticut banned the slave trade in 1774, and a gradual emancipation bill passed in the state legislature ten years later.

NEW YORK

Population: *319,000 plus 21,500 slaves*

New York was first permanently settled in 1624 by the Dutch, who called the colony New Netherland. Great Britain seized it in 1655 and renamed it New York. It had a diverse population from early on, consisting of Germans, French Huguenots, Jews, Scots, and Scotch-Irish, in addition to English and Dutch settlers. Some of these were migrants from New England. Farming was the main occupation; rice, wheat, grain, and indigo were the main crops. Manufacturing—of ships and iron—was a secondary concern. At the time of independence, New York City was the country's second largest city, with a population of nearly twenty-six thousand. Mills, factories, West Indian trade, and the importation of slaves all contributed to its growth. During the war and the continuing occupation of New York City by the British, the state was in the forefront of efforts to strengthen the Continental Congress. But after the departure of the British (November 1783), the longtime governor, George Clinton, managed to resolve the state's financial problems by confiscating the property of loyalists (in violation of the Treaty of Paris) and by levying duties on imported and exported goods. Because the bulk of these taxes were paid by out-of-state merchants (especially those in Connecticut and New Jersey), the tax burden on New Yorkers was proportionately lightened. New York then went from a state wanting to enhance the importance of the union to a state wanting to protect its own prerogatives.

NEW JERSEY

Population: *172,500 plus 11,500 slaves*

New Jersey was under Dutch rule until 1664, when the territory was conquered by England. The Dutch regained control in 1672, but the English took it back again two years later. The area was divided into East and West Jersey in 1676, because its proprietary owners disagreed over governance and land titles. New England Puritans were the principal settlers of East Jersey and English Quakers of West Jersey. The two Jerseys became a royal colony in 1702 and were governed by New York. Independence was restored in 1738 and the colony united. With no large urban centers, New Jersey's population was mostly agrarian and middle class. The farm economy concentrated on grains and livestock. Manufacturing developed in the eighteenth century, especially iron ore and lumber. The one college of note (and the alma mater of several of the framers) was the College of New Jersey (later to become Princeton University). New Jersey was a major battleground during the war, and the damage suffered by its farmers was reimbursed with federal certificates. By the time of the Constitutional Convention, these certificates had become next to worthless. That misfortune, plus the crop failures and economic recessions of the 1780s, plunged much of the state's population into poverty. New Jersey had its share of slaves, but it banned the slave trade in 1786.

PENNSYLVANIA

Population: *430,500 plus 3,500 slaves*

Pennsylvania was chartered in 1681 by King Charles II and founded by its proprietary ruler, William Penn. Penn established the colony as a refuge for members of the persecuted Society of Friends, known by their critics as "Quakers." Quakerism was a passive, egalitarian, and hope-filled faith, developed in reaction to the merciless gloom of Puritanism. Pennsylvania prospered under Penn's benevolent rule. His descendants, however, faced a challenge to their authority, as a rising merchant class in the 1750s and 1760s tried to have Pennsylvania converted from a proprietary to a royal colony. The economy was principally agricultural, growing rye, hemp, flax, and wheat. Flour, produced by river-powered mills, was the major export commodity. Manufacturing consisted of shipbuilding, iron works, textiles, tanning, and papermaking. Philadelphia was the nation's largest city as of 1750. Its deep-water port made it a hub of international trade and a center of cultural enlightenment. Many poets, painters, and writers were in residence; magazines, newspapers, and philanthropic societies abounded. Philadelphia also boasted the country's first library, hospital, public parks, police and fire departments, brick buildings, illuminated streets, and insurance cooperatives. The city's politics, though, had become quite factionalized on the eve of the Revolution. Independence from Great Britain divided the people into Tories, moderates, and radicals. Radicals produced the constitution of 1776 and largely controlled the government for a decade, when moderate republicans took over. Slavery was present from the beginning, but it never competed well against indentured servitude, and in the 1770s Quaker opinion turned against it. A gradual emancipation law was passed in 1780.

DELAWARE

Population: *50,000 plus 9,000 slaves*

Originally settled by Swedish immigrants in 1638, Delaware was taken over by the Dutch in 1655, and then conquered by the English in 1664. While under English control, both Pennsylvania and Maryland claimed the region. Pennsylvania eventually prevailed in this dispute, but its control was so uncertain that in 1701 it granted Delaware, commonly called the Three Lower Counties, its own assembly. Delaware became fully independent only with statehood in 1776. Tobacco was the original cash crop; wheat gradually replaced it. Fishing was also important to the colony, along with lumber, shipbuilding, and barrel-making (coopering). Wilmington was the most important city and a center of trade. But Delaware's "free" ports could not compete with the port of Philadelphia, through which much of the state's trade passed, and upon which heavy taxes were laid. Delaware prohibited the importation of slaves in 1776 and strengthened the ban in 1787.

MARYLAND

Population: *216,500 plus 103,000 slaves*

The colony of Maryland was founded during the reign of Charles I. The king gave a charter to Cecilius Calvert, the second Lord Baltimore, who wished to establish a haven for his fellow Catholics. While some Catholics did colonize the region, many Protestants from the Virginia colony also arrived, along with Quakers, Puritans, Lutherans, German Reformed, and other religious groups. Slaves were brought to Maryland to help planters cultivate their main cash crop, tobacco. When the price of tobacco fell in the mid-eighteenth century, planters switched mostly to grains. Shipbuilding and iron works were also major industries for the colony. Though largely rural, Maryland had two urban centers of consequence, Annapolis and Baltimore. Agitation to overturn an illiberal constitution (e.g., property requirements for voting and office holding) drew Marylanders toward revolution as much as opposition to British rule.

VIRGINIA

Population: *455,000 plus 292,500 slaves*

Founded by the Virginia Company in 1607, Virginia was the first permanent English settlement in the New World. England took up colonization to compete with Spain, hoping thereby to extract wealth from the continent and to spread the Protestant (as opposed to the Catholic) faith among the natives. But the settlement at Jamestown did not become a successful venture until John Rolfe introduced tobacco to the colony in 1612. Over the course of the seventeenth and eighteenth centuries, tobacco production grew to impressive proportions, reaching seventy million pounds by 1775. Such success was aided by the importation of slaves, whose numbers increased along with the increasing popularity of the crop. By 1740, blacks were 30 to 40 percent of Virginia's total population. Most Virginians were Anglicans. Dissident faiths included Quakers, Lutherans, Methodists, and German Reformed. Virginia's role in the Revolution was second only to Massachusetts's. After the war, Virginia soon discovered the difficulty of a confederated union composed of thirteen sovereign states, for sovereign Maryland controlled navigation on the Potomac, and sovereign Virginia controlled the ports along the Chesapeake Bay. Each state taxed the goods of the other, to the detriment of both. Fixing this problem proved to be the first step toward fixing the Articles of Confederation.

NORTH CAROLINA

Population: *293,000 plus 100,500 slaves*

Chartered by King Charles II in 1670, North Carolina was initially just Carolina, a single colony as yet undivided. Eight proprietary lords were its founders, and the philosopher John Locke was (possibly) the author of its constitution. In 1712, Carolina was separated into North and South, and in 1729, the two regions were given their own governments. North Carolina was not as aristocratic as its southern twin. In the western part of the colony, the population was more dispersed, and the region was more rustic. And even though the coastal residents were often slave-owning planters, the colony had no port city comparable to Charleston. Its largest religious groups, as of 1776, were Presbyterians, Baptists, Episcopalians (Anglicans), and Quakers. Tobacco, initially, was the main crop. Later the colony came to rely also on rice, tar ("tarheels"), turpentine, and lumber. After independence, the state developed a strong attachment to its own sovereignty. One of its delegates to the Continental Congress was responsible for inserting into the Articles of Confederation the provision that reserved to each state its "sovereignty, freedom, and independence." The merchant class, however, was more nationally minded.

SOUTH CAROLINA

Population: *142,000 plus 107,000 slaves*

South Carolina began as Carolina, undivided, in 1670; it became South Carolina in 1712. Most of the colony's original inhabitants were people who had already settled in other British colonies; those coming from Barbados brought with them their slaves. Other settlers were from Pennsylvania, Virginia, and North Carolina. Rice was the main crop, while indigo, cotton, tobacco, and cattle also contributed to the colony's prosperity. Some planters managed to make fortunes off of slave labor, and soon a wealthy, quasi-aristocratic class emerged, centered in Charleston. African slaves were the majority of South Carolinians by 1708, and largely remained the majority until the War for Independence depleted their number and white migration, for a time, accelerated. Charleston became a major trading hub after the war, with a port that rivaled those at Philadelphia, New York, and Boston.

South Carolina went through a series of wartime constitutions, shifting power among the branches and disestablishing the Anglican church. Presbyterians and Baptists were as numerous as Episcopalians (Anglicans), so generalized Protestantism became the new state religion.

GEORGIA

Population: *53,500 plus 29,500 slaves*

Founded by James Oglethorpe in 1732, Georgia was the youngest of the thirteen colonies. Its first inhabitants were convicted debtors, whose imprisonment in England was exhausting the pocketbooks of taxpayers and the consciences of humanitarians. In America, it was hoped, these debtors would become sturdy, yeoman farmers. Investors believed that the area would yield valuable products, such as wine and silk. And South Carolina, a colony since 1670/1712, wanted a buffer against Spanish, French, and Indian attacks. Thus philanthropic, financial, and military objectives lay behind Georgia's establishment. Aside from debtors, many other types of immigrants of different ethnicities and religions came to the colony. In 1754, Georgia switched from being a charter colony under proprietary rule to a royal colony under a crown-appointed governor. Most Georgians were small farmers, though the introduction of slavery led to the rise of an affluent planter class. Indigo, rice, lumber, and fur were the state's main products. Concern for security dominated the lives of Georgians, as many Spaniards lived among them and Creek and Cherokee Indians regarded the territory as their own.

Eleven of the thirteen colonies wrote state constitutions between the years 1776 and 1780. Rhode Island and Connecticut wrote no constitutions, but kept in effect their colonial charters, much altered, dating back to 1663 and 1662, respectively.

CONSTITUTIONAL FEATURES

Modes of Election/Appointment

STATE	HOUSE	SENATE	EXECUTIVE	JUDICIARY
New Hampshire (January 5, 1776; revised October 31, 1783)	Popular	Popular (by districts, with voting proportionate to taxes paid; unresolved elections settled by joint ballot of house members and elected senators)	Popular (unresolved election settled by house choosing two of top four vote-getters and senate choosing between them)	Executive and council
Massachusetts (June 16, 1780)	Popular	Popular (by districts, with voting proportionate to taxes paid; unresolved elections settled by joint ballot of house members and elected senators)	Popular (unresolved election settled by house choosing two of top four vote-getters and senate choosing between them)	Executive and council
Rhode Island	Popular	Popular	Popular	Joint legislative ballot*
Connecticut	Popular	Popular	Popular (unresolved election settled by joint ballot)	Joint legislative ballot†
New York (April 20, 1777)	Popular	Popular (by districts, with voting proportionate to population)	Popular	Special appointment council (executive + four senators nominated by assemblymen)
Pennsylvania (September 28, 1776)	Popular	No senate	Joint ballot of legislature and executive council	Executive council
New Jersey (July 2, 1776)	Popular	Popular	Joint legislative ballot	Executive council and house
Delaware (September 11, 1776)	Popular	Popular	Joint legislative ballot	Executive and joint legislative ballot

STATE	HOUSE	SENATE	EXECUTIVE	JUDICIARY
Maryland (November 11, 1776)	Popular	Popularly elected electors (tied elections repeated; then settled by lot if necessary)	Joint legislative ballot (tied elections repeated; then settled by lot if necessary)	Executive council
Virginia (June 29, 1776)	Popular	Popular	Joint legislative ballot	Joint legislative ballot
North Carolina (December 18, 1776)	Popular	Popular	Joint legislative ballot	Joint legislative ballot
South Carolina (March 26, 1776; revised March 19, 1778)	Popular	Popular	Joint legislative ballot	Joint legislative ballot‡
Georgia (February 5, 1777)	Popular	No senate	Legislature (electing one of its own as governor)	Popular**

* Superior court of judicature (above this the general assembly as final court of appeals).

† Superior courts (above these a supreme court of errors, consisting of the governor, lieutenant governor, and the senate, together called the council).

‡ Ordinary courts (above these a court of chancery, consisting of the lieutenant governor and a majority of the privy council).

** Superior or county courts (above these a supreme court, consisting of a chief justice and three county justices).

Terms of Office

STATE	HOUSE	SENATE	EXECUTIVE	JUDICIARY
New Hampshire	1 year	1 year	1 year	Good behavior
Massachusetts	1 year	1 year	1 year	Good behavior
Rhode Island	6 months	1 year	1 year	1 year
Connecticut	6 months	1 year	1 year	1 year
New York	1 year	4 years	3 years	Good behavior
Pennsylvania	1 year (no more than 4 years in 7)	No senate	3 years (4-year ineligibility)	7 years
New Jersey	1 year	1 year	1 year	7 years
Delaware	1 year	3 years	3 years (3-year ineligibility)	Good behavior
Maryland	1 year	5 years	1 year (3 successive and 4-year ineligibility)	Good behavior

STATE	HOUSE	SENATE	EXECUTIVE	JUDICIARY
Virginia	1 year	4 years	1 year (3 successive and 4-year ineligibility)	Good behavior
North Carolina	1 year	1 year	1 year (no more than 3 years in 6)	Good behavior
South Carolina	2 years	2 years	2 years	Good behavior
Georgia	1 year	No senate	1 year (2-year ineligibility)	1 year

Property Qualifications for Officeholders

STATE	HOUSE	SENATE	EXECUTIVE
New Hampshire	£100 estate, half in freehold	£200 freehold	£500 estate, half in freehold
Massachusetts	£100 freehold or £200 estate	£300 freehold or £600 estate	£1,000 freehold
Rhode Island	£40 freehold or 40s. annual rent	£40 freehold or 40s. annual rent	£40 freehold or 40s. annual rent
Connecticut	40s. freehold or £40 estate	40s. freehold or £40 estate	40s. freehold or £40 estate
New York	£20 freehold or 40s. annual income	£100 freehold	£100 freehold
Pennsylvania	None	No senate	None
New Jersey	£500 estate	£1,000 estate	Unspecified
Delaware	Freeholder	Freeholder	Unspecified
Maryland	£500 estate	£1,000 estate	£5,000 estate, £1,000 in freehold
Virginia	Freeholder	Freeholder	None
North Carolina	100 acres freehold	300 acres freehold	1,000 acres freehold
South Carolina	500 acres or £150 estate	£2,000 freehold	£10,000 freehold
Georgia	250 acres or £250 estate	No senate	500 acres and £1,000 estate

Suffrage Requirements

STATE	REQUIREMENTS
New Hampshire	£50 estate
Massachusetts	£3 annual freehold income or £60 estate
Rhode Island	£40 freehold or 40s. annual rent
Connecticut	$7 freehold per annum or $134 estate and good character (each person approved for voting)
New York	£20 freehold (house), £100 freehold (senate and executive)
Pennsylvania	Taxpayer or son of freeholder
New Jersey	£50 estate
Delaware	50 acres or £50 estate
Maryland	50 acres or £30 estate (house), electors with £500 estate (senate)
Virginia	50 acres or 25 acres with house or town lot with house
North Carolina	Taxpayer (house), 50 acres (senate)
South Carolina	50 acres or town lot or property tax paid in previous year or in present year
Georgia	Taxpayer with £10 estate or mechanical trade

Executive Councils

STATE	EXECUTIVE COMPOSITION AND TERM LIMITS
New Hampshire	Advisory; two senators and three representatives; joint ballot election; 1-year term
Massachusetts	Advisory; nine senators plus lieutenant governor; joint ballot election; 1 year
Rhode Island	Constraining; senate; ten members plus governor and deputy governor; popular election; 1-year term
Connecticut	Constraining; senate; twelve members plus governor and lieutenant governor; popular election; 1-year term
New York	No council
Pennsylvania	Constraining; twelve members; popular election; 3-year term and 4-year exclusion
New Jersey	Three or more senators
Delaware	Constraining; four members, each house electing two; 3-year rotating term
Maryland	Constraining; five members; joint ballot election; 1-year term
Virginia	Constraining; eight members; joint ballot election; indefinite term

STATE	EXECUTIVE COMPOSITION AND TERM LIMITS
North Carolina	Advisory; seven members; joint ballot election; 1-year term
South Carolina	Advisory; eight members plus lieutenant governor; joint ballot election; 2-year rotating terms
Georgia	Advisory; two legislators per county, half in residence with governor; legislative election; 1-year term; quasi-senatorial body

Religious Tests

STATE	RELIGIOUS REQUIREMENT
New Hampshire	Protestant officeholders
Massachusetts	Christian governor
Rhode Island	No religious tests
Connecticut	No religious tests
New York	Ineligibility of clergy; free exercise
Pennsylvania	Christian oath of office
New Jersey	Protestant officeholders; no established religion
Delaware	Christian oath of office; no established religion; ineligibility of clergy
Maryland	No religious tests
Virginia	No religious tests
North Carolina	Protestant officeholders; ineligibility of clergy; no established religion or compulsory support; free exercise
South Carolina	Protestant officeholders; ineligibility of clergy; Christian Protestantism as established religion
Georgia	Protestant officeholders; ineligibility of clergy; no established religion; free exercise

Sources: Francis Newton Thorpe, ed., *The Federal and State Constitutions, Colonial Charters, and Other Organic Laws of the United States*, 7 vols. (Washington, DC: Government Printing Office, 1909); Chilton Williamson, *American Suffrage from Property to Democracy, 1760–1860* (Princeton, NJ: Princeton University Press, 1960); Richard J. Purcell, *Connecticut in Transition: 1775–1818* (Middletown, CT: Wesleyan University Press, 1963), pp. 113–145; Paul Eidelberg, *The Philosophy of the American Constitution: A Reinterpretation of the Intentions of the Founding Founders* (New York, NY: Free Press, 1968), pp. 262–263; Irwin H. Polishook, *Rhode Island and the Union, 1774–1795* (Evanston, IL: Northwestern University Press, 1969), pp. 22–36; Patrick T. Conley, *Democracy in Decline: Rhode Island's Constitutional Development, 1776–1841* (Providence, RI: Rhode Island Historical Society, 1977), pp. 36–54; Willi Paul Adams, *The First American Constitutions: Republican Ideology and the Making of the State Constitutions in the Revolutionary Era* (Chapel Hill, NC: University of North Carolina Press, 1980), pp. 295–311; Jon J. Wakelyn, ed., *America's Founding Charters: Primary Documents of Colonial and Revolutionary Era Governance, 3 vols.* (Westport, CT: Greenwood Press, 2006).

APPENDIX E: ARTICLES OF CONFEDERATION

ARTICLES OF CONFEDERATION AND PERPETUAL UNION BETWEEN THE STATES OF NEW HAMPSHIRE, MASSACHUSETTS BAY, RHODE ISLAND AND PROVIDENCE PLANTATIONS, CONNECTICUT, NEW YORK, NEW JERSEY, PENNSYLVANIA, DELAWARE, MARYLAND, VIRGINIA, NORTH CAROLINA, SOUTH CAROLINA, AND GEORGIA.

Article I.

The style this Confederacy shall be "The United States of America."

Article II.

Each state retains its sovereignty, freedom, and independence, and every power, jurisdiction, and right, which is not by this Confederation expressly delegated to the United States in Congress assembled.

Article III.

The said States hereby severally enter into a firm league of friendship with each other, for their common defense, the security of their liberties, and their mutual and general welfare, binding themselves to assist each other, against all force offered to, or attacks made upon them, or any of them, on account of religion, sovereignty, trade, or any other pretense whatever.

Article IV.

The better to secure and perpetuate mutual friendship and intercourse among the people of the different States in this Union, the free inhabitants of each of these States, paupers, vagabonds, and fugitives from justice excepted, shall be entitled to all privileges and immunities of free citizens in the several States; and the people of each State shall have free ingress and regress to and from any other State, and shall enjoy therein all the privileges of trade and commerce, subject to the same duties, impositions, and restrictions as the inhabitants thereof respectively, provided that such restrictions shall not extend so far as to prevent the removal of property imported into any State, to any other State, of which the owner is an inhabitant; provided also that no imposition, duties or restriction shall be laid by any State, on the property of the United States, or either of them.

If any person guilty of, or charged with, treason, felony, or other high misdemeanor in any State, shall flee from justice, and be found in any of the United States, he shall, upon demand of the Governor or executive power of the State from which he fled, be delivered up and removed to the State having jurisdiction of his offense.

Full faith and credit shall be given in each of these States to the records, acts, and judicial proceedings of the courts and magistrates of every other State.

Article V.

For the most convenient management of the general interests of the United States, delegates shall be annually appointed in such manner as the legislatures of each State shall direct, to meet in Congress on the first Monday in November, in every year, with a power reserved to each State to recall its delegates, or any of them, at any time within the year, and to send others in their stead for the remainder of the year.

No State shall be represented in Congress by less than two, nor more than seven members; and no person shall be capable of being a delegate for more than three years in any term of six years; nor shall any person, being a delegate, be capable of holding any office under the United States, for which he, or another for his benefit, receives any salary, fees or emolument of any kind.

Each State shall maintain its own delegates in a meeting of the States, and while they act as members of the committee of the States.

In determining questions in the United States in Congress assembled, each State shall have one vote.

Freedom of speech and debate in Congress shall not be impeached or questioned in any court or place out of Congress, and the members of Congress shall be protected in their persons from arrests or imprisonments, during the time of their going to and from, and attendance on Congress, except for treason, felony, or breach of the peace.

Article VI.

No State, without the consent of the United States in Congress assembled, shall send any embassy to, or receive any embassy from, or enter into any conference, agreement, alliance or treaty with any king, prince or state; nor shall any person holding any office of profit or trust under the United States, or any of them, accept any present, emolument, office or title of any kind whatever from any king, prince or foreign state; nor shall the United States in Congress assembled, or any of them, grant any title of nobility.

No two or more States shall enter into any treaty, confederation or alliance whatever between them, without the consent of the United States in Congress assembled, specifying accurately the purposes for which the same is to be entered into, and how long it shall continue.

No State shall lay any imposts or duties, which may interfere with any stipulations in treaties, entered into by the United States in Congress assembled, with any king, prince or state, in pursuance of any treaties already proposed by Congress, to the courts of France and Spain.

No vessel of war shall be kept up in time of peace by any State, except such number only, as shall be deemed necessary by the United States in Congress assembled, for the defense of such State, or its trade; nor shall any body of forces be kept up by any State in time of peace, except such number only, as in the judgment of the United States in Congress assembled, shall be deemed requisite to garrison the forts necessary for the defense of such State; but every State shall always keep up a well-regulated and disciplined militia, sufficiently armed and accoutered, and shall provide and constantly have ready for use, in public stores, a due number of field pieces and tents, and a proper quantity of arms, ammunition and camp equipage.

No State shall engage in any war without the consent of the United States in Congress assembled, unless such State be actually invaded by enemies, or shall have received certain advice of a resolution being formed by some nation of Indians to invade such State, and the danger is so imminent as not to admit of a delay till the United States in Congress assembled can be consulted; nor shall any State grant commissions to any ships or vessels of war, nor letters of marque or reprisal, except it be after a declaration of war by the United States in Congress assembled, and then only against the

Kingdom or State and the subjects thereof, against which war has been so declared, and under such regulations as shall be established by the United States in Congress assembled, unless such State be infested by pirates, in which case vessels of war may be fitted out for that occasion, and kept so long as the danger shall continue, or until the United States in Congress assembled shall determine otherwise.

Article VII.

When land forces are raised by any State for the common defense, all officers of or under the rank of colonel, shall be appointed by the legislature of each State respectively, by whom such forces shall be raised, or in such manner as such State shall direct, and all vacancies shall be filled up by the State which first made the appointment.

Article VIII.

All charges of war, and all other expenses that shall be incurred for the common defense or general welfare, and allowed by the United States in Congress assembled, shall be defrayed out of a common treasury, which shall be supplied by the several States in proportion to the value of all land within each State, granted or surveyed for any person, as such land and the buildings and improvements thereon shall be estimated according to such mode as the United States in Congress assembled, shall from time to time direct and appoint.

The taxes for paying that proportion shall be laid and levied by the authority and direction of the legislatures of the several States within the time agreed upon by the United States in Congress assembled.

Article IX.

The United States in Congress assembled, shall have the sole and exclusive right and power of determining on peace and war, except in the cases mentioned in the sixth article; of sending and receiving ambassadors; entering into treaties and alliances, provided that no treaty of commerce shall be made whereby the legislative power of the respective States shall be restrained from imposing such imposts and duties on foreigners, as their own people are subjected to, or from prohibiting the exportation or importation of any species of goods or commodities whatsoever; of establishing rules for deciding in all cases, what captures on land or water shall be legal, and in what manner prizes taken by land or naval forces in the service of the United States shall be divided or appropriated; of granting letters of marque and reprisal in times of peace; appointing courts for the trial of piracies and felonies committed on the high seas and establishing courts for receiving and determining finally appeals in all cases of captures, provided that no member of Congress shall be appointed a judge of any of the said courts.

The United States in Congress assembled shall also be the last resort on appeal in all disputes and differences now subsisting or that hereafter may arise between two or more States concerning boundary, jurisdiction or any other causes whatever; which authority shall always be exercised in the manner following. Whenever the legislative or executive authority or lawful agent of any State in controversy with another shall present a petition to Congress stating the matter in question and praying for a hearing, notice thereof shall be given by order of Congress to the legislative or executive authority of the other State in controversy, and a day assigned for the appearance of the parties by their lawful agents, who shall then be directed to appoint by joint consent, commissioners or judges to constitute a court for hearing and determining the matter in question: but if they cannot agree, Congress shall name three persons out of each of the United States, and from the list of such persons each party shall alternately strike out one, the petitioners beginning, until the number shall be reduced to thirteen; and from that number not less than seven, nor more than nine names as Congress shall direct, shall in the presence of Congress be drawn out by lot, and the persons whose names shall be so drawn or any five of them, shall be commissioners or judges, to hear and finally determine the controversy, so always as a major part of the judges who shall hear the cause shall agree in the determination: and if either party shall neglect to attend at the day appointed, without showing reasons, which Congress shall judge sufficient, or being present shall refuse to strike, the Congress shall proceed to nominate three persons out of each State, and the secretary of Congress shall strike in behalf of such party absent or refusing; and the judgment and sentence of the court to be appointed, in the manner before prescribed, shall be final and conclusive; and if any of the parties shall refuse to submit to the authority of such court, or to appear or defend their claim or cause, the court shall nevertheless proceed to pronounce sentence, or judgment, which shall in like manner be final and decisive, the judgment or sentence and other proceedings being in either case transmitted to Congress, and lodged among the acts of Congress for the security of the parties concerned: provided that every commissioner, before he sits in judgment, shall take an oath to be administered by one of the judges of the supreme or superior court of the State, where the cause shall be tried, *well and truly to hear and determine the matter in question, according to the best of his judgment, without favor, affection or hope of reward,"* provided also, that no State shall be deprived of territory for the benefit of the United States.

All controversies concerning the private right of soil claimed under different grants of two or more States, whose jurisdictions as they may respect such lands, and the States which passed such grants are adjusted, the said grants or either of them being at the same time claimed to have originated antecedent to such settlement of jurisdiction, shall on the petition of either party to the Congress of the United States, be finally determined as near as may be in the same manner as is before prescribed for deciding disputes respecting territorial jurisdiction between different States.

The United States in Congress assembled shall also have the sole and exclusive right and power of regulating the alloy and value of coin struck by their own authority, or by that of the respective States; fixing the standards of weights and measures throughout the United States; regulating the trade and managing all affairs with the Indians, not members of any of the States, provided that the legislative right of any State within its own limits be not infringed or violated; establishing or regulating post offices from one State to another, throughout all the United States, and exacting such postage on the papers passing through the same as may be requisite to defray the expenses of the said office; appointing all officers of the land forces, in the service of the United States, excepting regimental officers; appointing all the officers of the naval forces, and commissioning all officers whatever in the service of the United States; making rules for the government and regulation of the said land and naval forces, and directing their operations.

The United States in Congress assembled shall have authority to appoint a committee, to sit in the recess of Congress, to be denominated "A Committee of the States," and to consist of one delegate from each State; and to appoint such other committees and civil officers as may be necessary for managing the general affairs of the United States under their direction; to appoint one of their members to preside, provided that no person be allowed to serve in the office of president more than one year in any term of three years; to ascertain the necessary sums of money to be raised for the service of the United States, and to appropriate and apply the same for defraying the public expenses; to borrow money, or emit bills on the credit of the United States, transmitting every half-year to the respective States an account of the sums of money so borrowed or emitted; to build and equip a navy;

to agree upon the number of land forces, and to make requisitions from each State for its quota, in proportion to the number of white inhabitants in such State; which requisition shall be binding, and thereupon the legislature of each State shall appoint the regimental officers, raise the men and clothe, arm and equip them in a solid-like manner, at the expense of the United States; and the officers and men so clothed, armed and equipped shall march to the place appointed, and within the time agreed on by the United States in Congress assembled. But if the United States in Congress assembled shall, on consideration of circumstances judge proper that any State should not raise men, or should raise a smaller number of men than the quota thereof, such extra number shall be raised, officered, clothed, armed and equipped in the same manner as the quota of each State, unless the legislature of such State shall judge that such extra number cannot be safely spread out in the same, in which case they shall raise, officer, clothe, arm and equip as many of such extra number as they judge can be safely spared. And the officers and men so clothed, armed, and equipped, shall march to the place appointed, and within the time agreed on by the United States in Congress assembled.

The United States in Congress assembled shall never engage in a war, nor grant letters of marque or reprisal in time of peace, nor enter into any treaties or alliances, nor coin money, nor regulate the value thereof, nor ascertain the sums and expenses necessary for the defense and welfare of the United States, or any of them, nor emit bills, nor borrow money on the credit of the United States, nor appropriate money, nor agree upon the number of vessels of war, to be built or purchased, or the number of land or sea forces to be raised, nor appoint a commander in chief of the army or navy, unless nine States assent to the same: nor shall a question on any other point, except for adjourning from day to day be determined, unless by the votes of the majority of the United States in Congress assembled.

The Congress of the United States shall have power to adjourn to any time within the year, and to any place within the United States, so that no period of adjournment be for a longer duration than the space of six months, and shall publish the journal of their proceedings monthly, except such parts thereof relating to treaties, alliances or military operations, as in their judgment require secrecy; and the yeas and nays of the delegates of each State on any question shall be entered on the journal, when it is desired by any delegates of a State, or any of them, at his or their request shall be furnished with a transcript of the said journal, except such parts as are above excepted, to lay before the legislatures of the several States.

Article X.

The Committee of the States, or any nine of them, shall be authorized to execute, in the recess of Congress, such of the powers of Congress as the United States in Congress assembled, by the consent of the nine States, shall from time to time think expedient to vest them with; provided that no power be delegated to the said Committee, for the exercise of which, by the Articles of Confederation, the voice of nine States in the Congress of the United States assembled be requisite.

Article XI.

Canada, acceding to this confederation, and adjoining in the measures of the United States, shall be admitted into, and entitled to all the advantages of this Union; but no other colony shall be admitted into the same, unless such admission be agreed to by nine States.

Article XII.

All bills of credit emitted, monies borrowed, and debts contracted by, or under the authority of Congress, before the assembling of the United States, in pursuance of the present confederation, shall be deemed and considered as a charge against the United States, for payment and satisfaction whereof the said United States, and the public faith are hereby solemnly pledged.

Article XIII.

Every State shall abide by the determination of the United States in Congress assembled, on all questions which by this confederation are submitted to them. And the Articles of this Confederation shall be inviolably observed by every State, and the Union shall be perpetual; nor shall any alteration at any time hereafter be made in any of them; unless such alteration be agreed to in a Congress of the United States, and be afterwards confirmed by the legislatures of every State.

And Whereas it hath pleased the Great Governor of the World to incline the hearts of the legislatures we respectively represent in Congress, to approve of, and to authorize us to ratify the said Articles of Confederation and perpetual Union. Know Ye that we, the undersigned delegates, by virtue of the power and authority to us given for that purpose, do by these presents, in the name and in behalf of our respective constituents, fully and entirely ratify and confirm each and every of the said Articles of Confederation and perpetual Union, and all and singular the matters and things therein contained: and we do further solemnly plight and engage the faith of our respective constituents, that they shall abide by the determinations of the United States in Congress assembled, on all questions, which by the said Confederation are submitted to them. And that the Articles thereof shall be inviolably observed by the States we respectively represent, and that the Union shall be perpetual. In Witness whereof, we have hereunto set our hands in Congress.

DONE at Philadelphia, in the State of Pennsylvania, the 9th day of July, in the Year of our Lord 1778, and in the third year of the independence of America.

New Hampshire: Josiah Bartlett; John Wentworth Jr.

Massachusetts Bay: John Hancock; Samuel Adams; Elbridge Gerry; Francis Dana; James Lovell; Samuel Holten

Rhode Island and Providence Plantations: William Ellery; Henry Marchant; John Collins

Connecticut: Roger Sherman; Samuel Huntington; Oliver Wolcott; Titus Hosmer; Andrew Adams

New York: James Duane; Francis Lewis; William Duer; Gouverneur Morris

New Jersey: John Witherspoon; Nathaniel Scudder

Pennsylvania: Robert Morris; Daniel Roberdeau; John Bayard Smith; William Clingan; Joseph Reed

Delaware: Thomas McKean; John Dickinson; Nicholas Van Dyke

Maryland: John Hanson; Daniel Carroll

Virginia: Richard Henry Lee; John Banister; Thomas Adams; John Harvie; Francis Lightfoot Lee

North Carolina: John Penn; Cornelius Harnett; John Williams

South Carolina: Henry Laurens; Will Henry Drayton; John Mathews; Richard Hutson; Thomas Heyward Jr.

Georgia: John Walton; Edward Telfair; Edward Longworthy

The aforesaid articles of confederation were finally ratified on the first day of March 1781; the state of Maryland having, by their members in Congress, on that day acceded thereto, and completed the same.

APPENDIX F: BIBLIOGRAPHY

GENERAL REFERENCE

Greene, Jack P. and J. R. Pole. *The Blackwell Encyclopedia of the American Revolution,* Cambridge, MA: Blackwell Reference, 1991.

Lloyd, Gordon. *The Constitutional Convention as a Four-Act Drama.* Available at http://teachingamericanhistory.org/convention/attendance.

Vile, John R. *The Constitutional Convention of 1787: A Comprehensive Encyclopedia of America's Founding,* 2 vols. Santa Barbara, CA: ABC-CLIO, 2005.

RECOMMENDED READINGS

Banning, Lance. "The Constitutional Convention." In *The Framing and Ratification of the Constitution.* Eds. Leonard Levy and Dennis Mahoney. New York: Macmillan, 1987, 112–131.

Beard, Charles. *An Economic Interpretation of the Constitution of the United States.* New York: Macmillan, 1913, 1935.

Beeman, Richard R., Stephen Botein, Edward Carlos Carter, and the Institute of Early American History and Culture, eds. *Beyond Confederation: Origins of the Constitution and American Identity.* Chapel Hill: University of North Carolina Press, 1987.

Brown, Robert E. *Reinterpretation of the Formation of the American Constitution.* Boston: Boston University Press, 1963.

Coby, John Patrick. "The Long Road toward a More Perfect Union: Majority Rule and Minority Rights at the Constitutional Convention." *American Political Thought* 5 (winter 2016): 26–54.

———. "The Proportional Representation Debate at the Constitutional Convention: Why the Nationalists Lost." *American Political Thought* (forthcoming 2017).

Diamond, Martin. "Democracy and the Federalist: A Reconsideration of the Framers' Intent." *American Political Science Review* 53 (1959): 52–68.

Eidelberg, Paul. *The Philosophy of the American Constitution: A Reinterpretation of the Intentions of the Founding Fathers.* New York: Free Press, 1968.

Jillson, Calvin C. *Constitution Making: Conflict and Consensus in the Federal Convention of 1787.* New York: Agathon Press, 1988.

Johnson, Calvin H. *Righteous Anger at the Wicked States: The Meaning of the Founders' Constitution.* Cambridge: Cambridge University Press, 2005.

Klarman, Michael J. *The Framers' Coup: The Making of the United States Constitution.* New York: Oxford University Press, 2016.

Levy, Leonard. *Essays on the Making of the Constitution.* New York: Oxford University Press, 1987.

McDonald, Forest. *E Pluribus Unum: The Formation of the American Republic, 1776–1790.* Boston: Houghton Mifflin, 1965.

———. *Novus Ordo Seclorum: The Intellectual Origins of the Constitution.* Lawrence: University Press of Kansas, 1985.

———. *We the People: The Economic Origins of the Constitution.* Chicago: University of Chicago Press, 1958.

Rakove, Jack N. *Original Meanings: Politics and Ideas in the Making of the Constitution.* New York: Knopf, 1996.

Robertson, David Brian. *The Constitution and America's Destiny.* Cambridge: Cambridge University Press, 2005.

Roche, John P. "The Founding Fathers: A Reform Caucus in Action." *American Political Science Review* 55 (1961): 799–816.

Wolfe, Christopher. "On Understanding the Constitutional Convention of 1787." *Journal of Politics* 39 (February 1977): 97–118.

Wood, Gordon. *The Creation of the American Republic, 1776–1787.* Chapel Hill: University of North Carolina Press, 1969.

Zuckert, Michael P. "Federalism and the Founding: Toward a Reinterpretation of the Constitutional Convention." *Review of Politics* (spring 1986): 166–210.

Zvesper, John. "The Madisonian Systems." *Western Political Quarterly* 37 (June 1984): 236–256.

NOTES

1. The Hartford Wits were Joel Barlow, John Trumbull, David Humphreys, and Lemuel Hopkins. The *Anarchiad* was a twelve-installment collection of poems, songs, and speeches published in the *New-Haven Gazette* between October 1786 and September 1787. Quoted in Kenneth Silverman, *A Cultural History of the American Revolution* (New York: Thomas Y. Crowell, 1976), p. 514.

2. John Fiske, *The Critical Period in American History* (Boston: Houghton, Mifflin, 1888).

3. James Wilson in the Pennsylvania Convention, November 24, 1787; in Max Farrand, ed., *The Records of the Federal Convention of 1787*, vol. 3 (New Haven: Yale University Press, 1966), p. 141.

4. George Washington to Bushrod Washington, November 10, 1787; in William B. Allen, ed., *George Washington: A Collection* (Indianapolis: Liberty Fund, 1988), p. 373

ACKNOWLEDGMENTS

I wish to express my gratitude to the Mellon Foundation, the Teagle Foundation, and the "Reacting to the Past" Advisory Board for grants underwriting summer research. I wish also to thank my student assistants, especially Amelia VanderLaan, who compiled three volumes of bibliographical material and provided a preliminary sketch of one of the role descriptions. Helping also with the role descriptions and with the histories of the states were Sarah Schwartz, Lillian Lamboy, and Bethany Singer-Baefsky. All served as invaluable critics during the two years of initial composition.

Much appreciation is due to those faculty who graciously volunteered to review the manuscript for Norton. These include Nathan Camp of the University of Georgia, Mark Higbee of Eastern Michigan State University, Paul Fessler of Dordt College, Scout Blum of Troy University, Greg Rose and Wendy Closterman of Bryn Athyn College, Betsy Powers of Lone Star College, Montgomery, Sean Taylor of Minnesota State University, Moorhead, and Colleen Sheehan of Villanova University. I benefited greatly from their comments and suggestions. Other faculty provided helpful feedback after use of the game. These include John Moser of Ashland University, Jeff Hyson of Saint Joseph's University, Paul Otto of George Fox University, Jeffrey Ostler of the University of Oregon, Leslie Rubin of Duquesne University, Bridget Ford of California State University, East Bay, Catherine Borck of the University of Hartford, Carol McNamara of Utah State University, Kelly Brown of Easthampton High School, and Elizabeth Taylor of the Masterman School of Philadelphia. My thanks to them as well, and to Norton editors, Scott Sugarman and Justin Cahill, who provided essential assistance with the book's layout.